CW01507851

ACKNOWLEDGMENTS

Some fine folks helped to make this book what it is and I will always be grateful for their assistance. To my friends in the field - Alana Atterbury in NYC, John DuMond in Albany and Bonnie Graham in Philadelphia thank you for the leg work (or should I say, "Legs" work?) *Merci beaucoup* to Mario Gomes, Bill Helmer, Allan May and Tom Prior for the materials they shared. Kudos also to Robert Hudovernik and Angela Troisi for their assistance with some great photos. To Rose Keefe, your skill as a computer artist is second only to your talent as a writer. Thank you also to John Colasanti for the numerous interviews, photos and emails regarding your uncles and Vincent Coll. Thanks also to the New York State Archives, Albany County Hall of Records, Catskill Municipal Building, New York City Municipal Archives, New York Public Library, Philadelphia Municipal Archives, Philadelphia Public Library, Monmouth County Public Library, New Jersey State Archives, Lake Saranac County Clerk's Office. Finally, a great big thank you to Tom Hunt for averting the apocalypse.

LEGS DIAMOND

GANGSTER

PATRICK DOWNEY

Dedicated to the usual suspects.

Life is good.

CONTENTS

FOREWORD

Upon his return from discovering the origin of the Orinoco River in South America, explorer Dr. Herbert Spencer Dickey was questioned about the dangers he and his team faced while on their exploration; first and foremost, were there hostile Indians? Dr. Dickey assured the press that other than mosquitoes and flies there were no dangers and that any natives they met up with were friendly. Talk then turned to the fact that the team carried a radio and, after a mere sixty minutes of doodling around with the dials, the party was able to tune in each night to the *New York Times* radio signal and keep up with current events while sitting on the rainforest floor. The current events were mostly about crime. "You people talk about the terrors of the jungle," Dr. Dickey told the press. "Do you know that the people down there, after hearing all about Al Capone and Legs Diamond over the radio, have an idea that the Americans are just a race of bloodthirsty bandits? They ask us about the dangers of life in the United States, just as you ask about the dangers of the jungle."[1]

"…After hearing all about Al Capone and Legs Diamond…" The former needs no introduction. His name is synonymous with Chicago gangland, where over the course of a dozen years nearly one thousand gunmen were wiped out by gangster bullets. His story has been told numerous times in books, movies and TV programs. Legs Diamond, on the other hand, over the past eight decades, has pretty much fallen to the wayside of history. Part of this is due to the fact that Legs never came close to attaining the gangland prominence of Capone. Al was the President and CEO of the largest criminal

organization in the USA, while Legs was one of many racketeers getting by in New York City. However in 1930 and 1931,
Jack's fame was on par with or, in the East anyway, eclipsed
that of Al Capone. Not because he could marshal hundreds
of hoodlums to war, not because he managed a multi-million
dollar organization. No, as will be seen, Jack was famous for
getting shot, beating the rap and cheating on his wife with
his Ziegfeld Girl mistress. But he was heralded as a top gangster and, since his name was trumpeted louder than any other
New York hoodlum, he was the Capone of the East. Of course
gangland knew better, so did Jack, but he would use that fame
to his advantage.

If crime is your industry, notoriety is bad for business.
Diamond received enough press to force dozens of gangsters
to fold up their tents and head for greener pastures. Jack's
fame in the last year and a half of his life cannot be overstated.
He was a bonafide celebrity on both sides of the Atlantic. His
recognition was that of a movie star, and that was without the
help of a publicist (though there would be accusations that he
did actually employ one). Like other stars, people sought his
autograph, and he received fan mail. During the summer of
1931, police confiscated a package mailed to Jack from Reading, Pennsylvania, believing that it was some nefarious parcel.
It turned out to be a "healing lotion" sent by an eight year-
old girl. "I read in the papers about Diamond being shot so
many times," she told detectives, "and how his arm is paralyzed
and I thought the healing lotion might help him."[2] Film studio
M.G.M. even considered making a film based on his life while
he was still alive.

In the final eighteen months of Jack's life, hardly a day
passed when he wasn't in the news. In 1931, he appeared in
the pages of the *New York Times* on 103 occasions, including
nineteen turns on the front page – modest numbers, considering that the *Times* only discussed Jack when there was actually
news fit to print. The tabloids like the *Daily News*, *Daily Mirror*
and *Evening Graphic* weren't so choosy. If Jack didn't do anything worthy of mention, they invented stories for him. If there

LEGS DIAMOND

GANGSTER

1

YOUNG MR. DIAMOND

Police Officer Herman Schulte was walking his beat on the Bowery when his attention was drawn to three young guys and a girl standing in front of a pawn shop. One of the guys went inside while the other three loitered out front. A few minutes later, the young man slipped out and the foursome headed up the street. His curiosity aroused, Schulte entered the shop and asked the proprietor what transpired with the fellow that just left. The shopkeeper said the young man offered to sell him some gold chains. Since the chains looked brand new, he asked the lad where he got them. The answer was evasive. Assuming that the merchandise had been stolen, the pawnbroker refused to buy them.

Smelling something fishy, Schulte ducked out of the shop and jumped onto a northbound streetcar. He spotted the quartet a few blocks up and stepped off the trolley. Another cop was nearby, Schulte called him over and together they cowed the group into a store and arrested them.

The officers escorted the foursome to the Clinton Street Police Station where the guys were searched. Each had exactly $1.45 in cash in their pockets and one of them had thirty-five gold chains. Two of the young men, James Burns, sixteen, and John Doyle, twenty, confessed to stealing the chains. The girl, Burns' fifteen year-old girlfriend Anna Schick, said she knew nothing of the robbery. The third man, John Diamond, age given as eighteen, admitted nothing.

Burns and Doyle stated that, earlier that day, they were passing the Strauss jewelry store in Brooklyn and noticed the chains and some rings on display in a window. Smashing the window with a brick, they grabbed the loot and ran. A cop stationed nearby heard the glass shatter and gave chase, but they outran him and returned to Manhattan.

The only thing incriminating Diamond was the fact that, like Burns and Doyle, he had $1.45 in his pocket. The other two men said that the reason everyone had the same amount of money was because of an even split of the proceeds of some jewelry they managed to sell.

Robberies were a daily occurrence in New York City and not every one of them received attention from the press. Though there was nothing especially interesting about this theft, the crime reporter working for the *New York Evening Telegram* wrote up the story and sent it in. Perhaps it was a slow news day and the editor needed something, anything, to fill space, and this was all they had. Whatever the reason, a brief article relating the story appeared on page eighteen of the February 4, 1914, edition of the *Evening Telegram*. By the time New Yorkers were reading about the crime, the young men had been transferred to Brooklyn, and John Diamond had admitted his participation in the robbery.

Little did any of the players involved in this little drama realize but both the apprehension of John Diamond and the subsequent article were historic events. It was the first of what would amount to over twenty arrests for the young hoodlum, as well as the first of what would be thousands of newspaper appearances for the man who would become New York's most famous gangster, Jack "Legs" Diamond.

☼ ☼ ☼

On February 15, less than two weeks after pleading guilty to robbery, Diamond found himself on a prison ferry cutting through the choppy, frigid waters of Long Island Sound on its way to Hart Island. The transfer took place the day after one of the worst blizzards in recent history had pummeled New York City. The sky was overcast, and the mercury hovered around eight degrees, as the teenager trudged down the gangplank to what would be his home for the next seventeen months: the New York City Reformatory for Misdemeanants. The following day, he received his second newspaper mention when the *Brooklyn Daily Eagle* listed the sentencing of about two dozen criminals by County Judge Dike.[ii]

Hart Island is a patch of land in Long Island Sound about one mile long and a third of a mile wide at its broadest point. The reformatory itself was an old insane asylum sandwiched between New York City's official potter's field (already the final resting spot for about two hundred thousand of the Big Apples forgotten with new arrivals being planted every day) and another prison which housed five hundred drug addicts and aging inmates.[7] Law enforcement officials couldn't have asked for a better "crime doesn't pay" visage: *Keep up your wicked ways young man and you'll end up in the other two places as well.*

The reformatory was unique in that it housed only first time offenders. Officials felt that if these non-professional, embryonic hoods were segregated from hardened criminals serving time in the city's other prisons, they would have a better shot at rehabilitation. Though the goal was lofty, the truth was that, like New York's other prisons, the reformatory was an outdated and violent institution in dire need of modification. The inmates had more to fear from the guards than they did from other prisoners, as torture from those in charge was a daily occurrence.

Conditions on the island were no secret, and if Jack[iii] read the papers he would have known that reform was in the air.

---

ii James Burns was sent to the House of Refuge and John Doyle was shipped off to the prison at Elmira.

iii Though he was named John and everybody who knew him called him that, Diamond is famous as Jack and that is how he will be referred to throughout the remainder of the book.

At the beginning of the year, Dr. Katherine Davis was appointed Commissioner of Corrections. She wasted no time in pointing out the need for updated prisons. In the week that Jack was awaiting transfer to the island, she discussed a special plan she had for the reformatory. She argued that first time offenders needed not only to get away from professional criminals but needed to get out of New York City altogether. To that end, 610 acres of farmland was purchased in New Hampton, New York where a farm colony was to be built. There would be no cells, no bars, no guards; superintendents would live and work with the youthful offenders on the farm raising their own crops. Eventually all of the 370 inmates on Hart Island would be moved there, but as Diamond shuffled through the front door that cold February morning the planned reform was still about a year away.[8]

Once Jack was processed, he no doubt became acquainted with the prison's sadistic overseer Martin Moore. Moore was the worst offender when it came to prisoner abuse. Typical inmate punishments at the time Diamond was there included the "stand-up." One inmate described how, every night for two weeks, he was forced to stand on a line from the start of bedtime, eight o'clock in the evening, until eleven o'clock. He was then allowed to sleep until two in the morning, at which time he was awakened and forced to stand on the line for another hour and a half before being left alone. He then had to get up in the morning and spend the entire day in the workhouse.

Another prisoner told about being in solitary confinement or "the cooler" as they called it. "They only give you one glass of water a day," he recalled. "They never empty the slop buckets (toilet) until the boys finish their stay, and they give you a blanket like a piece of Swiss cheese there are so many holes in it." A third testified that, while in the cooler, he went two days without a drink of water. He went on to say that he was forced to kneel for four hours and whenever he leaned over he was beaten with a billy club. A prisoner also told of overhearing Overseer Moore ordering five guards to beat up one of the boys.[9]

It's possible that Jack knew the victims quoted above and he surely endured his fair share of these abuses for his first year on the Island, but things began to change in the spring of 1915. Charged with torture, Overseer Moore was removed from duty in mid-March, and the first of the inmates were sent to the new farm at New Hampton. Over the course of that year more would be sent, but Jack would not be among them. There was a transfer in Jack's future, but it was not to the bucolic fields of New Hampton. Instead on July 26, 1915, two weeks after his seventeenth birthday, he took a boat ride down river to Blackwell's Island (also known as Welfare Island and now as Roosevelt Island) and checked into the New York County Penitentiary.

What the teenager did to earn a ticket to the Pen while other first time offenders were being shipped off to pitch hay and pick vegetables is unknown. Perhaps there was rebellious behavior to the substandard treatment he received at the hands of the guards at the reformatory. Whatever the reason, if Jack thought getting off of Hart Island was a step up, he was sorely mistaken. A report published by the State Prison Commission the summer prior to Diamond's transfer described his new home thusly, "The cells are not fit for the confinement of human beings…At the present time there are several hundred more inmates in the penitentiary than cells…From four (inmates) in the smaller cells, [to] up to thirty or more in the larger cells the inmates are crowded in together for at least twelve hours each day." For the foreseeable future this was seventeen-year- old Jack's reality.[10]

✵ ✵ ✵

How did a teenager originally from the City of Brotherly Love end up in a New York City prison cell unfit for humans? Information leading up to Jack's being sent to hell as a teenager is sparse. The story begins in Philadelphia at the close of the Nineteenth Century, when his parents John Diamond and Sarah Hart exchanged wedding vows on June 17, 1896. Though they were the children of Irish immigrants, both John and Sarah were born in Philadelphia - he, the son of a grocer, on August 20, 1871, and she on February 9, 1872.[11] They were parishioners of St. Anne's in what is now known as the Kensington District of northern Philadelphia. At the time of their marriage, the area was booming with jobs in the textile industry, and John obtained employment as a glass packer.[12]

Toward the end of 1897, Sarah became pregnant. The following summer, the doctor was summoned, and on July 11 the baby that would be christened "Legs" by the New York City press thirty years later was born. His parents called him John Thomas.[13]

Living with the family at the time was John Sr.'s younger brother Thomas, who worked as a machinist, and their younger sister Annie, who was employed as a hosiery mender. With a houseful of employed people, the Diamonds weren't hurting for cash.[14]

Almost four years to the day after Jack took his first gulp of air, John and Sarah welcomed another son into the world on July 9, 1902. They called him Edward Joseph.[15] As the young couple settled into domesticity in an era of horse drawn carriages and oil lamps, they couldn't have conceived of a world of newsreels, expensive cars, Thompson machineguns, international drug trafficking or national Prohibition, but these would be realities for their children.

Jack attended school at St. Anne's, where we're told that although he wasn't a very good student he did enjoy recitations. His favorite was a quatrain by Henry Wadsworth Longfellow:

Lives of great men all remind us,
We can make our lives sublime,
And departing leave behind us,
Foot prints on the sands of time.[16]

One can picture the sisters at St. Anne's explaining the significance of the piece to a second grade class. If this was indeed young Diamond's favorite poem to declaim, it makes one wonder how the lad thought that he might make his mark on the world.

Perhaps one of the reasons Jack did poorly in school was because his life began to turn upside down when he was about eight. Like most good Irish Catholic families of the day, John and Sarah continued to multiply. Another son, Thomas, was born on August 31, 1904. Hardly a year went by before Sarah was again pregnant in the early autumn of 1905. Sadly this pregnancy was marred by tragedy. At one and half years of age Thomas developed acute bronchitis. A doctor was called in but there was nothing he could do. After two days, it developed into pneumonia. The toddler passed away at ten o'clock in the morning on February 6, 1906.[17]

About three months later, Sarah gave birth to a little girl; they called her Margret. Like her brother Thomas, her time on earth would be tragically cut short. Eleven months after burying their son and brother the Diamond family bid farewell to their daughter and sister who died on January 4, 1907.[18]

A few months prior to Margret's death, Sarah was diagnosed with cardiac dilatation, a condition that, in time, could prove fatal. If that wasn't bad enough, the following April 28, 1907, Sarah visited a physician. She had contracted tuberculosis. A little over a month later, on June 6, she too was gone.[19] In a mere fifteen months, half the Diamond family was buried.

It would be convenient to say that the loss of his mother and two siblings started Jack on his road to crime. Although they did play a part, the tragedies do not excuse Jack's later choices. Early death was much more prevalent at the beginning of the Twentieth Century, and the losses that the Diamonds suffered were not uncommon. In fact, Jack's own father lost his mother at a very young age. Neither the elder John nor his siblings turned to lives of crime.[20]

Unlike most of the underworld figures Jack would grow to rub elbows with, he didn't live in an overcrowded squalid tenement nor did he have to face the problems and confines that those new arrivals from Europe who didn't speak English had to face. Subsistence wasn't a problem. So how does a working class kid get on the road to become one of the nation's most infamous gangsters? "Legs had a streak in him as a kid," His cousin Richard Diamond told a reporter in 1931. "He was light fingered, couldn't resist stealing things. The family doctor said an operation would cure him, but his mother wouldn't let him operate."[21]

According to his cousin, the seeds of criminality were planted as a young child when his mother was still alive, but she was able to keep him in check. Well, if not in check at least in school and in church. Once she was gone, however, he began to spend less and less time in each. Not long after his mother's death, Jack was sent to a Catholic Protectory because of delinquency.

School didn't hold much interest for Jack. Bored with books, the youngster took to hanging out in Hitner's junkyard with a group of other truants from St. Anne's. Together they would crawl around in the lot's many boilers that lay about rusting away. This resulted in them being called the Boiler Gang. Playing hooky seems to have been the Boiler Gang's chief occupation. A couple of the boys would stand guard keeping a look out for the local truant officer, Mr. Truax. If he was sighted coming in their direction, one of the sentries would shout, "Jiggers!" and the band would scatter around the yard, hiding in the many boilers. The story was told that one time Mr. Truax, a bit on the portly side, tried to follow Jack into one of the boilers and got stuck, which resulted in his having to be pried out.[22]

By 1910, the surviving Diamonds were living in a boardinghouse. The father was still employed as a glass packer but supposedly became a drinker and didn't manage the boys very well. Realizing that his eldest son wasn't interested in school, he obtained a job for him in a spinning mill. That lasted a week. He then got him a job at a steel mill. That didn't work either. At one point, he put his sons in a Catholic school for boys but, as cousin Richard went on to say, "My dad wouldn't stand for that, he said 'No Diamond's going to be in an institution while I'm alive' and took the boys out."[23] But Richard's father didn't take care of them either. The brothers first went to live with their aunt Annie. When they proved too unruly for her, they (or at least the eldest) were sent off to New York, where a chance sighting by a Bowery cop resulted in the frigid boat ride up the East River.

✳ ✳ ✳

The date Jack was released from the penitentiary on Blackwell's Island is unknown but he served less than a year. His time spent incarcerated had the opposite of the desired effect, and when he was released he had no intention of going straight. Instead of returning to Philadelphia upon his release, he traveled to the Chelsea district of Manhattan's West Side. At some point, Jack became involved with a gang of thieves headed by William "Baron Bean" Butler[iv] and was arrested again on May 12, 1916, for assault and robbery but released the same day. He went through the same thing two and a half weeks later, when he was arrested and released on May 31 for grand larceny.

About two months later, on June 28, 1916, Jack uncharacteristically joined the New York National Guard.[v] Whether he actually wanted to straighten out his life is unknown. Later he would claim he joined in patriotic fervor after reading the memoir "Over the Top" written by an American soldier named Guy Empey, who had fought in Europe prior to America's joining the war.[24] Trouble is that "Over the Top" wasn't published until 1917. On July 5, a week after signing up, he was arrested

---

iv The Butler clan was infamous on the west side. Baron Bean's dad was a former Tammany Hall assemblyman name Dick Butler who made the headlines a few years previously for breaking Harry Thaw, killer of Stanford White, out of the Matteawan State Hospital for the Criminally Insane.

v The previous day, June 27, another young hoodlum whom Jack would later do business with, eighteen year old Charles Lucania, who would later be known as Lucky Luciano, was arrested for the first time. He would spend six months in the reformatory on a narcotics rap.

for third degree assault. Perhaps he knew the arrest was coming and joined the Guard because he was trying to impress a judge or get out of serving some jail time. If so, the ploy worked. He was acquitted on July 14, three days after his eighteenth birthday.

Sadly a fire at the National Archives in 1973 consumed sixteen to eighteen million military personnel files, including Jack's, so we don't know exactly how bad a soldier he was. Fortunately journalist and author Fred Pasley researched it for a profile on Jack in 1931, preserving a brief outline of his service. According to the piece, Jack reported for duty on July 15, 1917, as a member of 20th Company in the Ninth Regiment, Coast Artillery. On November 5, he transferred to Battery A, First Trench Mortar Battalion, Coast Artillery Corps.[25]

Jack took to military life like a cat to water. In the five and a half months mentioned above, he went AWOL three times. One of the offenses, however, may have been an accident. Another tidbit from Jack's cousin Richard was that, while Jack was in the service he came back to Philadelphia to visit Eddie, who apparently moved back at some point and was lodged in a reformatory there. After the visit, Jack missed the train back and was listed as AWOL.

On one of his absences, he was back on Manhattan's West Side and on November 20, 1917, married a girl named Katherine Williams.[26] Jack was three years younger than his bride, so the nineteen-year-old claimed to be twenty-three on the marriage certificate.[vi] It appears to have been a short courtship and possibly an elopement. Jack wasn't introduced to her parents until after they were married. At their first meeting, Jack's new father in-law inquired about his habits. "Well, I smoke an occasional cigarette, like most of the other boys," Jack replied, adding, "But I can look any man on the West Side in the eye and tell him to go to hell."[27] To say the Williamses weren't very impressed with their new son in-law is an understatement. "Jack Diamond was the meanest husband in New York. He

---

vi At that time anyone under twenty-one years needed parental permission to marry.

treated my daughter like a dog," His ex-mother in-law would tell the press thirteen years later. "A week after my daughter and Diamond returned from their Philadelphia honeymoon, Katherine told me Jack beat her."[28] They didn't have to put up with him very long, however, as the couple only lived together for a week or so.

Years later, Katherine would say, "We were very young when we were married. It was a wartime romance. The war was on, and many young girls were marrying men in uniform. I liked him anyhow, and when he came around in uniform and asked me to marry, I consented. Soon after our marriage, Jack went to camp."[29] Was recaptured is more like it. As for their wartime romance, as will be seen, Katherine was singing a different tune when she went for an annulment a few years later.

After being picked up in New York, Jack was sent to and confined at Camp Merritt, New Jersey. No matter how hard Uncle Sam tried, however, he just could not turn Jack into a doughboy. On January 31, 1918, Private Diamond took another powder. This time, he stole a .45 and some clothes. A sergeant tried to get in his way, but Jack thumped him and successfully escaped back to New York City and his criminal ways.

About six weeks later, on March 13, Harold Agelikas was preparing his restaurant for the breakfast crowd. At four-forty in the morning, Jack and three cronies, Michael Culhane, William Tobin and Timothy Cleary, entered. Since the foursome weren't the working type, they were probably just ending their evening. They ordered their food, and Agelikas plated it up. The proprietor's gut correctly told him that the quartet was bad news, so he locked his cash register before heading into the kitchen to do some work.

A few moments later, Jack and the boys put down their forks and went over to the cash register. Culhane went behind the counter and tried to open it. While this was happening, Agelikas returned from the kitchen. Culhane drew his gun. "Don't move or I'll shoot," He ordered. Tobin also drew a pistol and told Agelikas to go back into the kitchen. Not wanting to get shot, the proprietor obeyed. Tobin followed him to the doorway and stood guard.

A minute later, Tobin stepped away. Agelikas returned from the kitchen and, seeing that the gang was gone, dashed out onto the sidewalk and saw them running east on Thirty-Sixth Street. Agelikas blew a whistle. The noise caught the attention of a beat cop, who saw the foursome running in his direction. The cop charged the quartet and managed to corral them all into a doorway at Thirty-Sixth and Broadway and arrest them. Back at the station, Jack gave "soldier" as his occupation and pleaded not guilty. A week later on March 21, the charge was dismissed.[30]

Less than a month later, on April 15, a man named Frank Plume returned to his furnished room on Twelfth Street to find that about eighty dollars worth of clothes and jewelry were missing. He inquired around the building, and two other residents noticed that they were missing some clothes and jewelry as well.

At around ten-thirty the next night, a cop was walking his beat and saw Jack hanging out at the corner of Twentieth Street and Eighth Avenue. Knowing Jack wasn't above breaking the law, the cop went up and searched him. He found a fully loaded .32 and arrested him. A thousand dollar bail was set, but before Jack had a chance to leave, the arresting officer informed Frank Plume about the arrest. Plume went to the station and identified the suit that Jack was wearing as one that had been stolen from him. Grand larceny was added to the charge, which added $5,000 to the bail. Once again, Jack gave "soldier" as his occupation and surprisingly pleaded guilty to the charges.[31] Even more surprisingly, the chargers were dismissed on May 1. This was most likely because the military caught up with Jack, and he was sent to Fort Jay on New York's Governors Island.[vii]

On July 10, 1918, one day shy of his twentieth birthday, Jack, along with the rest of his detachment, boarded the *S.S.*

---

vii The military may have gotten the charges dropped but Jack's relationship with the Butler clan shouldn't be over looked.

Toloa and sailed for Europe to take part in the "War to End All Wars." Eleven days later, he arrived in Brest, France. The army life in Europe didn't appeal to Jack any more than in the States, and he went AWOL again. He was arrested on September 7 and sentenced to three months' confinement.

During his incarceration, word reached his superiors that he was wanted back in New Jersey for the Camp Merritt business. He was sent back to the States arriving at Governors Island on January 5, 1919. On the following St. Patrick's Day, he faced a court martial on charges of desertion, carrying a concealed weapon, stealing and felonious assault on a sergeant. Found guilty, he was given a dishonorable discharge and sentenced to five years' hard labor.

On July 14, 1919, three days after Jack's twenty-first birthday and almost three years to the day he signed his name on the dotted line to join the service, he arrived at the disciplinary barracks at Fort Leavenworth, Kansas, to begin his sentence. He would end up serving only two years, however, because President Harding doled out a number of pardons to soldiers who were imprisoned during the war, and Jack was lucky enough to be the recipient of one.

Around this time, Jack's wife Katherine was working on getting a pardon from him. On December 29, 1920, she went before a judge seeking an annulment. In her testimony, she claimed that after they were married she learned that he was a drug addict- his narcotics of choice being cocaine, heroin and morphine. She also stated that he had been convicted of burglary. The judge understandably wanted to know why she married the guy. "Because he told me he loved me," she said, "and because he said he wanted somebody to nurse him if he got wounded in the war." Katherine was granted an annulment on May 29, 1921.[32]

In the first half of 1921, Jack returned to New York a free man. Free from the military prison at Leavenworth, free from the military itself and free from marriage. Now he was free to begin, along with his brother Eddie, his ascent to the upper echelons of New York's underworld.

Jack's first mug shot (Author's collection)

Eddie Diamond (Mario Gomes collection)

2

ROARING IN THE TWENTIES

With pardon in hand, Jack returned to his old haunts on New York City's West Side, taking an apartment at 360 West Twenty-Eighth Street. He wasted no time mixing with the law. On June 1, 1921, three days after his marriage was annulled, he was arrested for grand larceny but released the next day.

Prohibition had come into effect during Jack's incarceration and was proving a boon for hoodlums, so it didn't take Jack long to get his feet wet in the new racket. As a thief, Jack wasn't initially in the business of bootlegging, i.e. the buying, selling and distribution of the product, he simply stole from others. His first recorded venture took place in the early autumn of 1921.

On September 24, fifty-six-year-old John Gorman was preparing to leave his Bronx home at 1442 Commonwealth Avenue. He made sure to lock his cellar door as he had some valuable goods stored there, namely fifty-eight cases of Irish whiskey, three barrels of the same, three barrels of port wine and three barrels of sherry. The entire stock was valued at eight thousand dollars.

After Gorman left, Jack and Eddie, now nineteen years old, together with five others pulled up in a truck, broke into the cellar and liberated the spirits. A housewife neighbor of Gorman's witnessed the theft and told Gorman. He apparently knew by his neighbor's description that it was the Diamonds, and went to the police. A warrant was put out for Jack's arrest.

Meanwhile, Jack was arrested again on October 26 for assault and robbery. (The charge would be dropped on Halloween). Two days later, he was picked up in the Bronx for the Gorman robbery. He pleaded not guilty and was released on a $2,500 bail. A court date was set for November 15, which Jack blew off and his bail was forfeited. He managed to stay out of court for two years before finally having to answer for the Gorman theft. When the time came, the case was thrown out due to "insufficient evidence to convict the defendant."[33][viii]

As the Twenties began to roar, Jack and Eddie were beginning to make a name for themselves in gangland. The Diamonds formed a robbery gang that specialized in hitting lofts, stores and warehouses. Anywhere valuables, mainly silks, furs and jewelry, were stored they would pillage. Before long, they were one of the premier gangs in town. It was in the early years of Prohibition that the Diamond Brothers got involved with Arnold Rothstein. Popularly known as the Big Bankroll but most likely referred to as A.R. by his contemporaries, Rothstein was the money and brains behind much of New York City's underworld activities.

A.R. began the century as a gambler, and as his bank account grew so too did his position in the underworld. By the Twenties, he was the conduit between the gangsters and the politicians. He was Mr. Fix It. His wealth also made him the go-to guy for any enterprising young hood with a good idea but insufficient capital to see it through. Rothstein could act as a fence, help out with labor disputes and assist in getting the right candidate elected. If it was illegal and could turn a profit, he probably had his fingers in it.

---

viii This indictment, file 1149 from the Bronx, is most likely a "lost" Diamond case as it doesn't show up on his list of arrests. Listings of his police record show an arrest on Oct. 27, 1921 for assault and robbery. The arresting detective was listed as Moek and the charge was shown as being dropped four days later by a magistrate Brough. File 1149 lists the arresting officer as Reilly and the magistrates dealt with as Sweetser and March and the case lingering on until 1923 before being tossed out.

Exactly when and how the Diamonds became involved with Rothstein is unknown. It's possible that he acted as a fence for their pilfered loot. According to Rothstein's widow, they became acquainted in 1922 or 1923, when Arnold was acting as a mediator in a strike at a cloak and suit factory and the Diamond Brothers went to see him and offered their assistance in the labor conflict.[34] The move paid off and they acquired a powerful friend with good political connections.[ix] It has also come down through history that Jack was one of a string of gunmen who acted as a bodyguard for Rothstein. It's possible that Jack may have done this on occasion, but it appears that Diamond was too busy running his own enterprises to be a constant companion of the Big Bankroll.[x]

Regardless of how they met, during the early years of Prohibition, Rothstein was one of New York City's biggest importers of liquor, and Jack and Eddie went to work for him protecting his shipments. Jack got the idea that, rather than buy liquor, it would be much easier just to steal it, as in the case of John Gorman, from other bootleggers. He went to Rothstein with a proposition. If Rothstein would furnish the Diamonds with a few trucks and a drop-off point, they would be able to furnish him with cut-rate liquor. The thought of cheap booze appealed to Rothstein, so he set the brothers up with the means to begin their operation. Soon Jack and Eddie were hijacking liquor shipments meant for others.[35]

Jack gave marriage another shot in 1922, when he wedded Alice Kenney, whom a Diamond biographer described as being a "crass, nagging, beer guzzling ignoramus who could curse like a mule driver." Physically the New York Times described her as being five-foot-seven with a voice that was

---

ix Carolyn Rothstein also stated that hooking up with the Diamond Brothers was, "The real beginning of the end for Arnold."

x The story is told that A.R. hired Jack when he learned that Chicago hoodlum Gene "Red" McLaughlin was going to kidnap him. Jack was sent to Chicago to take care of the problem. Red was in fact tossed into a drainage canal with a few bullets in his head but this was a year and half after A.R. was dead.

"husky but penetrable." She liked to wear flashy clothes and adorn herself with numerous rings, bracelets and necklaces. There are reports that she drank but nothing to support or denounce the traits put forth by the aforementioned biographer. Unlike the first Mrs. Diamond, she loved Jack to a fault and was fiercely loyal to him. Ironically, though she knew exactly who and what Jack was, she took religion very seriously. Arrest-wise, 1922 was a slow year for Diamond. He was picked up only once as a material witness (for what is unknown), and was released the following day.

With his new-found wealth, Jack and Alice moved from the crowded streets of Manhattan to a bungalow in quiet Cliffside, New Jersey, which they decorated in gaudy fashion with a number of silks stolen by Jack and his gang. It has also come down that, as a gag, Alice had one of their chairs equipped with some sort of electronic apparatus. When Jack or one of his pals sat in it, she would flip a switch and give that person an electric shock. When the victim complained, she would laughingly tell him to get used to it because he was going to end up in the electric chair at Sing Sing anyway. The move to Jersey also resulted in a return to the newspapers.

After a while, the law abiding nine-to-five citizens of Cliffside became suspicious of their new neighbors, who didn't keep the same hours. Although Jack owned an expensive automobile, he never seemed to go to work. They also had other fancy cars showing up at their house at all times of the day and night. Across the river in New York City, the police knew that Diamond's gang was behind a number of the robberies plaguing the city and got in touch with the Bergen County, New Jersey, police and asked them to raid his house.

On Thursday, November 16, 1923, the police approached the house. Nobody was home, so they let themselves in and waited. Later that night, one of the gang showed up (presumably Jack, since it was his house) and the police tied him up and gagged him. Over the course of the evening, five other gang members and Alice showed up and also were arrested. The house was searched and, in addition to the expensive silks and furniture, police found Alice's bank book, which showed that she had deposited $3,000 over the previous two months. Besides Jack and Alice, the others arrested were Wallace Ackerson, Peter "French Pete" Burgess, John Monteforte, Salvatore Arcidiaco and John Hall. Ackerson, Hall and Alice were quickly released. Since none of the remaining four could give a reasonable explanation as to how they could afford all their pleasantries, they were shipped off to the Bergen County jail and held without bail while the New York City police tried to pin something on them. After five days, a lawyer was able to bail all four out at $50,000 per man.[xi] Nothing ever came of the arrests, and all were eventually released.[36]

After this run in with the law, Diamond realized that one doesn't stick out as much in a large city as one does in a small community like Cliffside. He and Alice moved to the Bronx, where he wouldn't have to worry about nosey neighbors. Back in his natural habitat Jack continued with his work. His next known job took place on Monday June 11, 1924. That morning, a truck containing a hundred-thousand dollars worth of diamonds and other precious stones left the midtown post office and was heading downtown to the U.S. Appraiser's Office for assessment of duties. Since the cargo was so valuable, the vice-president of the trucking concern was riding along with the driver to personally deliver the satchel of gems.

At ten-fifteen in the morning, the truck came lumbering down a West Side street into Greenwich Village. A Cadillac suddenly pulled alongside and forced it to the curb. As the truck came to a stop, another Caddy pulled up behind it and boxed it in. Four men brandishing .45's jumped out of the front car and ordered the men to get out of the truck and into the Cadillac. The driver complied, but the VP refused to get out or hand over the diamonds. Spurred by the delay, six other armed men jumped out of the rear Cadillac and hurried to the truck. One of the newcomers pistol-whipped the VP and

---

xi Chances are Arnold Rothstein was the only acquaintance of Diamond who could come up with $200,000 bail.

grabbed the satchel. The bandits returned to their respective cars and escaped uptown, where the truck driver was released at a subway station.[37]

Later that day, a guy brought the two Cadillacs to a garage and told the attendant (who had previously seen this fellow in the company of both Jack and Eddie) that he was leaving the cars there for the Diamond brothers. While this was happening, police already were considering Jack and Eddie as possible suspects in the jewel robbery and began to look for them. A few days later, the investigation led detectives to the garage and the cars. After speaking with the attendant, police went into action and on the morning of June 14 caught Jack and Eddie as well as two others, John Monteforte, who was previously arrested with Jack in Cliffside, and another bandit named Eddie Doyle. The four men were held without bail, although the Diamond brothers were represented by a lawyer. The truck driver, his boss and some other witnesses were brought in to look them over, but none could or would identify them. The Diamonds were released.[38]

On a personal note, 1924 also saw Jack in the role of best man for his brother Eddie, who got married on March 2 to a gal of Scottish descent named Katherine "Kitty" Donohue.[39] A couple years later, they welcomed a son. Eddie named the child John after his big brother. Being a family man, however, didn't stop Eddie from being a hell-raiser.

In her memoir, "A House Is Not a Home," famed New York City Madam Polly Adler tells of a visit to her establishment in the winter of 1926 by a very inebriated Eddie Diamond. With him was a gambler and underworld sort named George McManus and another man who remained anonymous. The trio proceeded to whip one of the girls with a belt until Polly stopped them, and then they proceeded to abuse her. After one of the revelers fired off a few shots from his pistol, the party broke up.

✳ ✳ ✳

Not satisfied with being one of many bootleggers in town, Rothstein began to fade out of rum running after a few years. It was a crowded and bloody industry that he couldn't control, and if he couldn't be in control he didn't want to be involved. Narcotics, however, was another story. By the end of 1923, A.R. was on his way to becoming the United States' largest drug importer. He set up a dummy corporation in Holland and sent buyers, including Sidney Stager and George Uffner, to the legitimate pharmaceutical companies in Europe to buy mass quantities of heroin, cocaine and morphine. Buying was simple. Getting it home was a bit more of a hassle, but not much. The stuff would be sent over in crates marked as toys or bowling pins. Drugs that were smuggled out of France made their way to America's gangsters via Canada.[40]

Stager and Uffner made a trip together in late 1923, returning on November 6 of that year. The latter returned in the spring of the following year and the former made another trip in the summer of 1925.[41]

Like Stager and Uffner, Jack eventually would get involved in drugs, but for the time being he was still up to his old tricks, which included hijacking booze. Had he stuck with ripping off small-time bootleggers, Jack would have fared better, but his penchant for big scores and fearlessness of consequences led to trouble with some formidable gangsters, namely "Big" Bill Dwyer, who along with his partner Frank Costello, was one of Manhattan's biggest bootleggers. At first, nothing was done about Diamond because Dwyer didn't want to tangle with Rothstein, but after a few more shipments disappeared, Dwyer and Costello quit worrying about Rothstein and sent a hunting party out for Jack.[42]

The attempt came just after four o'clock in the morning on July 1, 1925, as Jack was driving up Fifth Avenue. When he came to 106th Street, a sedan full of Italian gunmen armed with a shotgun and two pistols pulled up alongside him. There was a quick explosion, as sixty-four shotgun pellets peppered Jack's head and body and a .45 bullet clipped his heal. Luckily for Jack, there was a hospital on the avenue and attendants who heard the shooting ran out and found him unconscious.

The hospital workers turned off his car and carried him inside for treatment. Detectives were called, and Jack was arrested for carrying a gun. When they asked him who was behind the shooting, he simply replied, "Greasers."[43]

Jack recovered from the shooting. The buck shot apparently knocked some sense into his head, because he stopped ripping off Dwyer and Costello. Perhaps some deal was worked out regarding Jack's previous behavior as well, because Dwyer-Costello attempts on his life were halted.

Rising in the Rothstein camp began to pay dividends for Jack. The Dwyer-Costello matter aside, Jack was obviously more than just a booze hijacker by the latter half of 1925. His elevation in the underworld is evident by a passage in the *New York Times* a little less than three months after his run in with the "Greasers." That autumn, there was a Democratic primary for the upcoming mayoral elections and the candidates included incumbent Mayor Hylan and Tammany contender James J. Walker. When discussing support in the Bronx, a Hylan spokesman stated, "We are informed on reliable authority that arrangements have been made with men known as Jack Diamond, 'Frenchy' and 'Dutch'[xii] to steal the Seventeenth Assembly District for Walker by having guerrillas under command of these three men vote early on primary day upon the names of citizens who are entitled to vote and that when those citizens who are known to favor Mayor Hylan come to the polls they will be told they have already voted."[44] Tammany Hall was surely appreciative to Diamond and the others for their help on Election Day, and no doubt Jack earned himself some favors and prestige with the political machine.

---

xii Although only speculations can be made the Frenchy referred to may be a gangster named Francis "Frenchy" Dillon, who became a bootlegger in New Jersey and was later credited with being a Diamond pal, or possibly it was French Pete Burgess who was arrested with Jack in Cliffside, NJ. Dutch is no doubt Arthur Flegenheimer, a.k.a. Dutch Schultz, who was a Diamond thug at this time.

Favors and prestige, however, don't pay for fancy cars and fine hotel rooms, so it was back to business.

Rothstein must have seen something in Jack he liked because, following the election, he drafted Jack into his drug cartel and sent him to Europe to manage some deals. Jack went over for the first time in November. When his business was wrapped up, he boarded the *S.S. Berengaria* and sailed for home on November 25, 1925, arriving in New York on December 4. Interestingly, on the ship's passenger manifest, his address was given as 691 Broadway, Albany, New York.

✫ ✫ ✫

Every self-respecting Prohibition Era gangster owned a speakeasy, and Diamond was no different. His watering hole was known as the Bronx Theatrical Club. It consisted of three rooms "luxuriously furnished"[45] with twenty-five thousand dollars worth of wall tapestries[46] (no doubt hold outs from some of his robberies) and was located on the second floor of 378 East 149th Street, next door to a furniture manufacturer. It also contained an elaborate security system to thwart police raids. The main door was constructed of thick wood, and beyond that was an iron gate.

One of Jack's employees at the club was his pal and local hoodlum Arthur Flegenheimer, who went by the moniker Dutch Schultz. In 1925 Schultz managed to secure himself a deputy's badge, which made it lawful for him to carry a gun.

The Diamond speakeasy was not a secret to the Bronx authorities, and on January 22, 1926, a Federal prohibition agent, with a dozen Bronx cops in tow, raided the place. With axes and sledgehammers, the raiders hacked at the thick wooden door leading into the club. Inside, fifty or so people partied unbothered by the law. As the raiders chopped away, the band played and the patrons continued to dance, while taunting the police. Outside, a crowd began to gather to witness an event unique to that era.

Once the raiding party got past the wooden door, the agent and officers found themselves blocked by the iron gate. The crowd inside continued celebrating while deriding the police, as they went to work on the bars. When the cops finally cut through the gate, the crowd began to boo and heckle. Suddenly all went quiet as a whirring sound came from above. Much to the chagrin of the police and to the joy of the customers, yet another metal door descended from above, again separating the police from the revelers.

As the authorities went to work on this door the patrons rolled out two barrels and began pouring all their liquor into them. The raiding party managed to lift the door up a foot or so and they sent the smallest cop under. Instead of the verbal abuse he was expecting, the officer was relieved to hear a round of applause when he came through. All in all, it took the raiding party an hour to smash their way in. All the Prohibition agent got for his troubles was one bottle of champagne and the two barrels of mixed spirits. Before leaving however the cops busted up the security system. No arrests were made. [47]

Following the fracas, a police guard was placed out front of the club, but on February 6, Diamond was able to procure a court order having him removed. During this time, the Feds worked through the courts to have the place padlocked.[48]

The police had a legitimate excuse to return to the speakeasy on March 9, 1926. That morning the neighboring furniture factory was buzzing with activity as carpenters plied their trade. Next door at the club, patrons were simply buzzed and a fight broke out when "a fellow had spoken out of his turn."[49] During the melee somebody pulled a gun and fired a shot that pierced the wall and whizzed by the head of one of the furniture employees. The carpenter ran to the street and returned with the first patrolman he could find. By this time, a number of the speakeasy occupants had escaped by shimmying down the gutters, but about eight, including Dutch Schultz, remained inside.

Expecting trouble, those who stayed brought down new steel shutters over the door and rear windows. When the cop attempted to enter the club, he was refused admittance, so he called for reserves. In all a mix of twenty cops and detectives fell on the club. Like the first raid, a large crowd gathered to watch the action, so police reinforcements were brought in to keep them at bay and also to cut off traffic to the street. The raiding party tried to enter through the front door but, surprise, those inside wouldn't let them in. Realizing that entrance would have to be gained the hard way, the authorities headed over to the local fire house and procured some axes and a pick. They returned to the club but instead of banging away at the steel doors like last time, they entered the furniture factory and started hacking through the wall, while some other officers tried to chop through the metal sheets that covered the rear windows.

Dutch and the boys inside were no doubt surprised by the new entrance strategy and, as the first detectives began to come through the wall, they realized the futility of holding out any longer and opened the door. Schultz and the other seven were arrested. Schultz was forced to forfeit his deputy's badge.[50][xiii] After nine days in jail, all those arrested were released.[51]

The summer of 1926 found Jack making two more back-to-back trips to France to purchase drugs. When he arrived and how long he stayed are unknown, but on June 2 he set sail from Le Havre on the *S.S. Paris* and arrived in New York on June 9. The following month, he set sail from Cherbourg on the *S.S. Empress of France* on July 24. Instead of New York he sailed into Quebec on July 31,[52] no doubt taking care of business at the Canadian trans-shipment point.

Though his résumé now read bootlegger, drug dealer and speakeasy proprietor, Diamond still wasn't above robbery. On December 21, 1926, a car was driving through Central

---

xiii Schultz was arrested as Arthur Funsfler

Park. At the wheel was Charles Haffman. In the passenger seat was Albert Levy, who claimed to be an insurance broker. In his pocket was $8,000. As Haffman pulled out of the park and entered 105th Street, a sedan containing four gunmen pulled up next to them and one of the men yelled, "Pull over there. We got you know." Haffman hit the gas and raced ahead. One of the men in the sedan fired two shots which smashed through Haffman's rear window. Glass fragments flew into Levy's head as bullets slammed into his left wrist and his right arm. After that, Haffman pulled over. The four men from the sedan ran up to Levy and tried to get his money, but he put up a fight. While Levy and the bandits tussled, a crowd began to gather, so the gunmen jumped back in their car and took off.[53]

In the hospital, Levy told the police he knew the men who had tried to rob him. Haffman also knew the men. Twenty detectives were sent out and soon Jack, Eddie, Thomas "Fats" Walsh and Charlie Luciano were under arrest. Two of the four (which two wasn't mentioned) were brought to the hospital so Levy could identify them. Once the insurance man was face to face with the gangsters, he got cold feet. "There's some mistake," he told the detectives. "They aren't the men."

Back at the station, the four hoodlums were questioned about another shooting and then released. On the way out, Luciano was issued a summons to appear in traffic court to answer for a charge of attempting to procure a fraudulent registration card, and Eddie was re-arrested for a hold-up from the previous week.[54]

There is obviously more to the Levy affair than simple robbery. The victim knew the assailants by name, and they in turn knew he was carrying eight grand. How this came to be is anyone's guess. By this time in their criminal careers, the Diamonds, Luciano and Walsh didn't need to resort to sticking up citizens, but a sure $2,000 apiece for a few minutes work was probably too hard to pass up.

✵ ✵ ✵

Nineteen Twenty-seven would prove to be an unhealthy year for the Diamond brothers. Around April, Eddie was diagnosed with pulmonary tuberculosis.[55] Having seen their mother consumed by the disease, one can only guess at what emotions the brothers felt. Jack's turn at the business end of a doctor's probe would come the following autumn.

By this time, Federal narcotic agents were aware of Rothstein's drug operation and started raiding shipments in New York and arresting Rothstein men. On July 9, 1927, Jack fell into the net but was able to put the fix in. Contemporary journalist Fred Pasley stated that, before Jack surrendered, a bribe was offered to the agent in charge William Mellin. According to Pasley, Fats Walsh approached the agent with twenty-five crisp, new $1,000 bills and said, "Listen, can't you lay off John? I'm working for Rothstein now, but I like John and I know John knows he can't get away, but he'd rather go in for anything than narcotics. Be reasonable; here's the $25,000." Mellin, Pasley continued, refused the bribe and so Fats called Jack and told him the news. After hanging up, Walsh told the agent, "All right. Jack's willing, but he don't want to be taken to New York. He's afraid of the New York cops. They always sock him on the chin."[56]

It was arranged for Jack to surrender in Mt. Vernon, where he was arraigned and then released on, depending on the source, between $10,000 and $25,000 bail courtesy of Arnold Rothstein. Much to the chagrin of many he would never be called to court for the charge.[xiv]

It has come down through time that Rothstein actually set Jack up for that arrest and then bailed him out to cover up any hint of involvement. Rothstein reportedly wanted to get rid of both Jack and Eddie, as they were hitting him up

---

xiv Five years later, after Diamond's death, New York Congressman Loring Black would declare that federal agents protected Jack from the state and city police. According to Black, Diamond knew that federal drug agents were looking for him and that the NYPD was after him as well. He arranged it so he would surrender to the Feds in Mt. Vernon, New York, if they would keep him away from the New York cops.

for large loans which they never repaid. This account seems unlikely, however. If Rothstein wanted to get rid of Jack, why would he set up an arrest only to bail him out? Why not let him face the music or, cheaper yet, just have him bumped off?

☆ ☆ ☆

At some point, Jack struck up a relationship with the Lower East Side's top gangster, Jacob "Little Augie" Orgen. They most likely met through Rothstein, who worked with Orgen in the labor rackets. Jacob Orgen was born in 1894 and was known throughout gangland as "Little Augie". He had been the leader of his own small band, known as "The Little Augies," since circa 1911 and had the distinction of being gang leader "Dopey" Benny Fein's official gun toter during the latter's reign.[xv] Little Augie's ascension up the gangster ladder was put on hold in 1919, when he was sent to jail for robbery. In his absence, another hoodlum, Nathan "Kid Dropper" Kaplan returned from Sing Sing and proceeded to become the Lower East Side's number one gang lord specializing in labor rackets.

When Little Augie was released from prison in the early 1920's, he reformed his gang and a war broke out between his forces and those of Kid Dropper. On August 1, 1923, a number of Orgen's men were loitering in front of a building on the Lower East Side when a sedan containing five of the Dropper's men pulled up and opened fire on the group. The "Little Augies" scattered, with the exception of William Weiss who was wounded in the leg. Unable to run away, he was subsequently arrested. A half hour after the shooting, one of Orgen's lieutenants, Jacob "Gurrah" Shapiro, was dropped off at the hospital with a bullet wound to his face. This attack would prove to be the demise of Kid Dropper.

---

xv After passage of the Sullivan Law, which made it illegal to carry a gun, most gang leaders took to having subordinates carry their pistols for them in case they were stopped by cops.

The shooting of Weissman and Shapiro gave the "Little Augies" the break they were looking for, and they hatched a plan for eliminating the Dropper once and for all. First Shapiro would break the gangster code of silence and rat out Kaplan as the man who shot him. This would result in the gang leader being forced to appear in court to face the charge. Once they knew where and when the Dropper was going to face Shapiro, it was feasible that they could knock him off. All they needed was someone willing to shoot him and face the music, as escape would be impossible. Little Augie found the right candidate in a hanger-on named Louis Cohen, who had aspirations of being a gangster.

On August 28, 1923, the Dropper was brought to the Essex Market Court to be identified by Shapiro. The police had received a tip that the Little Augies were going to try to kill the gang leader, so there were between twenty-five and thirty officers spread out around the court house to keep the public away. To prepare Cohen for his big mission, Little Augie got him all coked up, gave him a gun and filled his head with lies about how famous he would become if he pulled off the murder.

The Dropper and various gang members were ushered into the courthouse and placed in front of Shapiro for identification. Shapiro told the court that, on second thought, he really wasn't sure who shot him after all. A short time later, a smiling Kid Dropper emerged from the courthouse with his wife and two officers. They approached a waiting taxi, and one of the cops climbed in the left side of the cab while the Dropper got in on the right and began to slide over so the second cop could climb in beside him. Before the second cop was all the way in, Cohen slipped through the crowd and ran up to the back of the taxi. Standing on his tip toes, he began firing through the back window of the cab. When the smoke cleared, the Dropper had a couple of bullets in his lungs. He died en route to the hospital. Cohen was immediately captured and practically carried into the courthouse.

After the shooting, the police went through the crowd and arrested "Little Augie" and two of his henchmen. Cohen, however, insisted that he wasn't a member of any gang and had acted on his own accord. Taking the rap himself, Cohen was sent off to Sing Sing feeling like a big shot, while Orgen was released and became the top labor racketeer on the Lower East Side.

Toward the end of the decade, Orgen started to expand his horizons. Moving his family to the Upper West Side, he joined Diamond in bootlegging and drug dealing, leaving most of the labor racket management to his lieutenants Louis "Lepke" Buchalter and Jacob "Gurrah" Shapiro, who were getting ideas about who should be running the show. The trio began clashing on contracts. During one strike, manufacturers offered Little Augie $50,000 to bring the labor strife to an end, but Gurrah argued that they could make more money by prolonging it and hiring out strong arm men. Wanting the quick money, Orgen ended the strike. Although Shapiro disagreed with the settlement, he went along with it.

That September, Jack packed his bags and sailed out for the last time while in the Rothstein camp. Instead of Europe, however, he traveled to Cuba. Why he went can only be speculated, perhaps for drugs or more likely for booze, maybe both. What is known is that he sailed from Havana aboard the *SS Toloa* on September 15, 1927, arriving in New York three days later.[57] [xvi]

By the end of the summer, narcotic agents were on to Little Augie and began trailing him as well. The shoe leather was wasted, however, because their investigation was cut short by a bullet. A Brooklyn union came to Orgen for strong arm men to fight strike breakers and, instead of cutting Shapiro and Buchalter in on it, he told the union to use Jack Diamond's mob. His lieutenants caught wind of it, and Shapiro informed Orgen that it was "his" strike and that Diamond had no business being there anyway since his gang specialized

---

xvi The cruise back must have held a certain bit of nostalgia for Jack. The *Toloa* was the ship he sailed to France on during the war.

in silk and fur robberies. Orgen told Shapiro that for various reasons loft robberies had come to a standstill and that the Diamond gang needed to venture into new territories.[58] Why Orgen went against his own gang is unknown, but chances are his relationship with Diamond was quid pro quo and since Diamond cut him in on the narcotic and bootlegging business he handed over some labor work in return. Whatever the reason, Shapiro and Buchalter decided that Little Augie had gone too far and it was time for them to run the show.

Lepke and Gurrah were aware that their soon-to-be former boss had a rendezvous with Jack planned for Saturday, October 15, 1927, at eight o'clock at night. They also knew that the duo would be meeting on the Lower East Side at the corner of Delancey and Norfolk Streets so arranged to have a welcoming party on hand.

A little before eight o'clock, a dark sedan with a handful of guys pulled up a short distance from the designated intersection and waited. Jack and Augie arrived at the agreed upon time and exchanged greetings. They began to walk north toward Rivington Street while the driver of the sedan pulled out into traffic and slowly pulled up behind them. Three armed men emerged from the car and walked up behind the duo. One of the killers put his pistol to the back of Little Augie's head and sent a bullet through the gang leader's brain. At the sound of the blast, Diamond instinctively turned around, and one of the gunmen fired into his abdomen. This shot was meant to neutralize Jack, if they wanted him dead he would have been so. With their victims on the ground, the men lowered their guns to their sides, tilted their heads down and calmly walked back to the car, which whisked them to safety.

As the gun smoke was still clearing, Jack lifted himself off the sidewalk. A few feet away, face down in a spreading pool of blood, Little Augie lie motionless. Grabbing at his wound, Jack staggered past witnesses and stumbled six blocks to a nearby hospital. Twenty minutes elapsed before the police learned that a shooting had taken place and only then after a little boy walked into the police station and said, "They croaked Little Augie. He's laying up there in Norfolk Street now."[59]

Orgen's body was taken to the police station and laid on the floor while cops questioned pedestrians. Other than the fact that three, possibly four, men were involved, the police were unable to learn anything else about the shooting. Diamond was no help either, he was transferred to Bellevue Hospital, where police questioned him relentlessly. Jack kept to the gangster code and said nothing of value. Who did he think shot them? He didn't know anybody who would want to do him or Little Augie any harm. What did Little Augie want to meet him about? How should he know, they got shot before they had a chance to start talking.[60]

Though Diamond was no stranger to newspaper ink, it was Little Augie's death that gave him his first real moment in the spotlight. As brief as it was, he was now front-page news. He was also christened with two nicknames. One, "Big Boy," disappeared by the next news cycle, but the other one was perfect for headlines and would stick with him. It most likely played a part in his becoming one of, if not the most famous New York gangster of the Prohibition Era: *Legs.*

As his fame increased, different theories arose as to why Jack was called Legs. Some of those being, he was a good dancer, he was fast on his feet and could steal from pushcarts without fear of being caught and, less flatteringly, he always ran out on his friends. The truth is Jack probably was never called Legs, Eddie was. When Orgen was shot, all the papers reported that Eddie Diamond was Little Augie's bodyguard but, for some reason, was unavailable for duty that night so Jack was filling in for him. Detectives familiar with the brothers stated that the slender Eddie was known to the cops as Eddie Leggie. A reporter most likely shortened the name to Legs, which had a fine ring to it that any newspaper editor could appreciate, and ran with it not really caring a hoot whether it was accurate or not.[61]

Early Mug Shots

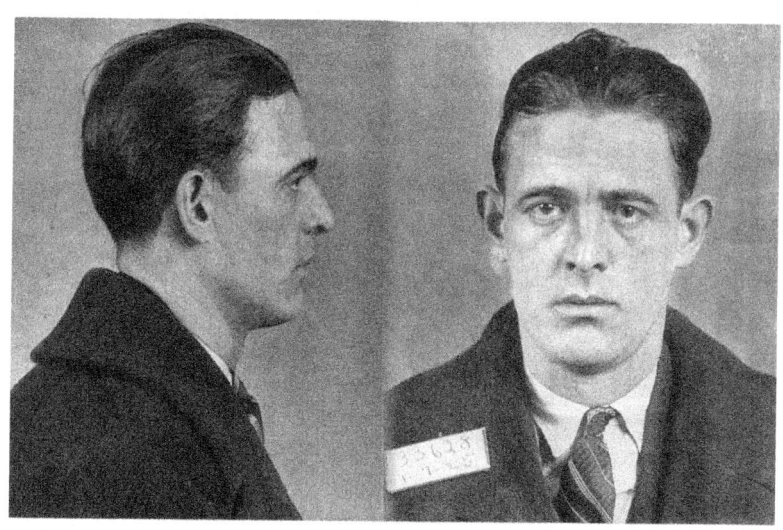

Arrested for the Levy robbery. L-R Eddie, Jack, Thomas "Fats" Walsh, Charles "Lucky" Luciano. (Library of Congress)

Arnold Rothstein (Harry Ransom Humanities Research Center, University of Texas at Austin)

3

DIAMONDS IN TROUBLE

Jack spent about two weeks in the hospital before being released to convalesce on his own. It appears that any animosity between him and Lepke and Shapiro was laid to rest with Little Augie, as there was no more trouble between them. Chances are he was finished with the labor rackets, but he still had some other irons in the fire.

Being a man of many endeavors, Jack needed a central location to conduct business and maintained Suite 1510 in the Paramount Building on Broadway, a stone's throw from Times Square. Though the name on the office door read, "Mackenzie Press Company," Jack was the tenant, and he paid $2,600 a year to be there. One flight down in 1408 was the "Kenton Importing Company," the front office for Jack's longtime pal Salvatore Arcidiaco.[62]

From this address, Jack managed his underworld activities, which now included drugs, bootlegging and kidnapping. For the latter, Jack and the boys liked to prey on crooked Wall Street brokers. They'd put the snatch on a guy and take him out of town and hold him until the ransom was paid.[63] Although he had his fingers in many underworld pies, it appears that he wasn't above his first calling, robbery, because that's what led to his next arrest, as well as another mention in the newspapers.

On January 31, 1928 a large sedan parked nearby the Gabbe & Bros. fur manufacturing plant in Brooklyn. Eight men slipped out of the car and took up positions in the shadows near the plant's entrance. After a while, a truck loaded with fifty-thousand dollars worth of leopard, silver fox and mole pelts pulled up to the plant. One of the men in the truck got out and rang the bell, while the driver remained inside the vehicle. As was custom, the night watchman, Herman Bermish, opened the door slightly and looked in both directions to make sure the coast was clear. Satisfied, he threw open the door, and the truck man began to carry in the first load of furs. Just as he passed over the threshold, five of the bandits sprung from the shadows and ran for the door. Bermish rushed to close it, but one of the bandits shot him and he dropped to the floor. The other three gunmen forced the driver out of the truck and took him to the garage next door for safe keeping, but he managed to run away. Next, three of the bandits jumped into the sedan and pulled out while their five confederates followed in the truck.

Before long, police were on their tail and the chase was on. Speeding down the streets, the cop car pulled up behind the truck and some officers opened fire. Realizing the futility of trying to out run the police car, the driver of the truck pulled over, and the five bandits abandoned their loot and jumped into the sedan and made their getaway. Bermish, who was thirty years old and engaged to be married the following month, died later that night from his wounds.[64]

Flipping through mug shots, witnesses were able to pick out two of the men who took part in the fur debacle. Police went searching for them at known haunts but then received word that the two men they were looking for could be found at the Paramount Building, in rooms 1510 and 1408. Detectives raided the offices at two o'clock in the afternoon of February 2 and found two guys, presumably Diamond and Arcidiaco. They were brought to the station house and the detectives returned and waited to see who else might show up at the offices. They didn't have to wait long. Gangster after gangster popped up at the suites and was brought down to the station. After each arrest, detectives would return to the Paramount Building and repeat the process. By nine o'clock that night, the

police had a total of fourteen known hoodlums in custody. In addition to Diamond and Arcidiaco, they also apprehended:
Salvatore Spitale, age given as 31;
Charles Entratta, 26;
Joseph Tedeceo, 37;
Max Kaplan, 35;
Frank Werner, 39;
Ben Marts, 21;
Charles Lagaeka, 33;
Sid Klein, 31;
Martin Barnet, 24;
Henry Jacobson, 28;
Herman Traeger, 30;
Ben Klein, 35;

Detectives declared that the arrests were some of the most important in months and that they would be able to link the gang to numerous robberies in Manhattan as well as Brooklyn. The gangsters were taken to police headquarters so they could appear in a lineup for the witnesses. While there the inspector in charge told Diamond, "Sooner or later, if you don't stop your criminal activities, you'll wind up like your former pal [Little Augie]."[65] If Jack had a response, it wasn't recorded. The inspector was wasting his breath anyway. Jack wasn't stopping his ways especially when, like every other arrest of the 1920s, nothing ever came of this one. Interestingly, this event took place three months after the Little Augie shooting and the name "Legs" still hadn't caught on yet. The press referred to him as either John or Johnny.

✦ ✦ ✦

Eddie Diamond's tuberculosis worsened in 1928, and he packed up the family and moved out west to Denver, Colorado, for the crisp mountain air. As will be seen, this wasn't simply a family venture to keep healthy. In addition to Kitty and little John, Eddie also was accompanied by a New York desperado named Dominick Bifano.

Jack remained in New York City. The fall of 1928 found him living in a suite of rooms at the Hotel Harding in the heart of Midtown Manhattan at Broadway and Fifty-Fourth Street. On October 5, a gangster known as Tony Marlow (real name Melillo), who lived next door to the Harding, was standing out front of the hotel smoking a cigarette when a casual acquaintance by the name of Bill White walked out and saw him. "Hello Tony," White said, offering his hand. Marlow took his hand and returned the greeting. While the two men were still gripping each other, two guys appeared from behind a parked car and shot Marlow five times. Still holding White's hand, Marlow fell to the sidewalk. A cop who was nearby heard the shots and turned to see the two gunmen hurry away. After a short chase, he lost them. Returning to the Harding, the police officer took Marlow to the hospital, where he refused to give any information on his assailants. "I'll take care of them myself when I get well," he told the police just before dying. After the shooting, Diamond vanished from his suite.

Since the police knew that Jack was living at the Hotel Harding, he was named as a suspect in the Marlow shooting. Whether or not he had anything to do with it is unknown, but he didn't bother turning himself in for questioning. He had other problems that needed settling. We are told that around this time, his relationship with Arnold Rothstein was falling apart. To make matters worse, just as Little Augie Orgen's lieutenants outgrew him, so too did Jack's former employee Dutch Schultz outgrow him in the Bronx. Together with his partner Joey Noe, Schultz began to squeeze Diamond out of the borough.

✳ ✳ ✳

Dutch Schultz was born Arthur Flegenheimer in Manhattan on August 6, 1901. Like Diamond, he lost a parent early on in life. The loss was not the result of disease or death, however. When Arthur was about eight years old, his father ran out on the family and his mother moved him and his sister to the Bronx, where she supported them with menial jobs like janitorial work and washing other people's laundry. Though he reportedly enjoyed school, Arthur dropped out after the sixth grade and took odd jobs to help support the family.

By the time he was seventeen, young Flegenheimer was hanging out with a delinquent named Marcel Poffo who, one year older than Arthur, was already a successful thief. Poffo is said to have taught Flegenheimer the tricks of the trade, but before his pupil could learn enough he was arrested for unlawful entry and sent to the penitentiary on Blackwell's Island for a short stay before being transferred to New Hampton Prison Farm. While at the farm, Arthur managed to escape. After a mere fifteen hours of freedom, he was captured and sent back to serve out a fifteen-month sentence. It was the only prison term he would ever serve.

Arthur returned home with a tough guy reputation. Since Arthur Flegenheimer is not a name that instills fear, he either was given or adopted the moniker of a turn of the century Bronx brute known as Dutch Schultz.

☆ ☆ ☆

At the dawn of Prohibition, Schultz went to work loading beer trucks for local bootleggers the Gass Brothers and by 1925 was working for Jack. As was mentioned, Diamond used his political connections to procure a Bronx deputy sheriff's badge for Schultz, which was repealed after the Dutchman was arrested in his boss's nightclub after the shooting on March 9, 1926.

As Jack recuperated from the Orgen shooting and spent more time in Manhattan, Schultz and Noe decided that they should work for themselves. Together they opened the Hub Social Club on Brook Avenue in the Bronx. They began importing beer from New Jersey brewers Frankie Dunn, Frenchy Dillon and William Culhane (all of whom would eventually be run out of the business by "Waxey" Gordon) before distilling their own suds.

Success came quickly for Noe and Schultz, and soon they were muscling former employers like the Gass Brothers out of business with a formidable mob of gunmen consisting of Bo Weinberg, Larry Carney, Bernard "Lulu" Rosenkrantz, Abe Landau, "Fats" McCarthy and the Coll Brothers, to name a few.

The duplicitous nature of Jack's character came out in his dealing with the Bronx gangsters. A deal had been made between the two parties where cash would be exchanged for territory and a meeting was scheduled for October 15 – the one year anniversary of the Orgen shooting - at seven in the morning at the Chateau Madrid on Fifty-Fourth Street.

Familiar with Diamond's treacherous nature, Schultz and Noe decided that it would be better if they split up. Noe, wearing a bullet proof vest, stayed outside the Chateau Madrid, while Schultz took a position in the second story window of a nearby building, which commanded a view of Fifty-Fourth Street. There may have been another gunman, possibly more, with Schultz. At the designated time that Jack was supposed to meet them, a blue Cadillac pulled up. As the Bronx duo had suspected, it was a double cross. As soon as the sedan came to a stop, Lower East Side hoodlum Louis Weinberg[xvii], a Diamond associate from the Little Augie days, jumped out and began firing at Noe. The Bronx bootlegger fell to the ground with a number of bullet wounds but managed to draw his pistol as Weinberg jumped back into the car.

As the Cadillac sped away, Noe and Schultz, and anyone else who may have been with the latter, fired at the car. Bullets from behind and above smashed into the Cadillac and one of them pierced Weinberg's neck under his left ear. With Weinberg bleeding to death in the back seat and bullets whizzing all around, the driver became unnerved and slammed into a truck, resulting in one of the Cadillac's doors being ripped off.

---

xvii Though called Louis Weinberg in the press his real name was Benjamin Greenberg

Regaining control of the car, the driver beat a hasty retreat back to the Lower East Side.

Noe was taken to Roosevelt Hospital where cops tried unsuccessfully to interrogate him. "I'll attend to this myself," he snarled turning his head away from his questioners. A half hour after the shooting, a guy pulled the blue Cadillac into a garage in East Thirteenth Street and asked the attendant to put a new door on it. Weinberg's body was in the back seat. "Pay no attention to that souse in the car," the driver told the attendant. "He's a good fellow, and I'll come back and drive him away."

Fifteen minutes later, the attendant received a call asking him to bring the car around the block. The attendant did so, but the caller wasn't there when he arrived, so he attempted to wake up Weinberg. Realizing that the souse was in fact a corpse, he called the cops. A search of the car turned up a handgun and, under the seat, a Thompson machine-gun wrapped in newspaper.

Examination of the car showed that five shots went through the back window. Those probably were fired by Noe. Others went through the car roof, lending credence to Schultz being in an upper window. Bullet holes in the rear door that was still attached to the car suggest a third gunman.

After Weinberg was identified, police returned to Noe and told him he was looking at a homicide charge if he lived. He told the cops that he acted in self-defense, as he thought he was about to be robbed. Noe was subsequently transferred to Bellevue Hospital and a rumor spread that rival gangsters were going to show up to finish the job. Guards were posted to his room to discourage any further bloodshed.[66] Knowing that the Dutchman would be striking back, Jack went into hiding.

✵ ✵ ✵

About a week after Noe was put on the spot, two guys checked into one of Denver's more affluent hotels. Though they claimed to be from Montreal, Canada, they were in fact from New York City. Despite their attempt to go unnoticed, the hotel staff would later say that the duo's comings and goings were a bit mysterious. The reason the two men didn't want to bring attention to themselves was because they were there to kill Eddie Diamond.

One of the killers was a gunman in the Schultz-Noe gang named Joseph Piteo and the other was a former model cum freelance gangster and sometimes employee of Arnold Rothstein named Gene Moran. In addition to riding shotgun on Rothstein's liquor trucks with the Diamond Brothers in the early 1920s, Moran also put in bodyguard duty the same as Jack. Moran, like Jack, also had his own criminal ventures on the side, one of which, stealing a quarter of million dollars in jewels from the wife of a millionaire, led to his second stay in Sing Sing. Considering his past working relationship with the Diamonds, Moran was no doubt there because he knew Eddie on sight and could put the finger on him.

In the three months that Eddie had been in Denver, he wasn't simply sitting in a sanatorium convalescing in the mountain air. He was living in a "fashionable" part of town with his wife and with the aforementioned Dominick Bifano. He had opened a boxing arena called the Olympic club and, with big brother Jack back East hip deep in dope and booze, it's likely there were some nefarious acts going on as well.

After a few days in town, Moran and Piteo rented three different apartments around the city and began to trail Eddie and study his daily routines. After trailing the younger Diamond for two weeks, the hit squad, actually containing three men, decided to make their move on the morning of November 5. [xviii]

---

xviii The third man was subsequently identified as another New York City gangster named Frank "Blubber" Devlin. How he became known as the third man is discussed in chapter 10.

Knowing the route that Eddie and Bifano took each morning to get home, the killers rented a Buick and parked on the corner of Eddie's street. The plan was to open fire on Diamond's Marmon when he and Bifano made the turn onto the street. Seeing Eddie's sedan approaching, the gunmen readied themselves. Eddie made the turn like he did every morning, but this time a half dozen bullets poured into his windshield. Miraculously, the bullets missed both men, although one hit the steering wheel causing Eddie to crash into the curb.

In a flash, Eddie and Bifano were out of the car and running for their lives. Bifano escaped between two houses, while Eddie ran up to the house nearest him. Three women and a toddler were standing at the door when a shot slammed into the house. "Let me in quick! They're after me," Eddie yelled as he pushed his way past the women and ran into the house. One of the gunmen ran up and, climbing the porch, saw that Eddie had run through the house and out the back door. Swearing, the killer took his frustrations out on the homeowner's dog and shot off one of its front paws. The gunmen then drove away and dumped the Buick.

Eddie and Bifano were arrested later that day when they returned to the scene. The police went to his house and took Kitty in for questioning. Inside the house, they found some pistols, rifles and ammunition for these, as well as some ammunition for machine-guns and shotguns. Eddie and Bifano (who gave the alias John Marino when arrested) were questioned overnight. "All I know is that Marino and myself were driving home when three men opened fire on us," Eddie told the police. "I did not recognize them and do not know why they would want to kill either of us." Both gangsters were then released.[67]

✳ ✳ ✳

A handful of hours prior to the attempt on Eddie's life, any troubles that the Diamond Brothers may have had with

Rothstein became moot. At twelve minutes after ten on the evening of November 4, A.R. was called to the phone at Lindy's restaurant. On the other end of the line was gambler George McManus. He was in Room 349 at the Park Central Hotel, just a short walk from Lindy's, and he wanted Rothstein to come over.

The previous September 8, McManus hosted a high stakes poker game with some out-of-town gamblers, and Rothstein attended. After nearly forty-eight hours of play, A.R. was out somewhere in the neighborhood of a quarter of a million dollars and, not having that kind of cash on hand, was handing out IOUs. None of the gamblers were worried about accepting Rothstein's markers, because they knew he was good for the money and had never welshed on a bet in the past, but as the days went by, A.R. kept putting off his payments. He said that he heard the game was rigged, but he likely was hoping that, if he stretched the wait out long enough, the players would willingly accept considerably less than what was actually owed them. He got greedy.

Of course this did not reflect well on McManus, who had hosted the game and whose obligation it was to see that the players received all monies due. It was bad enough that the other players weren't being paid off, but Rothstein was also saying that he heard the game was fixed, two things that could sink a gambler. With his reputation at stake, McManus got Tammany Hall big wig Jimmy Hines to go to bat for him and ask A.R. for the money. Rothstein told Hines that he would pay off when he was good and ready.

Handing his pistol to a sidekick, Rothstein left for the Park Central Hotel. He said he would be back in a few minutes. Chances are Rothstein probably thought that his waiting game had paid off and McManus was ready to settle on behalf of the other gamblers for a much smaller sum. That may have indeed been the case, but there was one factor A.R. wasn't counting on. McManus had been drinking and, as we learned from Polly Adler, he was an ugly drunk.

What was discussed between Rothstein and McManus is unknown. Perhaps A.R. called him a cheater, or perhaps McManus, a friend of the Diamond brothers, fueled by whiskey and fury, got into an argument with The Big Bankroll because of all the trouble he had put him through. Whatever the discussion, the result was that the drunken Irishman drew a handgun and fired a shot into A.R's belly.

McManus fled as Rothstein stumbled down the service stairs clenching his stomach. He was attempting to exit through the service entrance, when he was found by a hotel employee. He asked the employee to get him a cab, but instead the employee got the house detective. Though Rothstein continued to ask for a cab the detective called a cop, who then summoned an ambulance.

Adhering to the gangster code, Rothstein said nothing about who shot him. After lingering in a semi-conscious state for a few days, he died on November 6.

A search of Room 349 turned up many cigarette butts, two empty whiskey bottles and an overcoat with the name George McManus sewn into the lining. Subsequently, McManus was arrested for the shooting. No real evidence could be found against the well-connected gambler, and he was exonerated.

After a week and a half of living in fear, Eddie was able to breathe a sigh of relief when Denver police managed to capture his would-be assassins. Detectives uncovered the flats rented by the gunmen, one of which was at the Dresden Apartments. Three detectives were sent to check out the building and as they approached they saw Moran and Piteo sauntering out. The detectives hollered for the men to stop, and both went for their hip pockets. The officers had their guns out first, so the hoodlums took off in opposite directions. Moran ran between two apartment buildings and began to crawl into a basement window. Partially in, he changed his mind and crawled back out and ran down a nearby street where he was captured.

Piteo evaded his captors awhile longer. He managed to sneak undetected into the basement of a building, where a janitor was doing some work. He forced the janitor to change clothes with him and pretended to help him with his chores as reinforcements from the police department combed the neighborhood. Finally a contingent of officers came to the basement and knocked on the door. Piteo hid off to the side with his gun pointed at the janitor, while the latter told the detectives he hadn't seen anything. Sensing something was amiss, the law pushed the custodian aside and arrested the gangster without any trouble. With two of the gunmen under arrest, three detectives went back to the apartment and found an arsenal containing machine guns, an automatic rifle and two pistols. They stayed at the apartment for a while, hoping in vain that the third member of the murder party would show up.[68]

Back at the station, Moran gave his name as John Jackson and Piteo identified himself as James Nolan. The men were photographed and fingerprinted and the sets were sent off to New York City. Meanwhile, they were questioned about their arsenal. "Honest chief, we were going hunting. We were going to get our license tomorrow," they joked. The Denver police soon heard back from New York and learned the real identities of the gunmen. They showed Moran his dossier which read, "A racketeer of the worst type and has served jail sentences for the possession of explosives, carrying concealed weapons and grand larceny." When showed the telegram, Moran simply said, "It's a bum rap."

The fact that Piteo was a Schultz gun and Moran was a former associate of the Diamond's and employee of Arnold Rothstein raises a couple of interesting questions: After the Noe shooting, did Dutch Schultz and Arnold Rothstein unite to get rid of a common enemy and, since Legs was in hiding, they went after his brother? Or, if there was no Rothstein-Diamond feud, was Moran working freelance for Schultz? Since he knew the Diamonds from working with Rothstein, he would be able to identify Eddie on sight. Chances are that Schultz knew Moran as well. Later -in 1930- Schultz would admit to having known Gene's moll Anna Urbas. If he knew her, chances are he knew Gene.

Diamond was brought in to identify the two men who had tried to murder him. Both Moran and Piteo smiled at him while he nervously ran his fingers through his hair. "No, I don't know them," he told the police in a quivering voice, attempting to smile like his would-be assassins. "I've never seen them. Don't you see I'm nervous?" Police knew he was lying, but he was allowed to leave. Moran and Piteo, on the other hand, sat through numerous hours of questioning without showing any strain. The former chewed gum and smoked Turkish cigarettes, while the latter continually flicked dust, real or imaginary, from his shoes. Moran and Piteo were arraigned on November 24 and pleaded not guilty. Trial was set for December 17, and both were released on $5,000 bonds. Neither man stuck around Denver trying to clear his name. [69]

After more than a month in the hospital, Joey Noe succumbed to his wounds on November 21. About three weeks later on December 13, Bronx detectives received word that Noe's gang was gearing up for another hit on the Diamonds and raided what they referred to as the gang's headquarters, the speakeasy at 543 Brook Avenue. A handful of detectives stormed their way in, while another group waited outside. Standing at the bar were gang members John Jacoporo, Mike Basile and Joe Piteo freshly returned from Denver. Piteo later admitted that he was out on $5,000 bail for the Diamond shooting but insisted that he went to Colorado for a vacation not to bump off Eddie. The trio was arrested, and then the detectives made their way upstairs to the two-room apartment above the speakeasy. The rooms were sparsely furnished, containing only a table, a chair, three telephones and a safe. There they found another gang member named James Rose and made him open the safe. Inside were two handguns. A further search of the two rooms turned up fifteen hundred rounds of ammo for the pistols, five hundred shotgun shells and the drum to a Thompson machine gun.

As the detectives were discovering the arsenal inside, outside a sedan containing Schultz gang members James Russo, Dominic Dorelli and Charles Weisberg pulled up. When the occupants realized that the men loitering out front were detectives, they quickly pulled away. The detectives jumped into their car and caught the fleeing gangsters after a short pursuit. In the meantime twenty-year-old gang member Vincent Coll walked up to the speakeasy and, realizing a raid was in progress, stepped into a nearby doorway. When the sedan containing the detectives and their captives returned, Coll recognized Russo, Dorelli and Weisberg and tried to save his pals and their apparent companions from arrest. Approaching the car, Coll said, "Blow. The cops are here." The response was a pistol barrel pointed at him. "We sure are," a detective snapped. "Stick 'em up." Coll joined his seven confederates and was taken to the Morrisania station for booking.

Nineteen twenty-eight ended with Eddie back in New York. Seeing that the Big Apple wasn't safe for either of them, the brothers headed upstate. Jack scouted out the Catskill region and found a house in the hamlet of Acra near the town of Cairo. There are reports that he learned about this area from his old pal Salvatore Spitale, whose brother ran an inn in the area. Not only would the house be a safe haven but the mountain air would be healthier for Eddie. Calling themselves, Thomas and Alice Schiffer, Jack and Alice deposited some money in the Cairo bank in mid-December. On the twenty-eighth of the month, the house was purchased in Alice's name.[70]

On January 8, 1929, less than two weeks after Jack and his wife bought the house, Eddie went up to Saranac Lake, a town in the Adirondack Mountains that specialized in treating those suffering from tuberculosis and was put under the care of Dr. Francis Trudeau, one of the top physicians in his field. Though Jack bought the house in Acra for Eddie, his younger brother's stay there would be short-lived. Sometime around May, he made a permanent move up to Saranac Lake, taking up residence in the "cure cottage" at No. 6 Shepard Avenue.[71]

Jack decided to keep the house. Contemporary reports describe it as green with a red roof situated on little over half an acre of secluded land off of Route 23. Trees dotted the property and there was a small stream snaking through the back yard. Visitors had to travel up a drive way to get to the two-story abode. For security, Jack had two spotlights set up to illuminate the front yard and driveway. The bases of the trees were painted white so, in the event of attack, invaders wouldn't be able to use them as camouflage. One would stick out like a sore thumb standing next to a white tree in the glare of the spot lights. Two to three watchdogs also roamed the grounds.[72]

Behind the front door was the living room richly furnished with overstuffed chairs, ornate floor lamps and plush Turkish rugs. The walls were draped with dark red tapestries, and Alice adorned the chairs and sofa with fancy pillows and dolls that had squiggly arms and legs. One could extinguish a cigar or cigarette in one of the onyx ashtrays placed about the room. At the rear of the living room was a den. Across the hallway to the left was the dining room. The rear of the dining room let into the kitchen, which was stocked with every modern convenience and electrical appliance available. The *pièce de résistance* of the abode was a hidden stairwell inside a closet that led to the second story.

Upstairs were the bedrooms. Whether he was at home, a hotel or a rooming house, Jack always had his own bedroom. He generally slept separate from his women. At the house in Acra, his was the master bedroom facing the road. Painted in pink and orchid, it had a double-bed, a wardrobe, chest of drawers and four chairs of walnut. Alice's boudoir was next door and consisted of two twin-beds. Across the hall were two guest rooms, a room used for storage and the bathroom. In addition to the house there was a stand-alone garage and a separate one-room structure where Jack's men played cards and shot pool.[73]

As for Jack's true identity there were, undoubtedly, some locals in the know, but the average citizen believed that the affluent man who lived in the big house was Thomas Schiffer, real estate broker.[74]

A few weeks after moving to Acra, Jack brought some attention to himself when he got drunk and crashed his car. A local guy pulled him from the wreck, and Jack ended up in the jail at Catskill, a place that would become quite familiar in a couple years. He paid a fine and that was that.[75]

Drunk-driving aside, Jack was well received in his new home and one of the reasons was his tendency to spread his money around, putting plenty of local carpenters, plumbers and other handymen to work on his house. In addition to patronizing the local businesses, there are also examples of Jack opening his wallet for the greater good of his neighbors. He put up the lion's share of money that helped build Acra's church. A local woman who lost all her clothing in a fire found herself the recipient of a $100 charge account at a local department store, and some farmers with money troubles received some financial support that allowed them to keep their farms.[76]

✲ ✲ ✲

Two of Jack's hangouts in his new environment were the Aratoga Inn, a two-story roadhouse with a large bar and dining area as well as eight bedrooms for let on the second level. The Aratoga was owned by a guy named Jimmy Wynne, who would become good friends with Jack. Another watering hole of Jack's was the Hollywood Inn run by Paul Quattrocchi. Like Jack, Quattrocchi was a New York City transplant, having grown up on East 113th Street.

In April of 1929, one of Jack's gunmen, Peter Felice, moved into the Hollywood Inn while hiding out from the New York City police. Felice was a full-bodied brute carrying 238 pounds on a five-foot-seven frame. A career criminal, he was arrested at the age of thirteen for larceny and sent to the Catholic Protectory. He was sent to Elmira at the age of twenty for burglary, paroled and sent back in 1926 after being arrested for assault and robbery. According to police, on November 18, 1928, Felice got into a fight with a guy named Angelo Molicco and stabbed him to death and fled the city. He managed to dodge detectives until autumn of 1929, when detectives caught him at the Hollywood on October 20.[77]

Unlike Al Capone, Jack didn't have a standing army of gunmen ready to do his bidding, but he did have muscle. Jack's bodyguard and chief enforcer was a Brooklyn goon who went by the name of Gerry Scaccio. Born in Italy on January 25, 1901, Scaccio's real name was William Talomo. His family immigrated to the United States in 1905, settling in Brooklyn. Like Jack, Scaccio lost his mother when he was about nine years old. Also like Jack, Scaccio did a stretch in the reformatory for unlawful entry. This was followed in 1925 by a trip up the river to Sing Sing after being convicted of grand larceny in the first degree.[78] Another guy associated with Diamond, although the link wouldn't be known until both were dead, was a guy named Lefty Joe Burke. Jack and Lefty were confederates for ten years and when Jack began to operate upstate Lefty was part of the team.

Rounding out Jack's inner circle were James Dalton and Harry "Skunky" Klein. The former was Jack's chauffer and guy Friday. The latter, another New York City transplant, was the gang's gopher. Both stayed with Jack. Jack's cousin Jimmy Hart also spent time at the house as did a host of other guys.

Jack also became close with another bootlegger who was making a name for himself in Brooklyn. Where and how

Jack met Charles "Vannie" Higgins is unknown. Vannie's rise in the underworld is an enigma, though Owney Madden took credit for getting him started in bootlegging in 1926. Even though Higgins had a police record dating back to 1915, with the exception of a few shootings in the late 1920s, he managed to fly under the radar until he became famous in late 1930, early 1931. By that time, he was sarcastically referred to as the Police Chief of Long Beach, Long Island, because he was able to land all his liquor there with police escort. "I owned the whole department,"[79] Vannie told the press while leaving a courtroom after being exonerated for rum running. Newspaper reports stated that he gained his wealth through his speedboats. Bootleggers would bring shipments to within a few miles of shore, and his boats would go out and deliver them the rest of the way. He started out with one boat then, when the money started to come in, he expanded the Higgins Navy. Some of those he did business with were Diamond and Salvatore Spitale. As will be seen, it appears that the relationship between Jack and Vannie constituted more than just bootlegging.

✵ ✵ ✵

Though Jack enjoyed playing the country squire, his business was in Manhattan. It appears that over the course of the winter of 1929 a peace was made between him and Dutch Schultz. That spring Jack resurfaced in New York City to turn himself in for questioning about the Tony Marlow killing.[xix]

On May 20, Jack sauntered into the District Attorney's office and said, "I hear you want me. Why waste your time looking for me; here I am." The D.A. was a bit confused, as it was news to him that the gangster was wanted, but he took

---

xix It's interesting to speculate on how a peace was brokered between the two. Did they work it out themselves or did the local pols and somebody with much underworld power like Owney Madden dictate that shooting up midtown Manhattan was bad business for everyone?

Diamond's word for it, called police headquarters and told them to come and get him. Jack was taken back to HQ for pictures and then shuttled up to the Forty-Seventh Street Station where he was charged with, "acting in concert with another in the shooting and killing of Tony Marlow."[80] Jack admitted that he had a room at the Hotel Harding at the time of the shooting but denied having anything to do with the murder. He went so far as to say, "Marlow was only a beer loader, and I wouldn't bother with a mug like him."[81] In all, Jack spent four nights in jail during the investigation and was exonerated after both the cop who chased the gunmen and Bill White, the guy shaking Marlow's hand when he was gunned down, failed to recognize him.

With no threat from Schultz or the police to keep him in hiding, Jack was free to cater to his enterprises. One of which was running his Mid-town Manhattan speakeasy, the Hotsy-Totsy Club.

Jacob "Little Augie" Orgen (Harry Ransom Humanities
Research Center University of Texas at Austin

Arthur Flegenheimer AKA Dutch Schultz (Library of Congress)

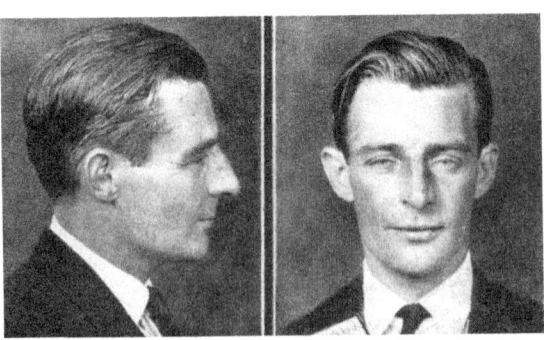

Eugene Moran was a former Rothstein bodyguard sent to Denver to kill
Eddie Diamond. (Mario Gomes collection)

4

EVERYTHING IS HOTSY-TOTSY NOW

July 13, 1929, daybreak was only a few hours away and the Hotsy-Totsy club was still jumping. The speakeasy was located in the heart of Manhattan on the second floor of 1721 Broadway, between Fifty-Fourth and Fifty-Fifth Streets. On the books, the owner of the club was Henry Boeckel. Off the books, he had a partner, Legs Diamond. It's possible that Legs' pal Charlie Entratta also had a piece of it. Either way, he was there that morning as was Diamond. The Hotsy-Totsy was an exclusive club in that one had to be invited to gain entrance.[82] As such, it was a watering hole for sports figures, newspaper reporters, celebrities and of course other gangsters. There were also some house rules to help deter trouble;

1) The girl you brought was the girl you left with.
2) No talking to another guy's girl.
3) No taking another guys girl.[83]

The talk along the Great White Way at that time was the gangland killing of gangster Frankie Marlow[xx], no stranger to the Broadway set, who had been bumped off less than three weeks before on June 24. He had been eating at a restaurant a few blocks away on Fifty-Second Street when he received a phone call and left the premises. He was last seen getting into a car at Fifty-Second and Broadway. Three quarters of an hour later, he was found in Queens with bullets in his head

---

xx Frankie Marlow's real name was Gandolfo Curto and was no relation to Tony Marlow

and neck. His funeral cortege contained a floral offering from Jack and Eddie.

Now, two blocks north of where Marlow took his last ride, between forty and fifty revelers were drinking, dancing and, probably more than few, discussing the status of the yet unsolved murder case. Business was such that Legs even took a turn behind the bar serving up drinks. Stunts like this were no doubt good for business. If word spread that a trip to the Hotsy-Totsy might result in the semi-famous Legs Diamond drawing your beer, those legitimate people who liked to rub elbows with gangsters would surely seek an invitation.

Among those delivering the drinks Legs was preparing for the patrons that night were Tony Merola, a singing waiter who also played the violin; William Wolgast, who had been arrested seven years earlier for being a rum runner; and a young guy from the Bronx named Tommy Ribler. Also on hand was the club's entertainment manager Hymie Cohen. Patrons imbibing Diamond's liquor included a young boxer named Ruby Goldstein, who had lost a fight earlier that evening, and his friend Nathaniel Jarvis. It was just another fun Roaring Twenties evening at the Hotsy-Totsy Club, but then the Cassidy Brothers showed up.

History recalls the Cassidy brothers, William or "Red" as he was known, age twenty-eight, and Peter, said to be thirty, as a couple of low-level waterfront thugs from Manhattan's West Side who were quick to use their fist. Though Peter fits that bill, his brother was a bit more. In fact, Red, who, by this time had moved out of the city to Long Beach, Long Island (described at the time as the Riviera of the East[84]), with his wife and two-year old daughter, owned his own speakeasy and was said to be an owner in a West Side brewery along with Owney Madden and Big Frenchy DeMange. As such, he no doubt had some sort of acquaintance with Diamond and Entratta.

The Hotsy-Totsy wasn't the Cassidy Brothers' first stop of the evening. Peter would subsequently say that prior to their getting there they had "plenty of drinks of gin in ten or twenty places."[85] They arrived sometime between two and three-thirty in the morning. In tow were about four or five of their friends. At some point, they joined Entratta, Ruby Goldstein and Jarvis at a table. Also present was a twenty-five-year-old ex-con named Simon Walker who had recently been released from Sing Sing after serving a sentence for robbery.[xxi] Though it can't be guaranteed, he was most likely a member of the Cassidy party. Red Cassidy and Goldstein were discussing that night's boxing match when Peter, inebriated and looking for trouble, began to insult Goldstein. Words went back and forth, and as voices rose, it was obvious that there was going to be a fight. As proprietor, Diamond most likely inserted himself into the fracas, if he wasn't already part of it. In an attempt to draw attention away from the argument, Hymie Cohen went to the band and told them to play louder. A few minutes later, approximately three-forty-five, gunshots were reverberating throughout the club, and everyone inside rushed for the exit.

In a matter of seconds, Walker lay dead in front of the bar with bullet wounds to the head. William Cassidy, three bullets in his back, was being hauled to the exit stairway by Peter and two other pals. Peter was then either smacked across the head with a pistol or grazed by a bullet and tumbled down the stairway leading to the front door. Red's two friends managed to get him down the stairs and rush him to the hospital, leaving Peter to his fate.

Police arrived on the scene and found Peter crumpled up in the stairwell unconscious. Upstairs they found Walker in front of the bar, his hand on a pistol that he never managed to fully draw out of his pocket. They caught up with Red at the hospital and questioned him in his final moments of lucidity. Instead of answers, they received only curses before he expired.

☆ ☆ ☆

Right away rumors began to circulate that the killings were a follow up to the Frankie Marlow murder or that they were a result of a fight over beer routes. Police Commissioner

---

xxi Though he went by Simon his real name was Harry.

Whalen was quick to say that it was simply a "drunken brawl"[86] and nothing more. The police managed to round up a couple dozen of the patrons who were at the Hotsy-Totsy at the time of the murders as well as some of the staff and began to piece together what happened. Singing waiter Tony Merola was arrested and held as a material witness. Diamond and Entratta were thought to have left the city immediately. This seems unlikely as there were some loose ends that needed to be taken care of, namely eliminating any of the Hotsy-Totsy staff that could corroborate anything that Merola might say that would put them in the electric chair.

Though his name never appeared in the press, it seems that the first one to go was the waiter Tommy Ribler. His mother and brother were interviewed by the district attorney's office eight months following the killings, when the police were trying to build a case against Diamond. Mrs. Ribler stated that every morning after work Tommy came home, had breakfast and went to sleep. On the morning of the Thirteenth, however, he came home about five o'clock, changed his clothes and told her that he was going to the baths. She never saw or heard from him again. His brother stated that someone had told him that they had an acquaintance who heard in a speakeasy that his brother "had been bumped off".[87]

While the police continued with their investigation, gangland bid farewell to William "Red" Cassidy on July 16. Any lingering doubts about whether he was simply a waterfront troglodyte or a successful bootlegger were laid to rest with him. Those wanting to pay their last respects to the beer magnate found him reposing at his mother's house in a $5,000 bronze coffin with silver trim. When it was time for the funeral, the fallen gangster was loaded into a white hearse and taken to his local church where a High Requiem Mass was held in his honor. The services complete, the hearse then transported Cassidy's remains to Brooklyn's Calvary Cemetery with fifty carloads of mourners in tow. Another eleven cars transported the floral tributes. Three more cars full of flowers remained at Ma Cassidy's house.[88]

Three days after Red Cassidy was buried, Police Commissioner Whalen announced that Diamond and Entratta had been indicted for the murders. Whalen said that detectives had built a strong case against the duo, adding, "I regard these as two very important indictments against two very notorious gunmen and racketeers. They [the indictments] will serve as a message to gangdom that the police will give them no quarter."[89] He also stated that the police were searching for the Hotsy-Totsy's entertainment manager Hymie Cohen, whom they wanted as a material witness.

While Police Commissioner Whalen was making his statements to the press, across the river a body was being taken to the morgue in New Brunswick, New Jersey. Earlier in the day, three guys were walking to work on the Bordentown Turnpike between the towns of Old Bridge and South Amboy when they came upon the corpse. He had been perforated by nine bullet holes, leading authorities to believe that he had been machine gunned. Fingerprints showed that his name was William Wolgast. The police were now down two witnesses. It would eventually be three, because Hymie Cohen, like Tommy Ribler, was never seen nor heard from again.

After a week had passed without any arrests, the NYPD turned up the heat on the underworld. Even though authorities believed Diamond and Entratta were out of town, they raided a total of thirty-three speakeasies and gambling joints in the Midtown area, arresting eighty-seven people while supposedly searching for their quarry. This disruption of business no doubt caused some animosity toward Entratta and Diamond from their underworld counterparts who were losing money.

Not until the last day of the month did the police get the idea to check Jack's house in Acra. With the assistance of some New York State Troopers, detectives made their way past three watchdogs and entered the house. Inside they found Jack's chauffer James Dalton, gang member Harry "Skunky" Klein and another guy named John Herring. They confiscated four rifles and some ammunition and also found some booze that the trio had been drinking. The three men were arrested for possession of the alcohol and sent to the jail at Kingston. All were questioned as to Jack's whereabouts but revealed nothing of value.[90]

☆ ☆ ☆

Less than two weeks later on the evening of August 10, 1929, Gene Moran was pacing around his bungalow in Brielle, New Jersey. He and some others had a score that night, and they were running behind schedule. His moll Anna Urbas sat by, as he smoked his cigarettes wondering where the rest of his crew was. At eight o'clock, two cars pulled up, one contained two men, the other three. Anna saw Gene to the door and watched him get into one of the cars. "We had better hurry up or we'll be too late for the job," she heard her boyfriend say as the cars began to leave.

Two hours later, the night watchman at the Newark, New Jersey, city dump saw two sedans pull in. One, containing two men, stayed by the entrance, while the other one, a Packard, pulled up behind a billboard. The guard knew the men weren't there to garbage pick. Without giving himself away, he crept up to sneak a peek at what they were doing. Two men, each carrying two gas cans, jumped out of the Packard and began dousing the car, inside and out, with petrol. They tipped the fourth can over so that the contents flowed under the car. One of them then struck a match and tossed it on the spilled gas. Flames shot up as the two men jumped into the remaining car and beat it. Wondering why guys would want to torch a perfectly good Packard, the night watchman approached the blaze and saw two human feet inside the inferno. By the time the fire department got there, the corpse was charred beyond recognition. The only clues left for identification purposes were the corpse's teeth and a key found on the body.

At one o'clock in the morning, Anna heard a car pulling into the driveway. Assuming Gene was back from his caper, she went to the door, where she was greeted by two of the guys he had left with. They informed Anna that her boyfriend was dead and that she had better leave town. Anna packed her things and headed to her mother's place in West Virginia. Before leaving town, however, she stopped on Manhattan's West Side to tell Eugene's father what had happened.[91]

☆ ☆ ☆

Back in Manhattan, the authorities were half-right when they said that Legs and Charlie Entratta left town. The latter and his wife Anna went on a mini-tour of New York State. First, they hit the Catskills and from there went to Albany. After that, it was Kingston and then Binghamton. Detectives arrived in Binghamton shortly after the couple departed and learned that they were heading for Chicago.

The investigation continued in the Windy City, where police learned that associates of Charlie's in New York City were going to wire him $1,500. On August 24, police staked out the telegraph office and arrested Charlie and Anna when they entered.

Anna would have been hard to miss. It was the dog days of summer, and she was wearing a silk wrap with a fox scarf. Just in case people didn't catch on that she had money, she also decorated herself with $20,000 worth of jewelry. She completed her outfit with two dogs on a leash. Charlie was the opposite. During questioning, he asked if he could send out for some smokes. Given permission, he let it be known that he only had a buck on him. The cops laughed at him for being broke but, not one to let her man look foolish, Anna opened her purse and flashed a roll of $1,200 and gladly offered to pay.

Entratta considered fighting extradition back to the Big Apple saying, "I don't want to go back to New York now. It's hot for me there. An election's coming on and the gangsters have got to go. I'd rather stay here."[92] Anna told him it would probably be best to go back and face the music. "Well give me until tomorrow so I can telephone my lawyer. He used to be district attorney in New York. Then probably I'll go back. Maybe."[93]

Two days later Charlie was in NYPD custody denying that he was even in the Hotsy-Totsy the night of the murders. As for being a friend and partner of Legs Diamond, he said that he only had a "nodding" acquaintance with the man. The next day, he was arraigned and charged with first-degree murder. He pleaded not guilty. In a police lineup, he was asked his occupation. "I'm a salesman,"[94] he said. When asked when he last worked at that job, he replied with, "I'll speak about that when my trial comes."[95] He was then whisked off to the Tombs to await his day in court.

The good news for Entratta was that, while this was taking place, the prosecutor's main witness, singing waiter Tony Merola, who had already spent more than a month in the Tombs, was starting to go a little batty. No doubt aware of what happened to Wolgast, Cohen and Ribler, he began to suffer "psychosis" and was sent to Bellevue Hospital.

With one of the killers in custody, the heat was on to find Jack. In an attempt to smoke him out, Police Commissioner Whalen went to the federal court and persuaded them to call Diamond to trial for the old narcotics rap from 1927. If Jack failed to appear, he would forfeit his $15,000 bail and be a fugitive. The court agreed, and the date was set for September 3. When the day came, Jack of course did not show up for the proceedings and so was declared a fugitive. The fifteen grand was forfeited but, since it was posted by Arnold Rothstein who had been dead for ten months and may have caused the arrest in the first place, Jack probably didn't lose too much sleep over it.

✧ ✧ ✧

So where was Jack hiding? Chances are he moved around a lot. After three months of dead ends, some detectives decided that his pal Charlie Luciano might know where he was hiding so paid him a visit on the evening of October 16. That night, Luciano went to a house that he owned in the Bronx and pulled his car into the garage. As he was pulling down the garage door, a couple of big detectives grabbed him and threw him up against the door and frisked him. "I was pretty sure they was cops the minute I saw them," he would tell a narcotics agent over a quarter century later, adding, "Then a car with two more guys pulls up to the curb. Each one of 'em takes hold of an arm and they hustle me to their car, throw me in face down in back and walk all over me getting into the back seat."[96]

Once inside the car, Luciano had his hands tied behind his back and tape placed over his eyes. The detectives started beating and kicking him, demanding that he tell them where Jack was hiding. Luciano said that he hadn't seen his former pal in over a year. The cops didn't believe him and worked him over some more. This went on for a number of hours before the detectives decided that they weren't going to get anything out of him. The ride concluded with a ferry trip to Staten Island, where they dumped the semi-conscious gangster on Huguenot Beach at about two o'clock on the morning of the Seventeenth.[97]

Assuming he was somewhere in New Jersey, Luciano gathered his senses and walked for about a mile before being approached by a cop. Hoping to avoid any unwanted attention, Luciano asked the officer to get him a taxi: "I'll give you fifty bucks if you do and let me go on my way."[98] The patrolman declined the bribe, brought him to the hospital and alerted the authorities. When questioned, Luciano said that he was at Fiftieth Street and Sixth Avenue the previous evening, when a limousine pulled up and three guys made him get in at gunpoint. The following day, the newspapers carried a story about Charlie surviving a one-way ride. In the years to come, this fraudulent newspaper tale would lead to one of the biggest myths regarding Luciano, that the nickname "Lucky" was tagged on him after he miraculously survived being taken for a ride by rival mobsters.

So, did Luciano actually know where Jack was at when the detectives were applying a black jack to the side of his head? "Hell, he was right there in my house when they put me against the garage."[99]

✵ ✵ ✵

Though in the final stages of consumption Eddie checked out of the sanatorium and returned to New York City to help run things for Jack while he stayed out of site. This was short term however, as Eddie's tuberculosis got the better of him and he returned to Saranac, New York, for his final battle. Dr. Trudeau checked in on Eddie for the last time on January 14, 1930. At around ten o'clock that night, Eddie died.[100]

The police were hopeful that Eddie's demise would be their big break. Everyone knew that the only person Jack really cared about was his brother and that it would be hard for him to pass up a last chance to say goodbye. Likewise, Jack knew that the detectives would be using Eddie's death to get him. There were two New York detectives stationed in Saranac keeping their eye on Eddie for months, so he wouldn't be able to go up to deal with the situation. Instead he sent his bootlegging buddy Charles "Vannie" Higgins to take care of things. Higgins arrived and supplied the necessary personal information for the death certificate and made the arrangements for Eddie's body to be returned to New York City.[101][xxii]

Having no luck in Saranac, detectives thought they might nab Jack at the mortuary in New York City, but according to

---

xxii The reason Higgins went and not Kitty can only be guessed. Maybe she was too distraught. The most interesting aspect of this is that it shows that Diamond and Higgins were apparently very close and not simply in the business sense. It would seem that the relationship must have been ongoing for some time if Higgins stepped up for this important responsibility. Another possibility is that Higgins wasn't sent but was already there. The *Brooklyn Daily Eagle* stated that when Eddie died he was surrounded by New York gunmen who made sure nobody came near him.

the *New York Evening Journal*, Legs outwitted the police by switching funeral homes at the last moment. They reported that a number of detectives were waiting at the West Side funeral parlor that they believed Eddie was being sent to while instead the body was delivered to one on the East Side. The *Journal* also stated that by time the coffin arrived, Legs had already said his goodbyes.

Whether or not the *Journal* story was legit, detectives took another stab at finding Jack by staking out Eddie and Kitty's West Ninety-Third Street apartment, where the gangster was laid out prior to his funeral. There they eyeballed a steady stream of visitors coming to pay their respects. Inside the flat, the mourners got to see Eddie in his casket lit by a candelabrum containing four candles. Flanking the coffin were the floral tributes which included two giant arrangements, one of which read "My Pal" and the other "9:30", denoting (so the purchaser believed) the time of Eddie's death. Jack didn't show up.

Still hoping that Eddie's distraught brother would try to sneak in a final goodbye, twelve detectives followed the twenty-eight-car funeral cortege to the cemetery. Thinking that Jack might try to show up dressed as a woman, the detectives went up to each lady wearing a mourning veil and peeked under it, each time apologizing for their intrusion. The service went on and, as Eddie was lowered into the ground, Kitty grabbed little John's hand, let out a scream and passed out. Some of those gathered there carried her back to her car and that was that. If Jack managed to show up, nobody was any the wiser.

☆ ☆ ☆

One of those who surely didn't show up for Eddie's funeral was Charles Entratta. He was still in the Tombs awaiting trial and none too happy about it, as was learned from a wiretap placed on his home phone. Authorities listened in on a call between Anna and one of Charlie's lawyers named Leavenworth. A memorandum dated January 28, 1930, contains a transcript of a call placed at nine-thirty that evening.

Anna:	Is Mr. Leavenworth there?
Leavenworth:	Hello.
Anna:	Hello. How are you?
Leavenworth:	Pretty Good. I was down to court when they were getting the panel. I have all the names and I also went down to see Charlie this morning and he is very crabby, fighting all the time, and this afternoon I received a rotten letter from him. I don't know what to do.
Anna:	Well, it is getting near the time now, don't mind him.
Leavenworth:	He gave me an address of the party that took those fellows to the hospital but it was a wrong address. I have the right one now. I am going to have a friend of his go and see him tomorrow.
Anna:	How many witnesses have they that saw it?
Leavenworth:	Two. The nut (Merola) and the other one.[xxiii] But we have a statement from the other fellow saying he was forced to make a statement. I want you to bring his mother and father there as there will probably be some Jews on the jury and it will help a lot. Also have some of the boys there in case we might want to send them out in a hurry. Have him dress in a dark suit and a dark tie.
Anna:	Will I send him down some other ties? He asked for six.
Leavenworth:	No, one dark conservative tie is enough. He don't want to dress to flashily before the Jury.
Anna:	Charlie is sure getting a rotten deal from those good friends of his. None of them are doing a thing for him.

---

xxiii Who "the other one" was is unknown.

Leavenworth:	Did you hear from Owney again?
Anna:	No but he is going to call me this week. Charlie told me to tell him I was going to sell my bracelet to pay you some money. You know Owney won't let me do that, so if he ask you, just say that you asked Charlie to get some money.
Leavenworth:	Where are you home?
Anna:	Yes.
Leavenworth:	Don't say too much over the phone.
Anna:	Don't worry I won't. I will call you tomorrow.[102]

Though it was a short call it contained some pretty interesting statements. For instance we learn that Entratta (and, more than likely, Jack) was close enough to Owney Madden that he would put up money for his defense instead of letting Anna sell her jewelry, whereas Jack and the rest of his inner circle weren't doing a damn thing for Entratta. Another telling statement is that Entratta somehow obtained the address of the friend of Red Cassidy who took him to the hospital and that the lawyer was going to send out one of Entratta's friends to talk to him. It doesn't take a stretch of the imagination to figure Entratta's friend was also a gangster and the talk they would have would boil down to lie or die.

About a week later on February 5, Entratta's trial started. The prosecution linked him with the murder in its opening statement but failed to produce any witnesses who would say that they saw Entratta fire a gun. Any angst Charlie may have had preceding the hearing melted away, as witness after witness who took the stand couldn't say who did the shooting. In fact, everyone blamed the fracas on the dead guys. All witnesses agreed that Peter Cassidy had insulted the boxer, Ruby Goldstein, and that Simon Walker took offense and went for his gun, leading Red Cassidy to go for him. After that, nobody saw anything. No one could explain how Red ended up with three shots in his back or how Walker ended up with a bullet through the head before he got his gun out. Even Peter

Cassidy couldn't shed any light on his brother's murder or how he ended up at the bottom of the stairwell with a head wound. He claimed to have little recollection of the events.

After three days, no witnesses fingered Entratta as a gunman, so the Judge ordered him acquitted. Charlie's joy was short lived, however. Before he made it out of court, a detective popped up and informed him he had violated his parole from 1923 and would be heading back to Sing Sing to serve the remaining eleven years of his sentence for robbery.

✲ ✲ ✲

On February 12, a few days after Entratta's acquittal, the New Jersey police received a phone call regarding the torched Packard from the previous summer. The tipster said that the charred corpse was Eugene Moran and that detectives should talk to his father William because he may know something. The police tracked down William Moran, who was a dockworker in New York. Mr. Moran admitted he knew that the man found in the Packard the previous summer was his son but didn't tell the police because he didn't want to get involved. He figured it wouldn't do any good and might end up getting him killed as well. He assumed Eugene's associates would mete out any justice that was to be had against his son's killers.

When asked about how he knew his son had been killed, Mr. Moran said, "About the middle of August this woman came to me and told me he had been killed in New Jersey. She didn't say how, but from reading the newspapers I could guess." He went on to say that the woman described the events surrounding the murder: how the five men picked him up and then the one o'clock morning visit. Mr. Moran said he didn't know the woman who stopped by but said that she and his son were staying at a bungalow in Brielle, New Jersey, at the time of his death. The police were able to locate the bungalow. The key found on Moran's body fit the lock on the door. A dentist from Brielle, New Jersey, was also able to confirm that the dead man was a patient of his known as Mr. Rice, who lived at the same bungalow where Moran's key fit.

Who placed the call to the New Jersey police? Possibly Eugene's moll Anna Urbas. At some point between August 1929 and February 1930, Anna defied those who had killed her man, and returned to the New York area. At first, she lived in New Jersey but then moved to Long Island City, Queens, on February 21, about a week after the police received their tip and the newspapers ran the Moran story on their front pages.

Those who put a bullet into Eugene's head and then put the match to him likely feared that the police would soon catch up with Anna or perhaps suspected she was the tipster. They decided that they should find her first. They succeeded, and the attractive young lady disappeared on February 26.[xxiv] On May 29, the body of a young woman broke free from the manhole cover which had kept her anchored to the bottom of the Harlem River for three months. Ninety or so days underwater made identification difficult. Acting on a hunch, police took dental pictures to the same Brielle dentist who identified Moran. He informed them that the pictures matched another patient of his, Mrs. Rice.[xxv]

✷ ✷ ✷

With Entratta acquitted and any witnesses to the Hotsy-Totsy killings dead or silenced, Jack decided it was safe to come out of hiding. On March 10, 1930, he donned a long black overcoat with matching derby, collected his lawyers and sauntered into the West Forty-Seventh Street Police Station.

---

xxiv This date comes from her death certificate. A newspaper account gives her disappearance date as March 24.

xxv According to Moran's father, Anna told him that two of the guys who picked up Gene the night he was killed were James Batto and Mortimer "Monkey" Shubert. New York police knew both of them. The former was killed about a month after Moran on September 11, and the latter two months later on November 14.

The group bypassed the front desk and went straight upstairs to the detective bureau. they approached Detective James Donnelly. "Hello Jim," Jack said, "I hear you want me. Well I'm here to surrender."

Jack was arrested and sent to police headquarters for questioning. During his interrogation, he was quite conversant whenever the topic was commonplace chitchat like Babe Ruth's salary for the coming baseball season, but whenever the topic came around to the Hotsy-Totsy case he clammed up.

Because he'd been knocked around by the police in the past, Jack let it be known that he took the precaution of having his picture taking before he came in, "Just to show I was okay before I surrendered in case I fall down the stairs or run into a door during the night."[103]

In those days, different police stations had different protocols when gangsters were questioned in a lineup by detectives. The lineup wasn't so much for gaining information as it was for letting the detectives get a good look at the gangster and hear his voice for future reference. The NYPD thought it prudent that gangsters shouldn't be able to see the faces of their detectives, so at some stations the detectives would cover their features with bandanas while the gangsters were paraded out. At headquarters, however, it was a little different. There was a stage-like platform for the hoodlum to stand on with a black screen in front of it. The hoodlum would be unable to see through his side of the screen, but the detectives would be able to see him.

When it was his turn, Jack climbed atop the platform and waited for the onslaught of questions to begin. Jack squirmed around uncomfortably as detectives discussed the Hotsy-Totsy affair during the pre-questioning banter. "They say the orchestra was right in the middle of a piece when the shots were fired," a detective said. "Do you remember that waiter who was arrested and went crazy thinking about the killings?" another asked.

After a few minutes of this, an Inspector Sullivan got the ball rolling:

"Were you in the Hotsy Totsy club on the night of July 13?"

"No," Jack answered.

"Where were you?"

"I refuse to answer on the advice of my counsel."

"Were you in or out of the city?"

"I refuse to answer for the same reason."

Jack then stated his age, said he lived at the Harding Hotel and worked as a clerk.

"Outside of being a clerk and a murderer what other occupations have you?"

"Several," replied Jack, "I had a lot of cabs and I run night clubs."

"Were you ever in a real fight in which you didn't shoot a person in the back?"

"I never shot anybody."

"Your brother died recently didn't he?"

"Yes, I'm the last of the family."[xxvi]

"Were you at the funeral?"

"No"

"It wasn't very nice of you to stay away from your own brother's funeral was it?"

Jack didn't respond at the blatant attempt to get his goat.[104]

On the way out a reporter from the *New York Evening Journal* asked Jack, "How does it feel to be a racketeer?" Flicking an imaginary ash from the end of his cigarette, Jack haughtily replied, "Call me an alleged racketeer if you please."[105]

After they were done with him at headquarters Jack was sent to the Tombs to await a hearing. While there, he was told that he was wanted downstairs in a lineup, so a witness to a major robbery in New Jersey could identify him as a participant. Jack refused to go, yelling, "I won't leave this cell, I know my rights." So the witness was instead brought up to view the

---

xxvi His father died in 1927.

gangster through the bars of the cell. Jack thwarted this by wrapping himself up in a blanket and holding a pillow over his face until they left. After spending a week and a half in prison, he was discharged on all the murder counts. Before he had a chance to leave, he was rearrested for the outstanding drug charge from 1927. Bail was promptly paid, and he was never troubled by the charge again. That night, he retired to a speakeasy on West Forty-First Street, where a celebration dinner was thrown in his honor. Among the guest who feted him were an assistant district attorney, and two judges, each of whom made a congratulatory speech.[106]

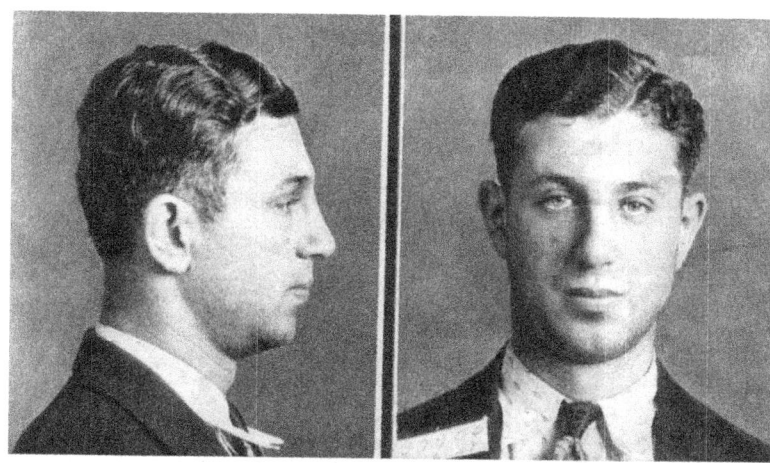

Charles Entratta, Jack's partner in the Hotsy-Totsy Club.
(Mario Gomes collection)

Jack turns himself in for the Hotsy-Totsy murders.
His lawyer is on the right. (Author's collection)

Charles "Vannie" Higgins was Jack's pal as well as
one of Brooklyn's biggest bootleggers. (Library of Congress)

Anna Urbas was the moll of Gene Moran and, like her
boyfriend, met a horrible fate. (Author's collection)

5

A STAR IS BORN

As the Hotsy-Totsy troubles were winding down, Jack found himself involved in an affair of different sorts. Less than a month before he turned himself in, a new musical comedy called *Simple Simon* opened to strong reviews at the Ziegfeld Theater. The star of the show was comedian Ed Wynn and one of the supporting players was a showgirl friend of Jack's named Doree Leslie. *Simple Simon* had all the trappings of a Ziegfeld show: music, comedy, extravagant sets and, as the *New York Times* described them, "a myriad of personable dancing girls and decorative creatures of stature and style."[107] One in that myriad was a friend of Leslie's named Marion Strasmick. (Actual spelling was probably Strasmich)[xxvii]

Marion was about twenty or so when she met Jack and had been a Ziegfeld girl going back to 1926. Her father Louis was a Jewish immigrant from Russia, and her mother Martha was French-Canadian. She was born about September of 1909[xxviii], and always dreamed of being a star. When she was thirteen, she came in eighth place in a beauty contest in her hometown of Boston. The prize included a contract with the Ziegfeld follies, but since she was so young the job had to be put off. By sixteen, she and her mother were living in New York, and she was dancing for Tex Guinan at the Moritz club. She also placed in an Atlantic City beauty pageant. Just after

---

xxvii This spelling comes from the U.S. Census

xxviii Her family was interviewed for the 1920 Census on January 7, 1920, and her age was given as 10 & 5/12.

turning seventeen, she became the envy of all aspiring star-
lets, a Ziegfeld girl.[108] She appeared in the musical comedy *No
Foolin'*, which ran from June 24 to September 25, 1926. This
was followed up in the fall by a road tour of the *Ziegfeld Follies of 1925*.[109] She appeared in another Ziegfeld show in 1927
called *Rio Rita*.

Marion didn't think Strasmick was good stage name so
vacillated between that and Roberts for a few years, finally
switching to the latter in 1928. Her friends and associates
however simply called her Kiki, a nickname she picked up at a
party from songwriter and future Hollywood producer George
"Buddy" DeSylva. "You look just like a little French girl," he told
her. "I think you need a nickname. You look just like Kiki and
I'm going to call you that."[110] The name stuck.

Following *Rio Rita*, Marion was in the hit musical comedy *Whoopee!*, which opened on December 4, 1928, at Broadway's New Amsterdam Theater. Produced by Florenz Ziegfeld
and starring Eddie Cantor, the show ran for 406 performances
before closing the following year on November 23, 1929. Also
in the cast was another dancing girl acquaintance of Jack's
named Agnes O'Laughlin, who would be a supporting player
in the Diamond saga of 1930.[111]

How Jack and Marion became acquainted is open to
debate. The only one of the two who described their meeting was Marion, and she gave two different versions. The first
account, and probably more accurate, given about seven
months after the fact, is that she was introduced to him by
her showgirl friend Agnes O'Laughlin[xxix] at the Club Abbey.
"Of course I knew that he was a gangster," she told the *New
York Evening Journal*. "I had heard a lot about him of course
and wanted to meet him."[112] Introductions were made, and "I
gave him my phone number. He called up often. We went out
together."[113] Mrs. Strasmick was none too pleased about her
daughter's new boyfriend. "My mother was quite upset when

---

xxix O'Laughlin would claim that Doree Leslie had introduced Marion to Jack back in 1928. That may be true, but it appears that they didn't
become a couple until March of 1930.

she heard I was going around with Jack. She was afraid of him because he was a gunman."[114]

The second version of their meeting was described after Jack's death in Marion's serialized account of her life with Jack. That account reads like a melodramatic romance novel. The timing was the same, but the facts conflicted with what she told the press a year before and, soap opera like dialogue was added. Jack was a dashing gentleman and Marion an innocent ingénue.

In the sugar-coated version of their meeting, it was a March night after a *Simple Simon* performance and Doree Leslie asked Marion to accompany her to a club to meet some people. One of those in the party was Jack. "How do you do Ms. Roberts, I'm glad to meet you,"[115] he said to Marion, who was immediately smitten with him. In this version, Marion claims that she didn't catch his name or possibly was introduced under an assumed name. At one point when the girls were alone, Leslie asked Marion, "Do you know who that is?" and Marion answered in the negative. "That's Jack Diamond. You've heard of him haven't you?"[116] Once again, Marion answered no. For the rest of that night, there was very little interaction between Jack and Marion as he spoke mostly to Leslie. However, when the party broke up, Jack hailed a cab and gave both the girls a ride home. When they got to Marion's hotel, Jack asked if he could call her and she said yes.

A few days later, he called using a fake name and asked her out. She said she couldn't, so he said he'd call her the next day. He invited her to meet him at the Club Madrid after her show, and she accepted. That night, seeing Marion approaching his table, Jack stood up and said, "You're right on time Marion. You look beautiful." Then he introduced her to the rest of the table, "How do you like this sweet kid I met a few nights ago." Jack ordered champagne for the table and toasted his new girlfriend: "Here's to a very beautiful Ziegfeld girl." Throughout the night, people stopped by the table, including famous performers of the time Jimmy Durante and Helen Kane. A good time was had by all and afterwards Jack and

Marion got into his chauffeured Lincoln and he dropped her off at her hotel. "I've had a very pleasant time and hope to see you every night from now on,"[117] he told her.

Though Marion's mother wasn't happy with the situation, she couldn't stop her daughter. There was, however, one obstacle to the budding romance. Marion was engaged to be married to band leader Eddie Elkins on June 2. Though Marion would later say that she and Eddie broke up right before she met Diamond, another version had it that Jack induced the bandleader to leave town.[xxx] Either way, Eddie took the band to California.

With the fiancée out of the way and Alice tending the house in Acra, Jack and Marion were a constant item. Jack called her every day, and there was always a telegram waiting for her at the theater saying something like, "Remember I'm seeing you tonight after the show."[118] He also tried to help her career along by having one of New York City's best choreographers give her private lessons. "I was devoting all my attention to Kiki Roberts," the Instructor remembered to a journalist eight years after the fact. "Legs Diamond had come to me and said I had to make a great dancer out of her. So I concentrated on Kiki. Diamond paid me more money than two dozen [dancers] could have afforded then. And Kiki got to be pretty good."[119]

✧ ✧ ✧

Now that he was in the clear for the Hotsy-Totsy murders and the drug charge against him was permanently stalled. Jack had two big projects at work during the summer of 1930. He was going to return to Europe to set up a drug operation and, closer to home, he was going to monopolize the booze and protection rackets in the Catskills. At some point, Jack

---

xxx In her tabloid memoir, Marion didn't mention Eddie by name but the *New York Evening Journal* did and reported that Diamond chased him out of town.

realized that the Catskill region was an untapped goldmine. During the spring and summer months, the area swelled with thousands of tourist who poured into the small towns and slaked their thirst at the many inns and taverns dotting Greene County. There were hotels, restaurants, every kind of business that catered to travelers, all operating freely and getting their booze from small-time bootleggers. He probably took notice sometime in 1929 but, because of the Hotsy-Totsy trouble, was unable to act. The summer of 1930 would be different.

While in New York City that summer, Diamond was staying at the Hotel President, and it was there that he was arrested yet again on July 15. This time, it was the Newark, New Jersey, police that asked that he be picked up, as they believed that he was responsible for a couple of bank robberies. Also picked up with Jack were two associates who were in his room at the time: Robert Miller, who was known as "Count" and had a long record as a confidence man; and Abraham Leimas, who said that he worked in real estate. The trio was locked in the Tombs, where Jack assured the authorities that he had gone straight and was making a living as a car salesman.

For two days, witnesses were brought over from New Jersey to see if they could identify the men. They couldn't. After spending forty-eight hours in lock up, Jack and his two associates were released. Interestingly the *New York Daily News* stated that the Newark bank robberies were just an excuse to get Jack behind bars, because the New York police had new evidence to implicate him in the murder of Eugene Moran and were hoping to indict him while he was in custody. Seeing that the Newark police really had no case to begin with, there may have been some validity to this angle. If it was true, chances are they wanted to avoid an encore of Jack's Hotsy-Totsy disappearance act.

Jack and Count Miller were released from the Tombs on July 17, and both men headed that night to the house at Acra to spend what would prove to be Jack's last weeks as a semi-anonymous gangster. [120] The following month, events would unfold that would catapult Jack into superstardom.

Back at Acra, Jack began his drive to monopolize the bootlegging and protection racket for Greene County. The exact date of his launch is unknown, but later testimony by saloon keepers indicated that he put the idea into action in August of 1930, possibly late July. His partner was Hollywood Inn proprietor Paul Quattrocchi.

So as to not seem like an outsider horning his way in, Jack wanted another local guy for his beer enterprise. He approached Angelo Benedetto, the owner of the White Bottling plant, a soda-water manufacturing business located in the town of Cairo. Within a few weeks, the numerous inns, hotels and saloons in the surrounding towns were buying their beer and liquor from Jack. A couple of weeks into the operation, Benedetto got cold feet and backed out. Jack let him go but kept using his plant as an office and operation center.[121]

Naturally, the local beer merchants like the Coglianese Brothers, who enjoyed a lucrative business before Jack's arrival, didn't like the idea of losing their customers. They also didn't have the nerve or muscle to stand-up to Jack, who called a meeting of the local beer purveyors at a saloon in Haines Falls called the Mountain House. It was presumably there that Jack laid down the law. All the bootleggers and inn-keepers accepted that Jack was now top dog, except a saloon keeper named Harry Western, who ran the Chateau Inn at Lake Katrine, located a few miles from the town of Kingston.

Originally from Jersey City, New Jersey, Western had moved to the Catskills around 1920. His family, consisting of two brothers, one of whom was a cop and the other a fireman, remained in New Jersey.[122] Western also had ties to Brooklyn, where he ran a night club during the winter months when there were no tourists to drink his beer at the Chateau. Western was the first holdout against Diamond, and Jack would have to do something if he was going to maintain his dominance over the rest of the pack.

Before he could deal with Western, however, Jack had to return to New York City. On Thursday, August 14, a plain-clothes detective saw him and three other men leave the

Hotel President, get into a car and drive off. Curious as to what one of the Big Apple's more infamous hoodlums was up to, the detective jumped into a cab and tailed them. Trailing the gangsters he learned that they procured passports as well as tickets for the German ocean liner *Bremer*, which was to set sail a week later on August 21. The detective went back to the station and reported his findings.

With preparations for his voyage settled, Jack returned to Acra that night. The following day, he went about getting more customers for his Greene County alky business. Arthur Pacini, owner of the Village Inn in the town of East Durham, was lounging on his porch when Diamond arrived with his entourage. With Jack's main enforcer Gerry Scaccio leading the way, the group barged into Pacini's place, passed through his kitchen and down to the cellar where the proprietor kept his beer. Two of the guys started to bust open his kegs, while Scaccio put a gun to Pacini's head. Jack pulled out his own gun and pointed it at his head as well and ordered the innkeeper not to tell anybody about the visit. Jack then had two barrels of his beer brought in and informed the terrified Pacini that, from now on, he would be getting his beer from Diamond.[123]

Unbeknownst to Jack, back in New York City the news about his passport and sailing plans had made its way to the press and, on August 20, the day before he was to set sail, the *New York Daily News* announced to its readers "European Travel Lures Legs Diamond, Racketeer." The *News* went on to say when and on what ship Legs would be sailing. It also mentioned that a dozen detectives would be waiting for him on board prior to departure to make sure no enemies would be gunning for him and his pals. The *New York Evening Journal* ran the same story verbatim for one of its issues.[124]

The surprising and unwanted attention from the press forced Jack to change his plans, a move that would change his life forever. Understandably, he skipped the *Bremer*, choosing instead to sail on August 23. With the extra two days, he went back to Acra to settle some local business, which resulted in the event that would launch his name around the world and ultimately lead to his death.

The murder of Harry Western, the stubborn saloon keeper who refused to bow to Jack, is still a mystery. What is known is that he received a phone call at the Chateau on Friday night, August 22, at about ten o'clock, demanding that he go to Diamond's house at Acra. He called his wife and told her he had some urgent business to take care of.[125] He was never seen again.

Six hours or so after Western had phoned his wife, gang gopher Harry "Skunky" Klein was woken up in his room at Diamond's house. Two men, whom he never identified by name, told him that there was a Buick coupe outside and he was to drive it to Brooklyn and run it off a pier. As Skunky was preparing to leave, he saw Jack packing for his trip and talking with Alice. She was asking why he was planning to travel under the name John Nolan. Jack told her it was because of the recent publicity. In fact, to avoid another foul up, he hadn't even booked passage yet, choosing instead to wait until just a few hours before shipping out. [126]

Klein made his way outside and found the Buick. Whether or not he noticed the bloodstains in the back seat is unknown. He drove the car to Brooklyn and parked it in a garage until he could find a good place to ditch it. Meanwhile, Diamond was chauffeured to New York City in his Lincoln by James Dalton. Dalton was ordered to the West Side where he dropped his boss off at the Nineteenth Street Pier, where the White Star Lines steamer *Baltic* was preparing to set sail. Dalton's other responsibility that weekend was to go to Brooklyn the following day and pick up a friend of Alice's named Anna Witcher and bring her back to Acra for a Catskill vacation.

After Dalton left, Diamond walked a block down to the Red Star Line's office and booked passage on the *Belgenland* for his first trip to Europe since 1926. The *Belgenland* raised anchor at eleven in the morning and headed out into New York Harbor. As the cityscape disappeared from view, Jack must have breathed a sigh of relief. The last thing he wanted was to bring attention to himself and this trip. He no doubt felt somewhat satisfied, knowing that he had slipped out of the city undetected by both the police and the press. He would be able to enjoy a leisurely weeklong cruise before landing in Europe to purchase hundreds of thousands of dollars worth of drugs. Little did he know that, before the *Belgenland* was halfway across the Atlantic, his name would be front page news on both sides of the ocean, and the passengers who were now passing him on the decks without giving him a second glance would be asking for his autograph.[xxxi]

✵ ✵ ✵

When Skunky Klein arrived in Brooklyn that Saturday he didn't know what to do, so he got in touch with Frederick Witcher, the husband of Alice's friend Anna, who would be going back to Acra with Dalton. He consulted with Witcher about how best to dispose of Western's car. How tight Jack and Fred Witcher were is unknown. Anna had spent the previous Memorial Day up in Acra, and obviously Jack's minions knew them as well.

In an attempt to ditch the car in the river, Skunky and Fred took it to a pier near where Witcher worked. Unable to get the car over the stringpiece, they took it back to the garage.

---

xxxi According to a *New York Times article* dated 8/30/1930 – The Department of Justice stated that, crossing with Jack were Charles Entratta, alias Green, [Salvatore] Arcidiaco, [Herman] Traeger and [Charles] Lucania (Lucky Luciano). The only one of the four that went to Europe for sure is Arcidiaco. As will be seen he discussed it openly with the police. Whether he sailed there with Jack is unknown. Passenger lists from Ancestry.com show that he returned from Europe via Southampton, England aboard the *SS Majestic* setting sail on October 1 and landing in New York City on October 7. A search for Entratta (Green), Traeger and Lucania and various spellings of their names in the passenger manifest of vessels arriving in New York turned up nothing.

They loaded some blocks inside for the gas pedal and agreed to find another spot the next day.

Early Sunday morning came and went, and the car was still in the garage. How Skunky spent his morning is unknown, but that afternoon three detectives were cruising around Brooklyn when they saw him standing on a corner. Knowing Skunky previously as a bootlegger, they decided to keep an eye on him. A short time later, Dalton pulled up in the Lincoln and leaned out the window to chat with him. After a short conversation, Dalton pulled away. Klein started to go his own way, but before he got very far the detectives pulled up and made him get in their car. Then they tailed Dalton to Witcher's apartment and watched him enter.

The detectives parked their car and went up to the apartment. Inside they found only Dalton and Anna and questioned them. Dalton admitted that he was Diamond's chauffer and that he dropped Jack off at the *Baltic* and was there to take Anna back to Acra. Satisfied that there was no monkey business going on, the detectives did a bit of snooping and were getting ready to leave when one of them spotted three large suitcases under the bed. "What's in those cases?" one of the detectives asked. "I don't know," Anna replied. "I asked my husband once and he told me, 'None of your damned business,'" Intrigued, the detectives opened the cases expecting to find a pistol or two. Instead, they were shocked to find an arsenal. The haul included:

Two black-powder bombs,
Three pipe bombs,
Three tear gas bombs,
Eighteen hand grenades,
Six dud grenades,
Five steel vests,
Three steel waist protectors,
Three signal guns,
Thirteen loads for the signal guns,
Four rifle silencers,
Two machine gun stocks,

Twenty-nine boxes of ammo ranging in caliber from .22 to .45,
A gallon of tear gas,
150 loose bullets of different sizes,
Sixteen, 25-round machine gun clips,
Twenty two fountain-pen pistols,
A manual for using a Thompson machine gun.

Needless to say, the detectives were now very interested in Klein and Dalton. They and Anna were brought to the station. Anna's husband Fred was picked up later at his mother's house. Fred claimed that he didn't know what was in the cases. When asked where they came from, he said that in March some sailor offered him $10 a month to keep them for him. He didn't know where the sailor currently was or his name. Unfortunately for Fred, Anna had told the police a different tale. She said that when she returned from her last trip to Acra (Memorial Day) they were under the bed but hadn't been there before she left.

To make matters worse, during the interrogation the detectives learned that Skunky was in town to ditch a car. The garage was named and the car retrieved. There was no license plate, so they got the engine number and traced it to Harry Western. By this time, Mrs. Western had alerted the Greene County authorities about her missing husband, so when the Brooklyn detectives called about the bloodstained car, Greene County wanted custody of Dalton and Klein.

Since two of Diamond's boys were found with Western's blood stained automobile as well as an arsenal, the Greene County authorities thought it time to visit the Diamond house at Acra. At three-thirty in the morning on August 26, a sheriff, two sergeants and six troopers advanced up Diamond's driveway and found themselves illuminated by the glaring floodlights. Inside the house they found only Alice, a friend of hers who was staying over, some house servants and a nineteen-year-old kid who did odd jobs around the property. Alice and her friend were questioned about Western and denied knowing anything. When it came to questions about her husband, Alice was tight-lipped. The authorities searched the house and found nothing, although they thought they hit the jackpot when they found the hidden stairwell in the closet, but it led to nothing interesting. Two days later, Dalton and Klein were released on the arsenal charge and were immediately rearrested at the behest of Greene County and sent up state.

When the story about the arsenal and Western's car broke, authorities understandably wanted to speak with Jack, but nobody was sure where he was. Some thought the story about him being on the *Baltic* was a hoax, as there were reports of him being sighted in the Catskills. Since Dalton said that he dropped him off at the *Baltic's* pier authorities wired the captain and asked if Diamond was on board. The captain responded with a message stating that a search of the ship proved fruitless. Unconvinced, the police wired Ireland, *Baltic's* destination, warning them a gangster was on the way. Not until August 30 was it discovered that Jack was sailing on the *Belgenland*. That ship's first stop was Plymouth, England. Word of Jack's impending arrival was sent to Scotland Yard. Though there was no arrest warrant for Jack back in New York, authorities in England labeled him an undesirable alien and refused him permission to land. Once the English papers caught wind that there was a bonafide American gangster on the way over, they had a field day and started printing stories about Jack. One tabloid went so far as to print a telephone interview they claimed they had with Jack stating that he was already in the country.

Although he booked passage as John Nolan, once Jack was on board he went by his real name. He spent most of his time in the smoking room playing poker but didn't win much. As the days passed, the passengers learned the true identity of the friendly guy staying in Cabin 50 on the A Deck. When Jack decided to partake in the skeet shooting that the *Belgenland* offered as an on deck activity, word spread that the notorious Legs Diamond was going to be wielding a shotgun. A number of people gathered about, assuming that they were going to be treated to some expert marksmanship. They were let down when Jack missed every shot.[127]

By the time the *Belgenland* arrived in England, Jack was famous. He was continuously approached by women asking him to autograph their menus, fans and passenger albums (a booklet listing those on board). The morning they landed in England, Jack was greeted first by members of Scotland Yard. They informed him that he wouldn't be allowed off the boat, which didn't bother him because his destination was the ship's second stop, Antwerp. Afterward a number of reporters were allowed into his cabin for an interview. When asked about whether he expected any trouble landing at his final destination, he responded, "Why they haven't got a thing on me. I don't mind about not landing in England but I hope I am not going to be stopped from landing anywhere on the Continent. I don't want to be sent back to New York. Maybe I'll go there myself someday, because I have a wife and kiddies at my home in the Catskills." He continued his lying by saying that the reason for the trip was solely for his health. "I intend going to Vichy to get the cure. I have stomach and liver trouble and have been told to come here and take the waters."

He laughed off questions about the arsenal. "I ain't got no house in Brooklyn, and I ain't got a chauffeur. The chauffeur belongs to my missus, and she sent him to bring Mrs. Witcher over to have a vacation with her in the Catskills. I don't know anything at all about the arsenal."

He went on to blame his troubles on the press: "It's these newspapers. All the time they are driving the police to do something and the police do it. They hold me for a couple of days and all the headlines scream about it. But when they let me go two days later they never say a word about it."[128]

When it was learned that Diamond was heading for Belgium, the New York Police urged the American diplomat's office there to tell Belgian police what kind of character was headed their way.[129] At nine o'clock the next morning, the *Belgenland* docked in Antwerp, and Jack headed down the gangplank without any fanfare. The lack of attention gave him a false sense of security. Belgian newspapermen were about but didn't know what the American gangster looked like until other passengers pointed him out. Once they saw him, the press closed in, but Jack told them that he would speak with them later. At about that time, a detective approached him and asked to see his passport. His luggage was given a quick once-over while he posed for some press photos. The detective informed Jack that there was no warrant for his arrest, which made the gangster happy until he saw his bags being loaded into a taxi and he was asked to accompany the detective to City Hall.[130]

The police weren't sure what to do with Jack, so they sent a message to the Minister of Justice, asking for guidance. While waiting for word back from the Minister, who was on vacation, Jack spent most of the day at City Hall and spoke with the press. "I do not understand what is going on," he told them. "I embarked from New York under my own name, and not for one moment have I concealed my identity. I wonder who imagined I was traveling under the assumed name of Knowland or Nolan." He also reiterated that he was there only to cure his stomach. After a long afternoon, a message finally arrived saying that Belgium considered Jack undesirable and he had to leave at once. He was told to pick any of the countries on the Belgian border as a destination. He chose Germany and was boarded onto a train with a Belgian escort for the journey.[131]

When the U.S. diplomat's office found out Diamond was headed for Germany, the American Embassy in Berlin was notified of the situation. The embassy, in turn, contacted the Berlin police and told them that an undesirable American was on his way. The Berlin police contacted authorities in the German border town of Aix-la-Chapelle. When Jack's train pulled into the station at midnight, he was arrested by the German Secret Service, under the pretense that the United States asked that he be extradited for the murder of Harry Western. He was questioned for over two hours before being placed into a cell. Most likely this was just an excuse to hold him until authorities could find a legal means to kick him out. Technically they had nothing on Jack as the American Embassy denied that they wanted him arrested, stating that they were just being courteous by passing on the information of his arrival. The NYPD also stated that he was not being sought by authorities in New York.[132]

A reporter was allowed to visit Jack. He asked him about all the stories from New York. "It's all lies," Jack yelled. "The New York Police pester me all the time. They arrested me twenty-two times in the last few years and always had to let me go for lack of evidence. I came to Europe to seek quiet. I want to go to Vichy and Wiesbaden to take the cure. My stomach is bothering me." Then, for effect, he grabbed his stomach and grimaced as if he was in much pain.[133]

Once it was cleared up that America didn't want Jack, the Germans decided that they didn't want him either and planned to deport him back to the U.S. Jack asked the U.S. Consulate in Cologne to intervene on his behalf. What, if anything, the consul did is unknown, but the Prussian Minister of the Interior called Jack's bluff. He set up a medical exam with some doctors. If they found he was as ill, as he claimed, he could stay for the cures he was seeking. If he checked out fine, he would get the boot.

After examining him the doctors declared that he was fit and Jack was soon on a train with an escort of two detectives and headed for deportation. The first stop was Cologne, where he and his escort stopped in a station restaurant for dinner before boarding an overnight express train for Bremen.[134]

Jack's train arrived in Bremen at six o'clock in the morning on September 4. He had a light breakfast and was then taken to jail, while the authorities looked for an America-bound passenger ship to place him on. Much to their chagrin, all passenger ships were filled up. Jack was released from jail and checked into one of Bremen's premier hotels. Although he was allowed to be alone in his room, there was a guard at the door. The next day, passage on a liner still couldn't be found. It was decided that Jack, who arrived in a first class cabin, would return to America on a freighter. The only other passengers on the ship were approximately five-thousand canaries.

In the meantime, Jack hired a lawyer in Berlin to work on getting his deportation overturned. He was unable to do so, and after his second night in Bremen Diamond was loaded into a car and driven to Hamburg. There, the freighter *Hannover* was waiting for him. Two hundred people were on hand to see the American gangster. As he was walked to the ship, one of them yelled, "How are you?" Jack responded that he didn't like Germany. He boarded the ship and took a room that one of the officers had given up for him. A Hamburg lawyer came aboard and consulted with him before the ship set sail. Diamond told him to file a complaint against the Prussian Government. That afternoon, September 6, the *Hannover* set sail for America, a trip that would take about two weeks. During the crossing, Jack had access to the wireless and was in contact with his Berlin lawyer directing him to do whatever was necessary to get the deportation nullified. There was a Germany-bound steamer that would be passing the *Hannover*, and Jack wanted to arrange a transfer. [135]

There would be no mid-ocean ship swapping however, and on September 22, after sixteen days at sea, the *Hannover* pulled into Philadelphia. Hundreds of people were waiting at the dock to catch a glimpse of their now infamous native son. Before reaching its pier, the ship stopped at Marcus Hook. It was met there by a cutter containing custom officials and two and half dozen reporters. The *Hannover's* captain barred the reporters from boarding the ship. However Diamond mistook the custom officials for newsmen. When the leading official, a man named Laughlin, approached him, Jack yelled, "The first newspaperman I see I will punch in the nose. They got me into all this trouble, although I ain't done nothing. You hear me, I'll punch the first one in the nose."[136]

Mr. Laughlin assured Jack he wasn't a reporter and was just there to make sure everyone on the ship was legitimate. While Laughlin inspected his documents, Jack droned on about his dislike for reporters: "I won't see a newspaperman. I won't see them at all. I'm just a respectable young fellow who's been away on a holiday and I'm not going to answer a lot of questions about whether I killed this guy or that guy and so forth."[137]

"I hear they want to talk to me about that fellow Harry Western who kept a beer joint up in the Catskills. I'm supposed to have bumped him off I suppose? Well I don't know Western and never heard of him until I was asked about it in Europe."[138]

Perhaps after two weeks with the canaries, Jack was glad to speak to a human, because he continued with his diatribe: "I don't care about the cops. Cops are the least of my worries. What I'm worried about five times as much as meeting the cops is meeting my wife." Why? "Well there it is newspapers again. The German papers went and published a story that I was playing around with a blonde over in Bremen, a dancer in a cabaret. Ain't that a nice thing for the Missus to read with her toast and coffee? Not a word of truth in it either. I don't go in much for blondes."[139]

Once the custom officials were done with their business, the *Hannover* steamed to its pier at the mouth of the Delaware River. The mass of gawkers would have to wait another two hours before they got a glimpse of Diamond, as he refused to leave the ship. Philadelphia detectives went aboard, and Jack told them that he wasn't going anywhere unless they brought a car up to the gangplank so that he wouldn't have to go through the crowd. A sedan was brought in and Legs, looking slick in a blue suit, blue shirt, blue tie, soft gray hat and black patent leather shoes, finally came down the gangway.[140] He was ushered into the car with his two lawyers, Dan Prior and Murray Rosenthal. He was also accompanied by both Philadelphia and New York detectives. Once the party was in the car, cops got on the running board and began to swing their billy clubs liberally as the sedan made its way through the crowd.

Diamond was taken to the local precinct at Twelfth and Pine Streets, where he was placed under arrest. "You have no right to arrest me. I was born and raised here in Philadelphia and you have nothing against me. I am getting a sleigh ride here and you know it. I have lots of friends here and I don't care for this publicity."[141]

At the station, Jack showed his passport and ID and began complaining. "I am going to Washington as soon as I get away from here and complain to the proper authorities about the way I have been treated."[142]

Jack's complaints fell on deaf ears. He was taken to the Bertillon rooms for mug shots, finger prints and measurements. Afterward, he was locked in a cell where he had a dinner consisting of coffee and mush. A hearing was scheduled for the next day at City Hall, and he was released at eleven o'clock that night. He reportedly spent the night at the home of an uncle, who had visited him earlier in the day. [143]

The next day, Jack arrived at City Hall wearing a brown suit, brown shirt and black tie, with his hair slicked back. In the hearing room, dozens of detectives crowded around to look Diamond over should they ever run across him in Philly.[144] After a handful of cases were heard, the court crier called out, "John Diamond. Diamond come forward." Jack approached with Rosenthal and Prior. Two detectives were witnesses against him. "We got orders to pick up Diamond on a charge of being a suspicious character," one of them told the judge, adding, "He agrees to leave Philadelphia, and as long as he gets out that's all we ask."

"How about it Diamond?" asked the judge.

"As soon as I can make arrangements I'll go. Say an hour or an hour and a half."

"All right. Discharged" the judge decreed and Diamond took off for New York.[145]

Marion "Kiki Roberts" Strasmich
(Courtesy Robert Hudovernik: Jazz Age Beauties)

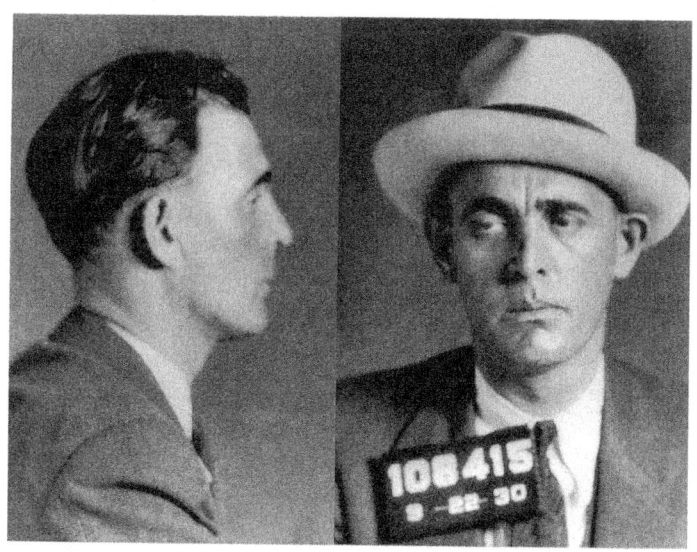

Jack's mug shot from the arrest in Philadelphia. (Author's collection)

6

A STAR IS SHOT

There was too much money involved in the European drug deal for Jack to give up on it, so the first order of business when he returned to New York was to figure out a way to get back to Germany. Those who invested in the trip, however, namely Salvatore Spitale and his partner Irving Bitz, wanted their money back pronto, but Jack stalled them. He would return to Europe and make the deals, end of story. His partners felt that he was too "hot" and simply wanted their investment returned.

On Wednesday, October 8, Count Miller received a cablegram from Germany which read,

"Unquestionably arrangements will be made for John to enter Germany. Send me $5000 as I need that amount to make arrangements and cover expenses."[xxxii][146]

The following day, Jack left his home at Acra and returned to Manhattan. Instead of the Hotel President, Jack got a room at the Hotel Monticello located at 35 West Sixty-Fourth Street. He had set up Marion there the previous August just prior to leaving for Europe. She was currently in rehearsals for a new musical called *Smiles*. Marion occupied Room 831, and Jack was given Room 829. Down the hall and around the corner in Room 825 lived the Monticello's manager Jacob Ginsburg and his family. Ginsburg and Diamond were friends, as the former used to be the manager of the Hotel Harding when Jack was staying there back in 1928. Also staying in the hotel was an

---

xxxii Some sources put the amount at $3,500

associate of Jack's named Harry Drescher. Drescher was a former Prohibition agent who now worked in bail bonds. He still had contacts with his former co-workers and was said to be a middle man who fixed bribes with Prohibition agents.[147] Also rooming at the Monticello was Count Miller, who delivered the cablegram to Jack.

On Friday, Jack's longtime confederate Salvatore Arcidiaco, just back from Europe himself, stopped by in the afternoon for a brief powwow. Later that night, there was a meeting consisting of four men. On Saturday night at about midnight, Marion returned from rehearsal and found Jack's hat and coat in her room but no Jack. A few minutes later, he popped in and said, "I'm across the hall in Room 829 with some people. I'll be in shortly." But he didn't return until two o'clock in the morning.

Eight hours after Jack hit the sack, Ernie Muller, who lived next door to the Monticello Hotel, was out front fixing his car when he noticed a new Chrysler pull up across the street. He saw two men get out and enter the hotel. He thought it odd that they left the motor running and a door open but he returned his thoughts to his own auto. A few moments after the two men entered the hotel, the phone in Marion's room rang and she rolled over to answer it. It was the hotel operator saying that there was a call for Jack. She handed the phone over. After a brief exchange, Jack said that there were a couple of guys coming up. He didn't bother getting dressed, there was no need, it was Salvatore Spitale and either his brother Joseph or his partner Irving Bitz.[xxxiii][148] Jack knew them well enough to greet them in his red silk pajamas. Jack told Marion that he was going to take them to his room and that he didn't expect to be back before she left for rehearsal. He gave her a one hundred dollar bill and told her that he had to go back to Acra later in the day but would be back by midnight. Marion started to run a bath for herself. A minute later there was a

---

xxxiii Witnesses would later identify Salvatore and Joseph Spitale as the two men who went upstairs. Jack would later say that Spitale and Bitz were the guys.

knock at the door. Jack opened it, and Marion heard him tell the two guys, "Let's go over to my room where we can talk."[149] After they left, Marion climbed into the bathtub and began to soak. A few minutes later, gunshots were echoing throughout the eighth floor. Back outside, Ernie Muller saw the two men run from the hotel and jump back into their Chrysler and speed off. The whole affair took about five minutes.[xxxiv]

While Ernie scratched his head outside the Monticello over the two guys and the Chrysler, upstairs Jack staggered out of Room 829 with blood pouring out of bullet wounds in his right shoulder, beneath the left armpit and near the center of his chest. The crimson liquid was also streaming down his face, the result of a bullet fired into his forehead. Luckily for Jack, he was falling backwards when that slug struck him. Although it creased his scalp, it didn't pierce his skull.

Jack made his way to Marion's room and told her to clear out. At the other end of the hall, Monticello manager Jacob Ginsburg and his family were preparing for a trip to New Jersey when they heard the shots. Ginsburg's wife was in another room, and he called to her to make sure everyone was all right. After he was sure it was safe, he opened his door and saw Jack, crouched over and holding his head, going toward the elevator. Ginsburg ran up to him. "What happened?" he asked. "I'm hurt. Please get your doctor right away. Take me to your room, and please get me the doctor in a hurry. I'm badly hurt."[150]

Diamond went into Ginsburg's room and lay on his bed. "My God, what can I do for you? Is there anything I can do for you right now?" Ginsburg pleaded. "Yes," Jack replied, "get me a big drink of whiskey." Ginsburg retrieved a bottle and gave it to Jack and then called the hotel operator and had him put a call through to a doctor named Babcock at the McAlpin Hotel. He asked Babcock to come right over. The doctor

---

xxxiv Since nobody was keeping minutes at the meeting, one can only speculate as to the reason for the shooting. It seems highly likely that Spitale, who'd probably been trying to get his investment back since Jack's return from Europe wanted his money back right then. Jack refused stating that the fix was in for his going back to Germany, but Spitale didn't want to hear it.

said he couldn't leave right away but would be over as soon as possible. Next Ginsburg called the lobby and had them send up Joseph Goldie, the assistant manager. After these two calls, Jack asked him to call Harry Drescher up from the sixth floor. While they were waiting for Drescher, Goldie showed up in his bathrobe and saw Jack on the bed. "Who shot you?" he asked. "Don't ask me any questions," Jack responded. "Get me a doctor. Somebody gave it to me. I don't know who it was." Ginsburg told Jack that the doctor wouldn't be able to get there right away. "To hell with the doctor. Get me an ambulance and take me to a hospital," Jack wailed, "They'll know what to do."[151] A call was made to the MacDougal Ambulance service, and a wagon was sent out. Oddly, it was the exact same ambulance and driver that was sent out to pick up Arnold Rothstein almost two years previously at the Park Central Hotel.[152]

Drescher entered the room just as Ginsburg was leaving to take his family to Jersey as planned. The manager told him about the shooting. Seeing his blood-soaked friend on the bed, he hurried over and asked Jack who shot him. Diamond waved the question aside and told him, "Harry I want you to take care of my wife Alice and see that nobody gives her the worst of it in Acra." He added, "Tell her to have Judge Prior in Albany take care of all her business up there. It looks like I am going. I've eight shots in me, four around my heart and one in my head."[153] [xxxv]

The ambulance arrived and both the driver and attendant were greeted in the lobby by Goldie, who took them upstairs. Doctor Babcock had arrived before them and was attending to Jack. "I'm coming to pieces," Jack cried. "It seems as though my arm is falling off. Can't you give me something Doc?" Babcock gave Jack a shot for the pain and then he was lifted onto a gurney. "Take it easy boys. It hurts," he told the driver and attendant. As they were wheeling Jack out, the driver told him that he "got it good." "Well," Jack replied, "it all

---

xxxv Jack was mistaken: he had been shot a total of four times.

goes along with it, you know."[154] Once inside the ambulance, Jack, like Rothstein, was taken to Polyclinic Hospital.[xxxvi]

The police didn't learn about the shooting until after Jack was in the hospital. Once they found out, guards were placed on Jack's floor and no non-hospital personnel were allowed entry. Guards also were stationed outside the hospital as well. When word made its way around town that Jack had been shot and was being treated at Polyclinic, the switchboard lit up. The hospital received in the neighborhood of two thousand calls inquiring about Jack. The underworld was even represented, when racketeer Larry Fay, who would be deemed New York City's Public Enemy No. 3 the following year, stopped in to inquire about Diamond's status.[155]

When Jack got out of surgery, Police Commissioner Mulrooney and District Attorney Crain were waiting for him. Jack lied and told them that he had just returned to the city the night before and went to bed at two o'clock in the morning after spending the evening reading in his room. Then, that morning, he was lying in bed at eleven-thirty when "the door opened and three men walked in. One of them said, 'Well here we are, let's go.' And all three blazed away at me over on the bed, and they ran out. After a while, I got to my feet and went along the hall as far as the elevator. Then I fell over again, and I don't remember anything until I came to in Ginsberg's room." Mulrooney asked him how he made it out of the room with such terrible wounds. "Well, I took two good shots of whiskey and I was able to make it."[156] Jack said he didn't know the guys who shot him. "He's lying of course," Mulrooney told the press. It was obvious to all that Jack was shot by guys he knew and didn't think he had any reason to fear.

The police learned that Room 831 was Marion's room and began searching for her. Later that night, they went to the

---

xxxvi The previous night the body of a gangster named Louis Figura was found on the outskirts of Harrison, NJ. In his pocket was a room key for the Hotel President. Since Jack was a recent resident of the hotel, New Jersey police tried to say that Figura was a Diamond lieutenant but Police Commissioner Edward Mulrooney said that the shootings were not connected.

apartment of her friend and fellow showgirl Agnes O'Laughlin. At first, Agnes refused to let the police in, but when they threatened to break down the door she acquiesced. The detectives searched the room and didn't find anything. Opening a closet, however, they saw a big pile of clothes on the floor. Underneath the garments was a much shaken Marion. Both she and Agnes were brought in for questioning.

When news of the shooting made it back to Acra, Alice chartered a plane to the City and arrived at the hospital at around nine-twenty in the evening. With her was Paul Quattrocchi. Earlier that day back in Cairo, as word of the shooting spread around town, he overheard the local beer runner Joe Coglianese say, "I hope Diamond dies." Not appreciating the slight on his friend Quattrocchi socked Coglianese in the jaw.

When Alice arrived at the hospital she was allowed to visit with Jack for twenty minutes. Money was one of the topics discussed. "Kid there's $400 in my pockets and a postdated check for $500. Get them; you'll need them," he told her. Unfortunately for Alice, the police got to the funds first and held them for evidence. They were especially interested in learning why someone had paid Legs Diamond $500.[157] After the visit, Alice was hauled off to the police station for questioning. When she arrived, Marion was already there, and the *New York Evening Journal* reported that the two women exchanged nasty looks with each other but no words were passed. When asked about Alice, Marion only said, "She has her troubles and I have mine. I don't want to say anything about her."[158]

After the police were done with Alice, she sped around town trying to collect money. Whether or not they kicked into the kitty is unknown, but the *New York Daily News* was able to print an exclusive interview with her. It was billed as, "The only interview she ever has granted" but other than she was trying to get up some money she didn't spill anything good in the piece. "Jack told Mulrooney that he'd tell who shot him if he knew. So would I," she stated. The paper, like its readers, knew she was lying.

"Do you know any of his friends?" the paper asked.

"He had many friends, but I'm not sure that I knew them."

"Did you know of any enemies?"

"He didn't have any enemies. Why should he have enemies?"

"Did you know the Roberts girl?"

"No." The interviewer noted that the last response was delivered coldly and with a narrowing of the eyes.

She said that she would pray for Jack and try to have a certain priest from Baltimore sent down. Then, nodding to her lawyer Murray Rosenthal, she closed with, "I'm sorry I can't tell you more. He won't let me talk."[159]

While Jack lingered somewhere between life and death, the police began to pull in suspects. Salvatore Arcidiaco was brought in and readily admitted having met with Diamond at the Monticello on Friday. "Diamond put up a proposition to me that I rejected," he told the police. "I was with him less than ten minutes and left." He also admitted that he went to Europe at the same time as Jack "to buy some rye whiskey." Dutch Schultz was brought in as well. He told the police that all he knew was what he read in the papers. Both men were then paraded in front of Marion to see if she could identify them. She denied having ever seen Schultz, and when Arcidiaco came in she was asked if she had ever seen him before and answered no. Having already told the police he had met with Jack, the gangster prompted her, "Don't you remember that I talked with Jack in your room at the Monticello Friday afternoon and you were there." "Oh yes, I remember now," she replied. [160]

Authorities also were interested in Jack's former pal Charles Entratta, who managed to get out of serving the remainder of his sentence. It was no secret that there was bad blood between them since the Hotsy-Totsy affair, so some detectives journeyed to New Rochelle, where Charlie, forbidden to enter New York City as part of his parole, was living at the Hotel Lafayette with his wife Anna. As the detectives were taking her husband out to their car, Anna, certain that the men were actually gangsters taking Charlie for a ride, began to scream. The detectives were able to convince her that her spouse was not going to be killed, and she settled down.

Entratta was brought into the city and questioned by Mulrooney. Satisfied that he had nothing to do with the shooting, Jack's former pal was sent back home.[161] Since Marion said that she remembered one of the guys who stopped by over the weekend was named "Maxy," Waxey Gordon was also brought in. He denied having anything to do with the shooting and he too was released.

As the days passed, Jack began to bounce back. Being a Broadway habitué, he would have appreciated that his life and death struggle became a wagering sport. When news first spread of the shooting, odds were 100 to 1 that he would live. By day four, with daily reports of his condition in the papers, the odds were down to 50-50.[162]

On Friday evening, October 17, the superintendent of Polyclinic Hospital received a phone call. "You better get some protection for all your hospital patients," the caller said, "because they are going to blow up the hospital to get Legs Diamond good tonight." In a panic, the superintendent called the police who, although they figured it was a prank, surrounded the hospital with cops.

Not caring for the possible danger or all the publicity resulting in having New York's most famous gangster in their care, the hospital asked that Jack be removed to another hospital. The police informed the Polyclinic that Diamond wasn't wanted for anything, so he was their problem. The powers that be at Polyclinic were able to fix it so Jack could be transferred to Metropolitan Hospital, a city-owned facility, on Welfare Island. Alice complained that Polyclinic wasn't giving Jack a "decent break."[163]

The following day, Jack was informed about the transfer and was none too happy about it. "I won't go," he yelled when the ambulance that would transport him had arrived. He kicked his feet at the orderlies who attempted to lift him on to the stretcher. "I've got five bullets in me. You can't move me anywhere," he snapped at them. Polyclinic doctors, however, all agreed that he was well enough to be relocated. Upon hearing this, Jack said, "First they said I'm to weak to take another X-ray and now they say I'm so much better I can be moved. I'm not and I won't go." Since Polyclinic was trying to dismiss him as a ward of the city, Jack whipped out a roll of bills and said, "Show 'em that. I've got plenty of dough."[164]

After a while, Alice showed up with their attorney Murray Rosenthal, and the latter held a meeting with the hospital officials. Afterward he had a discussion with Jack, and the gangster agreed to go.

Word of the transfer spread and by time Jack was wheeled out of the hospital, there was a crowd of about five hundred people gathered to catch a glimpse of the gangster. Though they saw the gurney they couldn't see Jack, as he had a towel placed over his head. With a car full of armed police for an escort, Jack was on his way back to Welfare Island for the first time in about fifteen years. When the ambulance reached the Queensboro Bridge, a group of motorcycle cops were on hand to clear all traffic out of the way. Midway across the bridge, the ambulance entered a special vehicle elevator and was lowered down onto the island.

Though no longer front page news, Jack's convalescence was still fodder for the newspapers. A few days after the transfer, he was described as sitting up in bed, smoking cigarettes and reading detective magazines while Alice sat at his side. "These stories are the bunk," he said, regarding the pulps, "and they hand me a laugh."[165]

The district attorney continued to question Jack to no avail. "You could go out and pick up one thousand men on my description of the gunmen." He told the D.A. "I couldn't identify their pictures because I didn't get a good look at them after the first shot." Of course nothing turned up about the three imaginary shooters that Jack described, but there was irrefutable evidence that Jack was visited by two acquaintances just prior to the shooting. Spitale and his companion had yet to be identified, and Jack assured the D.A. that the two men had nothing to do with the shooting and refused to name them.

He did tell the D.A., however, that he would have them contact his office but only if he agreed not to arrest them as they both had criminal records. In frustration, the D.A. asked Jack if he could shine any light as to why somebody would want to kill him. "It is as much a mystery to me as to you," Jack replied.[166]

Not all hospital visits were official. Society matron Cordelia Biddle and her husband were touring the penitentiary on Welfare Island and asked if they could stop in and visit Jack. Jack consented, and the couple was brought in. Readers of the *New York Times* read of a reserved, polite Legs:

"How do you feel, Mr. Diamond?"

"Pretty good, thank you."

"Do you like it here?"

"Yes, it's all right."

"And you'll be out of here soon, won't you?"

"I guess that's up to the doctors."

Ms. Biddle then wished him a quick recovery and said she was glad to meet him.

"I was glad to meet you to," he replied in kind.

New York Daily News readers were treated to a more colorful Legs.

"How do you feel, Mr. Diamond?"

"Pretty good kid."

It was noted that during the conversation Jack had grimaced.

"Oh, it pained you then didn't it?"

"Well those were no love taps those guys gave me."

"I do hope you get better soon."

"I hope so too."

"Goodbye Jack, lots of luck."

"Thanks kid, come again."

After a number of weeks Doctors determined that it would be too risky to remove two of the bullets lodged in Jack's body, so he would have to carry around a constant reminder of Spitale's ire. Finally, after two and a half months in the hospital Jack was discharged on New Year's Eve 1930.

Knowing that his release would be a media event, Jack dressed in snappy attire. When it was time to leave, a gaunt Legs emerged from the hospital sporting a gray overcoat, new checkered cap, blue pinstriped suit and spats to match his coat. Alice flanked him in a fur jacket and thwarted the photographers on hand by covering her husband's face with a crime pulp. With them walked some detectives and Steve, the male nurse who would accompany them to Acra.

They boarded the one o'clock ferry that took them over to Eighty-Sixth Street where his cousin Paul -"Paulie" to the family- Hart was waiting for them with Alice's car. With police cars in front and behind, they drove to the 125th Street railroad station for the two-fourteen train that would take them to the Catskills. There was a large crowd waiting for them at the station, so they drove around until departure time. When Jack finally appeared on the platform, the station lit up like a Hollywood film premiere as flashbulbs of fifty photographers began to pop. There was also a movie camera rolling, but it quickly broke down, which brought a smile to Jack's face.[xxxvii]

Jack spoke to the press in the few minutes before boarding. Somebody asked about the shooting. "I don't know what it was all about," he responded. "I've only been in New York for thirty days in the past two years, as the police know. I'd be lying if I said I knew who shot me." He lied.

He told the press that he didn't mind having his picture taken but didn't care for liberties that the reporters took. "Newspapers create a character for you and if you don't live up to it the public thinks you're no good. They want to see horns actually sprouting out of my head. They want me to talk tough. (Did he mean statements like "Those weren't love taps those guys gave me"?) I never said 'yiz' or 'youse' in my life."

Someone questioned Steve about the safety of his new job. "There'll be no trouble," he assured them. Jack smiled and then mentioned that Alice gave him some instructions should

---

xxxvii Fortunately there was another on hand and footage exists today of Jack making his way through the crowds and boarding the train.

he be shot at again: "Don't be too brave in case of trouble. Get behind the biggest piece of furniture in sight."[167]

Jack went on to say that he was looking forward to getting back to Acra. "You know, we're six miles from electric light there and it's a good place to rest."

"Better than the Monticello anyways," one of the reporters quipped. Appreciating a good line, Jack grinned.[168]

A party of five plainclothes cops boarded the train with Jack and escorted him to the city limits and then got off. When Jack's party arrived in the Catskills, Dalton was waiting for them in a Cadillac and drove them back to Acra, where Jack continued to convalesce as well as make headlines.

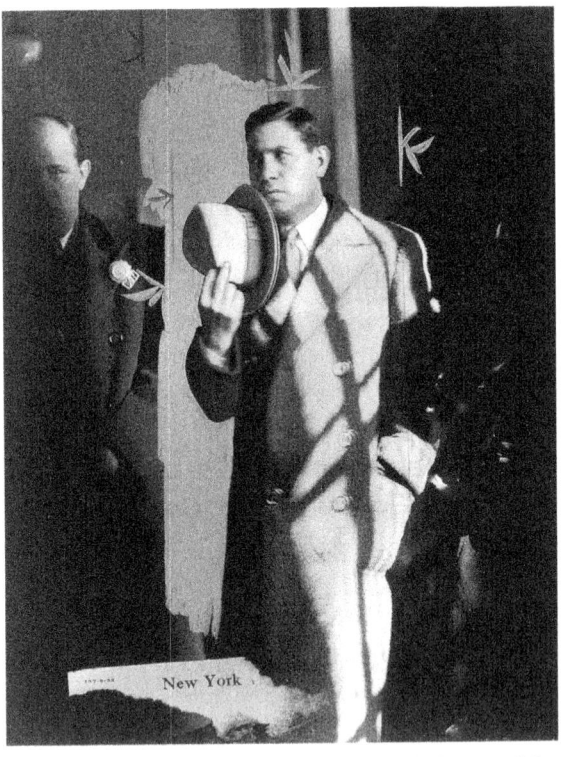

Jack's friend turned enemy Salvatore Spitale. (Library of Congress)

Jack's release from the Metropolitan Hospital on
Welfare Island. (Author's collection)

7

THE PERILS OF FAME

Diamond's first order of business when he arrived home from the hospital was to take a nap. He woke up at three o' clock in the morning and rang in his final New Year with a welcome home party. The *New York Daily News* reported that his boys could be heard singing throughout the day. When one photographer ventured too close to the driveway, he was approached by a guard. "I wouldn't come around with that camera or anything that looks like a gun," the photographer was warned, "because there might be an accident up there."[169]

A week later on January 6, business took a hit when Scaccio and Dalton were arrested and charged with attempted extortion for trying to shake down a trucking contractor named Hoy for $1,500. Dalton was released for lack of evidence, and Scaccio was never bothered by the charge.[170]

While Jack convalesced, the underworld carried on without him. With nothing much else to do but read the papers, Jack probably kept himself informed on the goings on back in New York City. He surely read about a vice investigation being led by Judge Samuel Seabury which was aimed at members of the New York City Police Department and their legal counterparts who worked in tandem to extort money from women. The police would arrest women on the pretense of prostitution. The women would then be forced to pay a lawyers fee (bribe) in order to avoid jail. It was a lucrative racket that had gone on for years. Following the story, Jack would have had no idea that he would eventually get dragged into it.

On January 26, he would have read a story in which he was familiar with both the locale and some of the main characters. On the previous night, Dutch Schultz and some cronies, Marty Krompier for one, showed up at the Club Abbey. Also there was another gangster, Charles "Chink" Sherman, who in addition to bootlegging was also a drug dealer and most likely a pimp - two occupations the Dutchman looked down on. Over the course of the evening, some unkind words were passed between the two hoodlums resulting in Sherman drawing a pistol and shooting Schultz. Krompier responded by breaking a bottle and stabbing "Chink" about the head and body. Some more gunshots went off, and soon everybody vacated the premises.

A girl in Sherman's party piled Chink into a taxi and took him to the hospital. The police showed up a short time later and the gangster lied to them saying that he was worked over outside the club. They knew he was lying but could do nothing. Meanwhile, the Dutchman was taken to the apartment of gang member Edward Popke, known throughout gangland as "Fats McCarthy." Police eventually showed up, and although they found the Dutchman's bloody coat, as well as two sawed off shotguns, the gang leader had already moved on to another hideout. [171]

While Sherman lingered between life and death, Schultz remained out of sight, waiting to learn if he would be dealing with a murder rap. The police were eager to bring him in and so left no stone unturned in their hunt for him. Since Jack had a history with Schultz, he was one of those stones. On February 2, detectives headed up to Acra to question Jack about the affair. However, as the *New York Daily Mirror* reported the following day, the detectives were unable to question Jack, as he was dying from double pneumonia as well as "…three bullets festering in his body and two lungs far gone from tuberculosis." Of course Jack wasn't dying. This was only one of the many fabrications the *Daily Mirror* would print about Jack during the winter of 1931.

✮ ✮ ✮

On the morning of February 26, 1931, about a month after the Club Abbey incident, a Bronx man was walking through Van Cortland Park on his way to work and came across the body of a woman. The corpse would be identified as that of extortion queen Vivian Gordon and her murder case would prove to be one of the biggest stories of the year. In addition to being an extortionist, Vivian was also supplying information to the D.A.'s office for its use in the aforementioned Seabury investigation. That led to the belief that cops bumped her off to keep her from talking. After a few days, it was established that the police had nothing to do with the murder. While the investigation was in progress, the *Daily Mirror* printed its own unsubstantiated findings regarding the case. What better way to sell more papers than drag Legs Diamond into the fray? At first Legs and Gordon were simply underworld acquaintances, but, on March 6, after a week without any arrests, the *Mirror* ran the headline "Diamond's Enemies Killed Vivian."

"This fact was definitely established yesterday," read the *Mirror* article, which indicated Gordon had been killed because Jack was going to use her testimony to "crush" his foes. In the same story, the *Mirror* also established that Gordon was at the Club Abbey the night of the Schultz-Sherman bout and had a ringside seat. They also stated that she was friends with Brooklyn beer lord Vannie Higgins as well. Readers were treated to all their favorite gangsters in one yarn.

Tying Legs Diamond, as well as Dutch Schultz and Vannie Higgins, with the Gordon murder was no doubt a good way to get customers to plunk down their pennies. Taking advantage of a good thing, someone at the *Mirror* was struck with an even better idea. If the public ate up the fact that Gordon was killed because of Jack, just imagine how they would react if they found out that she was killed *by* Jack. So three days after they headlined that Jack's foes killed Vivian, a new headline stated, "Legs Diamond Put Vivian On The Spot." The "definitely established facts" from three days previous were exchanged for "Underworld says…" What did the underworld profess? That Jack hired a couple of killers for $15,000 to do away with Vivian. Why? Take your pick: One reason was that he owed her sixteen grand and didn't want to pay off.[xxxviii] Another was that Vivian was going to expose secrets of his love life since he wasn't paying off on the money owed. As for Dutch Schultz and the Club Abbey incident, that was Jack as well trying to have his enemies bumped off. Again the price was $15,000. According to the piece, the Dutchman, who in actuality was hiding out and recovering from his wound, was now at the bottom of the Hudson River.

Jack may not have been aware of the *Mirror's* pieces. While the papers were being hawked on New York City street corners, he was in Chicago. A few weeks before the articles ran, Jack received a call from Marion, then performing in the road tour of the musical comedy *Flying High*. On February 22, the show began a three-week run in Chicago. It was during this time that she "could not resist an impulse to telephone him at his country home in Acra." This call, in addition to making Jack "the happiest man in the world," also rekindled the relationship which ended with the Monticello shooting. Jack began to call her three times a week. The calls ended up with a trip west.[172]

Jack returned to Acra around March 8, so probably saw that the *Mirror* had labeled him as Vivian's killer. Chances are he didn't care for the publicity, but it was the paper's next move that really got him. Someone at the *Mirror* managed to convince police that not only was Legs the instigator of the Vivian Gordon murder but he was currently hiding the actual killers at his house.

---

xxxviii Though the perpetrator was incorrect the reason was dead on. Gordon was rubbed out by a couple of goons at the behest of her lawyer John Radeloff who owed her a considerable sum of money.

Word of this made its way to New York Governor Franklin Roosevelt, who gave the order to raid Jack's home. A squad of fifty state troopers was chosen from twelve different counties to take part in the raid. At midnight on March 11, the troopers gathered in the town of Troy in preparation. Even though all telephone communications were cut off with the police so that there would be no leaks, Jack was tipped off two hours earlier, and he and Dalton fled the premises.

At four o'clock in the morning troopers armed with rifles and teargas took off for Acra. When they arrived at the town of Cairo, three of their cars took off with special orders. One went three miles past Acra to commandeer the road there and block anyone coming or going. Another car was sent to Paul Quattrocchi's Hollywood Inn. The third went to the Aratoga Inn.

As the sun began to rise, six carloads of troopers, including a reporter from the *Mirror* who had been posing as a detective, advanced on Jack's house. As they headed up the driveway, the flood lights snapped on and the troopers froze, expecting the rat-a-tat-tat of a Tommy gun to break the silence at any moment. They were relieved when nothing happened and approached the house. They knocked on the door, and a servant answered. He informed them that Jack wasn't home and that Alice had been gone for about two weeks. (She had left Jack after he rekindled his relationship with Marion.) Snooping around, the fake detective found some morphine in a cigarette box and helped himself to that, as well as to some of Jack's mail and private letters. Police also grabbed a list containing twenty of Jack's booze clients. Upstairs in one of the bedrooms they found not the two killers of Vivian Gordon but Jack's cousin and another guy sleeping off a drunk. In Jack's room they came across his luggage, which showed that he had returned from Chicago only three days earlier.

Jack was incensed by the raid, and the following day he broke the gangster commandment of "Thou shalt not bring unwanted attention to thyself." The man who just six months previously in Philadelphia threatened to beat up any reporter who approached him set up an interview with a reporter from the *Albany Evening News* to publicly complain about the raid. The journalist, who was expecting a tough-talking, knuckle-dragging hoodlum, was impressed with Jack's appearance and demeanor,

"It was evident from the pauses in his conversation that he meant to choose his words carefully. A well-fitting, dark blue suit, black shoes and his general conversation give scant support to the figure he has been represented to be."

With the ear of the press bent to him, Jack let loose: "My house was ransacked. My personal mail was taken. Even medicine [the morphine] which was prescribed by my physician was taken." He continued his rant with, "I won't know all that was taken until Mrs. Diamond returns home. She is visiting her sister. [He couldn't really tell the truth on that one.] No one showed any warrant. Entrance was made at the point of rifles."

In discussing the raid, Jack said, "The most outrageous thing about it is the supposed federal agent, who assumed to direct a captain, a lieutenant and about twenty state troopers. The fake federal agent," he continued, "I have learned is none other than a special writer for a sensational New York sheet, putting over a hoax on the New York state authorities. It has filled its pages with false and absurd stories about me. The articles had no regard for truth. It strikes me that having libeled me and having feared I would take legal steps to call it to account, it hoodwinked someone powerful enough to stage a sensational stunt for its first page."

Jack ended by striking a blow for the common man: "I intend to see to it that no one, no matter how powerful or influential, shall use the sovereignty of the State of New York to violate the privacy of one's home."[173] Nothing ever happened.

By springtime, Marion was back in New York. After her show closed in Chicago, she went to Albany, and Jack checked her into a hotel. The two picked up where they had left off. They spent time together dining, dancing and taking pleasant drives in the country. With Alice gone, Jack moved Marion into the house. [174]

As Jack was rebounding both physically and financially that spring, he found himself down a man. On April 5, Peter Felice was back in the Bronx attending a "racket" at the Winter Garden. As he was standing in the foyer, somebody came up and shot him in the back of the head and then fired another bullet into his left eye. A cop, who happened to be nearby, hailed a taxi and rushed the wounded gangster to Fordham Hospital where, despite predictions to the contrary, he eventually recovered.[175] The police assumed that it was friends of Angelo Mollica getting revenge. It was also a sign of things to come.

William Talamo AKA Gerry Scaccio was Jack's
body guard and chief henchman. (Harry Ransom
Humanities Research Center, University of Texas at Austin)

8

A STAR IS SHOT – AGAIN

In the spring of 1931, Jack still had a shot at being a successful gangster. He was done in New York City - all the press he received from his ill-fated trip to Europe and the subsequent shooting at the Monticello, not to mention the men who still wanted him dead, saw to that. His infamy also meant no more trips to Europe to set up drug deals, but he still had the liquor and extortion enterprises up in the Catskill regions. That is, until a chance encounter on a dark road with a small time booze hauler brought it all crashing down.

The evening of April 15 found Jack touring some local speakeasies with Kiki, Dalton and Scaccio. Since they were social visits, Jack had no qualms imbibing. A few miles away in Cairo, truck driver Grover Parks was returning from a job in Albany and pulled onto his farm. Though it was eleven-thirty his night wasn't over. He moonlighted as a rumrunner for a local still and had a delivery to make. After a late dinner, he headed over to a neighboring farm owned by a family named Duncan. He got another truck and, together with nineteen-year-old James Duncan, went to Catskill to pick up an order of hard cider. With the hooch on board, Parks and Duncan headed back to the Duncan farm. Driving on the same road was the Diamond party, returning from their night of partying.

Looking into his rearview mirror, Parks noticed a Ford sedan speeding toward them with its headlights turned off. The car pulled up right behind them and after a few moments fell back before again darting forward. This time, the sedan pulled up right alongside the truck and Parks saw two men, one in the front passenger seat and the other in the back seat each pointing a pistol at him. One of them yelled for him to pull over and get out of the truck.

Both vehicles came to a stop, and Parks climbed out. He was approached by a man he had seen in Cairo many times before and knew as Mr. Schiffer.

"Throw up your hands!" Jack barked at Parks. When Parks didn't immediately comply, Jack punched him in the face. After that, the truck driver put his arms up. "Keep your hands up or have your block knocked off," Jack threatened.[176]

Since Jack was in the midst of monopolizing the Catskill booze industry and he knew it wasn't his stuff on the back of Parks' truck, he had some questions for the alky runner. With their caps pulled down over their eyes, Parks and Duncan were forced into the back seat of the Ford. Jack and Marion climbed into the front seat with Scaccio, who was now at the wheel. Dalton jumped into Parks' truck and drove it back to Jack's house, followed by the Ford.

The caravan pulled up Jack's driveway, and Marion went into the house while Parks and Duncan were ushered into the garage and told to sit on the floor. Jack began to interrogate Parks, demanding to know what they were hauling and where they were taking it. Parks, however, wasn't in a talking mood and remained tight-lipped during Jack's questioning.

"I'll make you tell," Jack finally said.

Some matches were retrieved, and Parks had his shoes removed. Jack and Scaccio lit the matches and applied them to the bottoms of the truck driver's feet but still he refused to talk.

"He's tough," Jack told Scaccio, "go get a rope."[177]

Minutes later Parks had a noose around his neck and was being dragged through Jack's back yard to a tree that stood near the creek. The end of the rope was tossed over a tree limb, and Parks was hoisted off the ground. He managed to save himself by grabbing the branch. Jack lowered him to the grown.

"Hold his hands," he told Scaccio.[178]

Scaccio pulled Parks' hands behind him, and Jack once again pulled him off the ground. This time, Parks blacked out and Jack let him drop to the ground. Next they got a bucket of water and dumped it over the unconscious truck driver. Once Parks had his senses back, a gun was placed in his ear and he was told he had one more chance to talk. To show they meant business five shots were fired off by his feet. Parks still refused to answer. Frustrated but not willing to kill, Jack let him go. The truck driver went home, and his wife administered aid to his swollen face and bleeding wounds.[179]

Perhaps it was the booze coursing through Jack's veins that was responsible for this episode or perhaps he was just in a bad mood. Whatever the reason, his poor decision-making during his run in with Parks would prove to be his downfall.

The following day, Parks went to Greene County Judge William E. Thorpe and applied for a pistol permit. The judge asked the truck driver why he wanted to carry a gun. When Parks finished his story, the seeds of Jack's demise in Greene County were sewn.[180]

Judge Thorpe ordered Parks to relay his story to other Greene County authorities. On Sunday, April 19, Sheriff Harold I. Every was brought into the loop. Warrants were issued for both Jack and Dalton, and early Tuesday morning, April 21, Sheriff Every, together with a deputy and a state trooper, headed to Acra to pick them up.

Jack was still in bed when the authorities arrived and began knocking on his door. The pounding woke him up, and he came down to meet them, groggy, but amiable, in his pajamas. The sheriff handed Jack the warrant, and the three officers stood by as Jack read it.

"Those guys are crazy," Jack said, handing back the warrant.

Dalton, Jack informed them, was in New York City. Then saying no more, Jack got dressed and was taken to the county jail at Catskill.[181]

Jack was placed in a cell to await arraignment. In another cell sat Skunky Klein, still waiting for his trial eight months after his arrest for possession of Harry Western's car. Paul Quattrocchi showed up and hung around the courthouse in the event that Jack needed a person on the outside for anything that might pop up. Word of the gangster's arrest spread around town, and by the time Jack arrived for his arraignment the court room was packed with gawkers.

Jack faced the judge alone and declined counsel, stating that he'd been in touch with his own lawyer. He pleaded not guilty to the charge of second degree assault. He also asked that bail be set. Before agreeing, however, the judge wanted to see Jack's police record because, "It might make a great difference in the amount of bail." The Catskill district attorney didn't have a copy of the record, so Jack was taken back to his cell until the judge was able to decide on bail.[182]

The next day, Jack was back in front of the judge with his lawyer, a bondsman and $20,000 in cash. After researching Jack's past, the judge shocked the trio by setting bail at $25,000. Jack was escorted back to his cell, while his team went about trying to scare up the additional five grand.

After spending two more nights in jail, the bail was finally raised, and Jack was released early in the morning of April 24. He returned home to a find that Marion had set up a welcome home party for him. After a short time, he went upstairs to rest, and his guests moved the party to a nearby roadhouse. While Jack's friends were celebrating his release, other people in the locale also were congregating on Jack's behalf, but for a less jovial reason. Local business owners who were being shaken down by Jack and could easily see themselves hanging from a tree or having their feet scorched were starting to talk to the Catskill district attorney. Others, like the local American Legion, who didn't take kindly to having their neighbors tortured by gangsters, formed a vigilance committee and decided that they would take action should Jack or any of his gang cause any more trouble.[183] There were still others planning on ridding society of Jack permanently, but they weren't taking their troubles to the authorities or making statements to the press.

☆ ☆ ☆

On the evening of April 26, Jack and Scaccio went to the Aratoga Inn arriving at ten-thirty. This wasn't a simple drinking mission, however; Jack was expecting an important phone call. The inn's phone was in a little room just past the foyer. Chances are the caller was an underworld business associate, and Jack did not want to take the call at home since there was always the chance his phone was being tapped.

Jack and Scaccio had some drinks, while Jack made numerous trips to the phone room. After more than ninety minutes, Jack decided that his important call wasn't going to happen. Checking the time, he called to the Aratoga's owner James Wynne,

"If he calls, tell him I waited until 12:12 will you?"

With that, Jack put on his cap and walked past the phone room and on to the enclosed porch. Scaccio was still inside the bar when everyone heard the first blast from a twelve-gauge automatic shotgun. The front glass shattered as shot peppered the wall. One of the pellets blew the cap from Jack's head.

Jack turned his body just as the gunman pulled the trigger for the second time. Though most of the shot missed, four pellets slammed into Jack's body and he dropped to the floor. For the second time in six months, the fourth time since 1925, Jack was prostrate with burning lead in his body. "Gerry, I'm hit," he yelled to Scaccio. "Come and get me."[184]

As the front of the Aratoga was being sprayed with pellets, innkeeper Jimmy Wynne doused the lights and everyone hit the deck. Scaccio crawled to his fallen leader and dragged him back into the barroom.

"Bum shooting; better luck next time," Jack reportedly said as the shooters fled in their car.[185]

Either by luck or by a phone call placed by Wynne, a man named M. F. Butler, said to be the undertaker for the village of Cairo, came along and Scaccio loaded Jack into his back seat – after all it wouldn't have been prudent to hit the road in their sedan while the shooters were still in the vicinity - and climbed into the front seat with Butler, telling him to head for the hospital in Albany. Butler made the fifty-plus-mile trip as Jack's blood seeped into the rear cushions. Butler pulled up in front of the hospital at about one-thirty and both he and Scaccio lifted Jack out of the car and carried him into the lobby. They set Jack down in front of a shocked nurse and Scaccio said, "Take care of this man." Then he and Butler took off.[186]

Back at the Aratoga, the patrons were questioned by police, but nobody could offer any information. A search of Jack's sedan turned up a 25.20 pump-action rifle, along with nine shells of the dum-dum variety but no clues as to the identity of the shooters was found.[xxxix] Police also headed over to Jack's house and questioned Marion.

"I told him not to go," Marion sobbed when told the news. "I begged him to stay at home where he would be safe."[187] [xl]

Also questioned were Jack's cousin George Hart and gang affiliates Ben Greco and Harold Alton. The police learned nothing.[188]

News of the shooting filtered down to New York City just before sun-up. Alice caught wind of it somehow, possibly

---

xxxix The fact that Jack had a rifle and dum-dum bullets in his car leads one to believe that he knew he was in trouble either with locals mad about Parks or other gangsters or both.

xl In her newspaper expose released after Jack's death Marion stated that she had been picked up and taken to the Catskill police station that night to be questioned about the Parks and Duncan case and that upon her return two of Jack's "friends" told her that Jack had hurt his arm and was in Albany. They drove her to the hospital early that morning and it was there, through the newspapers, that she learned of the shooting. There may be some validity to her statement as the *Albany Evening News* reported that Jack had two young female visitors early that morning who "filled the hospital corridor with their giggles," and treated the whole affair in a non-serious manner. The girls left after a short visit.

from a reporter, and called the editor of the *New York Evening Journal* to verify the story. Of course the paper printed the conversation in the morning edition.

Editor: Hello?

Alice: This is Mrs. Diamond. Where's Jack? What hospital?

Editor: Albany General.

Alice: Is he hurt?

Editor: Four shotgun slugs. Are you going to see him?

Alice: As fast as I can get there.

Editor: What about the girl [meaning Marion]? Are you going to overlook her?

Alice: Of course I'm going. I belong with him. At times like this her kind don't count.[189]

Just as it was after the Monticello shooting, the news from Jack's doctors was grim.

"He is very, very bad. I doubt he can make it," attending physician Dr. T.M. Holmes told the press. One pellet had fractured his left arm. He had one pellet each in his right lung and liver, as well as one in his back. The doctors didn't think it a good idea to go probing for the ones in his lung or liver, so he would end up carrying them around as souvenirs along with Spitale's slugs. Dr. Holmes' prognosis wasn't the only bad news for Jack. It turns out that less than forty-eight hours before the shooting, Governor Roosevelt, who had been receiving complaints about Jack and his gang, issued an order for New York State Attorney General John Bennett to eliminate the Diamond gang from Greene County. What had originally been a local problem and probably fixable from a bribery standpoint was now statewide and national news. A local judge could be had; the governor of New York was another story.

Bennett jumped into action by moving into Catskill with twenty plus state troopers in his party to protect the witnesses he intended to have speak to a grand jury. When the townsfolk saw the caravan of police arrive, they welcomed them with applause and shouts of approval. Bennett and his team wasted no time in attempting to build a case against Jack.[190]

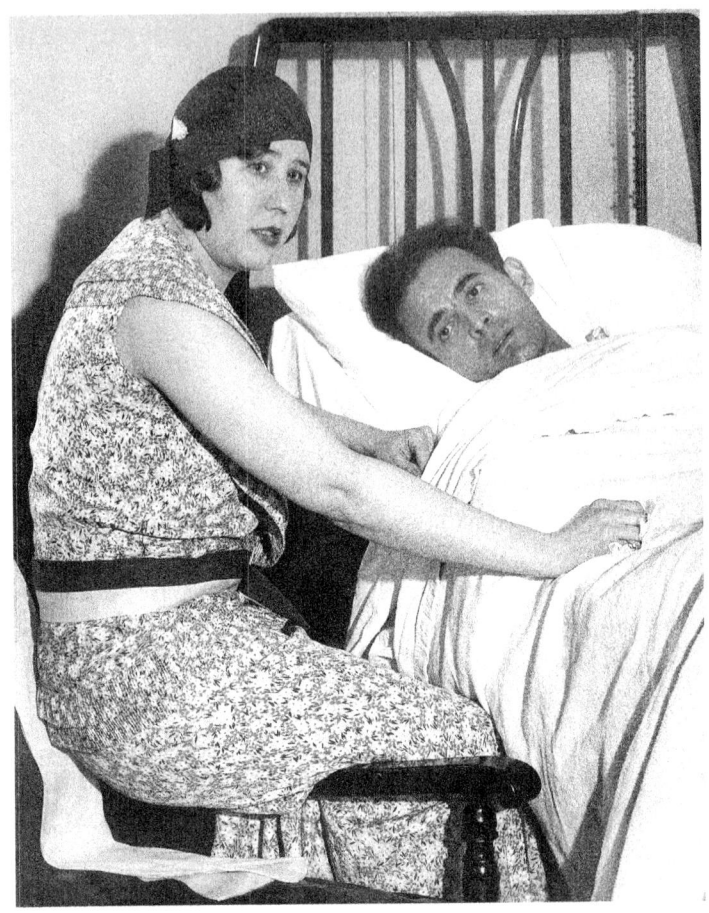

Jack and Alice turn it on for the camera at Albany
Hospital following the Aratoga shooting. (New York Daily News)

9

ENOUGH IS ENOUGH

As Attorney General Bennett's investigation was getting underway, the citizens of the Catskill region were thrown into a frenzy on the night of April 28 as Grover Parks' eighteen-year-old son Donald told police that three gangsters forced his truck to the side of the road outside the town of Cairo and then hung him from a tree. Afterward two of the hoods took off in a car bearing Brooklyn license plates, while the third left in his truck.

Troopers were immediately directed to stop any car with Brooklyn plates. Two attacks on their neighbors was too much for the locals to stand, and once word spread about the second ambush rumors began to circulate that the farmers were considering arming themselves, attacking Diamond's gang and even burning down the house at Acra. Just as the flames of vigilance were being fanned, however, the younger Parks broke down and recanted his story, telling police that he was jealous of all the attention his father had received and was looking for some for himself. Police thought perhaps he was lying out of fear of retribution, but they believed him after he took them to the spot where he had hid his truck. The second Parks story quickly disappeared, but there was plenty more forthcoming Diamond news.

Earlier in the day, police raided Jack's house yet again. Arrested on the premises were his cousin George Hart, Nick Fusco, Harold Alton and Ben Greco. Attorney General Bennett wanted Marion brought in for questioning, but she had

disappeared after her interview following the Aratoga shooting. Scaccio and Dalton, likewise, took a powder. With keys
procured from one of arrestees, the police let themselves into
the house and ransacked it in their search for evidence. Any
locked bureau, drawer or desk was broken into and papers
taken.

Paul Quattrocchi's Hollywood Inn was also raided in the
search for incriminating evidence. Paul, having been named
in the Governor's executive order along with Jack and James
Dalton, was arrested for assaulting local beer runner Joe Coglianese, whom he clocked the previous October right after the
Monticello shooting when he overheard Coglianese say, "I
hope Diamond dies."[191]

Also of interest that day was the discovery of a blue Buick
sedan found in the town of Catskill containing two sawed off
Browning automatic repeating shotguns, a Luger, two Colt
automatics and a Smith & Wesson .38. The car also contained a
New York City driver's license made out to a non-existent person. Since Catskill was a sleepy little burgh, with little in the
way of an underworld, it was determined rather unanimously
that this was the car and weapons used by Diamond's would
be assassins.

Though Jack knew better, he blamed locals for the
shooting in a statement released by one of his lawyers, Isaiah
Leebove:

"It must have been a farmer who pulled the trigger." Jack
said, "The newspaper stories were responsible. They got my
assailant all steamed up. I have no grudge against whoever it
was who shot me."

He went on to say that he didn't see the shooter (or
shooters) but added that most farmers in the region owned
repeating shotguns, implying that it could have been any
number of people.

"Do you believe New York gunmen tried to get you?"
Leebove asked.

"No. They've nothing on me," Diamond answered.

Leebove then went the local gunman route. "What about the vigilante committee made up of farmers who are supposed to be determined to drive you from the county?"

Again Jack held the media responsible for all his troubles. "Blame the papers for their uprising. I'm no menace," he lied. "I've done more to help the community than most of those who would attack me."

Then, looking ahead to his future trial, he took the opportunity to do some self-promotion:

"I have tried to lead a peaceful life since coming here. I'm not guilty of the crimes pinned on me. I'd have to be half a dozen fellows to have committed one-tenth of the jobs I'm accused of doing. I was doing pretty well in the beer racket, but I never went in for extortion and shakedowns. Anyone is welcome to investigate. I'll cooperate with any official. They've nothing on me." [192]

The following day Attorney General Bennett received a phone call from the Albany hospital. The consensus was that Jack wouldn't live to set foot in a court room. He had a temperature of 100.2 and a rapid pulse. They were expecting pneumonia to set in and once it did he would have, according to Dr. Holmes, a, "very slim chance of recovery." [193]

If having both the Grim Reaper and Attorney General Bennett breathing down his neck wasn't enough, Jack got another bit of news that day: the federal government was also getting in on the act. Prohibition agents wanted to bust him for bootlegging. Agents from Washington, D.C., came into town and conferred with Bennett and then headed to the town of Kingston, where they were issued a number of warrants that would allow them to raid a number of stills and speakeasies as well as arrest members of Jack's gang.

One of the first finds was a fifteen-hundred gallon applejack still found on a Catskill farm owned by a couple of brothers named William and Fred Hanna. The farm had been leased to one Harry Costello, which was an alias for Gerry Scaccio. [194]

Although she said that she would go to Jack "as fast as I can get there," Alice actually didn't pay her first visit until

April 30, when she showed up with some flowers. She stayed for about ninety-minutes before taking off. Instead of heading back to the house at Acra, Alice moved in with some friends in Albany so she could be closer to Jack.[195]

First Bennett, then the Feds, and the following day Jack was in the crosshairs of another group, the Catskill Chamber of Commerce. While not as formidable as the two former outfits, the mouse's roar was loud enough to splatter Jack onto the front page of the *New York Times* for the fourth straight day. Like Bennett, the Chamber of Commerce received numerous complaints from boardinghouse proprietors and innkeepers regarding the Diamond gang. With Jack reportedly knocking on Heaven's door and the county crawling with local, state and federal authorities, the Chamber leadership figured it was safe to go public. However, the Chamber members felt differently.

Trying to set one hundred nervous members at ease, the chairman opened a Chamber meeting by telling reporters that they couldn't take notes or name names. He went on to say that if the business community did not stand with Attorney General Bennett, gangsters would win the day and Greene County would be forever under their influence. He moved that the Chamber adopt a resolution stating, in part, that "the Catskill Chamber of Commerce pledges itself and its members to the support of the attorney general and his staff in every possible way in driving all racketeers from Greene County, and we call upon the businessmen and the boardinghouse proprietors of Greene County to give all information which will lead to the indictment and conviction of all men who now are or have been engaged in the business of racketeering in this county." He then asked that other members speak up. A hundred men, who could easily envision themselves evaporating like Harry Western or at the very least being the guest of honor at a Legs Diamond foot-warming party, remained mum. In the end, one guy got up and seconded the motion. The resolution was quietly adopted, and the meeting was adjourned.[196]

May 1 brought more bad news for Jack, both personally and professionally. Personally, Doctor Holmes said that his condition took a turn for the worse. In his daily status report, the doctor said, "One third of his right lung has partly collapsed and there is danger of pus entering the cavity made by the slug. This slug," he added, "about the size of a marble, is in the right lung. Diamond has a severe case of pleurisy, which had resulted in the collection of fluid in the right side of the chest. Diamond, however, remains conscious at all times, although he talks very little. He speaks only when spoken to."[197]

On the professional side government agents found $5,000 worth of Jack's beer, wine, champagne and liquor hidden in an outhouse behind the Aratoga Inn. Down the road a piece was a summer inn called the Villa Pedro and on the property was a large white barn. Inside authorities found stacks and stacks of empty beer kegs, as well as eight large kegs containing brew and some cases of bottled beer as well.

There was also more trouble brewing with the Feds. William Mellin, the federal narcotics agent who busted Jack back in 1927, came to town to make arrangements to have Jack moved to New York to face trial for that arrest. And, last but not least, following the lead of the Catskill Chamber of Commerce, the Cairo Chamber of Commerce also passed a resolution to assist District Attorney Bennett in wiping out racketeering in Greene County.

The following day, as Jack went through a painful operation to have a shotgun pellet removed from his left arm, the investigation intensified. Papers taken from his house and the Hollywood Inn showed that Jack's business wasn't limited to Greene County. Operations ran into a dozen and a half counties between New York City and Albany. Twenty state troopers also returned to the Villa Pedro after receiving a tip that they could find Harry Western's body somewhere on the grounds. The search turned up nothing.

Quattrocchi was the big loser for the day. He was being held without bail for second-degree assault (for hitting Coglianese) and Jack's lawyer, Daniel Prior, who was also representing Paul, argued that he had a right to bail. Bennett, who wanted the Diamond lieutenant to remain behind bars until

May 11 when the grand jury was scheduled to deliver its report on the Diamond gangs' racketeering, argued that he should remain in jail for the time being: "Abundant testimony has been given to [me] in connection with the investigation now being conducted into the activities of the defendant to show that he is one of the principal leaders of the gang headed by John Diamond...Intimidation and coercion have been practiced by the defendant and [I am] of the opinion that to admit him to bail would seriously harm and prejudice the investigation into activities of the defendant and of Jack (Legs) Diamond due to fear in which the defendant is held by many in the County of Greene."[198] Bennett also argued that the federal government wanted Quattrocchi as well and that if he were released the Feds would try him outside Bennett's jurisdiction and they would lose him. They also tossed in the fact that he harbored Diamond's gunman Peter Felice for about half a year.[199] The judge decided that Paul could stay in jail another week or so, while he mulled over Bennett's argument.

It was also reported that Bennett intended to get any safe deposit boxes held by Jack, Alice and Quattrocchi. For safety reasons, Pinkerton detectives were assigned to the bank executives of the financial institutions where the trio did business.[200]

On May 4, knowing that the D.A. was going after safe deposit boxes, Alice went out to try to beat them to their prize but lost. She hurried to the First National Bank in Cairo to get the contents from Jack's box but was informed that the authorities had just been there and took it. "He'll [Bennett] be sorry for it,"[201] she snapped and then sped off. It was the second time in as many days that investigators beat her to the banks. She also tried previously to get some cancelled checks from a bank only to find out they had been there before her.

While Alice was failing at her attempts to collect incriminating evidence, back in Albany detectives and state troopers paid a visit to the New Kenmore Hotel after receiving a tip that they would be able to find Kiki there. They didn't. The law did score one point, however. Since Jack was still out on bail and could conceivably leave the hospital – and conceivably intimidate potential witnesses - Bennett was able to get an arrest warrant signed out for him for carrying concealed weapons. Armed with the warrant, two state troopers paid a visit to Jack in the hospital. He was told that he was under arrest and that a doctor of the attorney general's choosing would be examining him to see if he was fit to be moved. "It's ok with me," Jack said.[202]

After raiding Jack's safe deposit box, the investigators, together with a couple of state troopers, headed over to the Aratoga Inn with a search warrant. Proprietor Jim Wynne wasn't on the premises, so they broke down the door. Waiting on the inside were two large dogs that had to be forced outside. In addition to two rifles, two shotguns and a pistol, the investigators found some evidence that showed that Wynne had business contacts all across the country and that he was buying his beer from Harry Western up until just before the latter disappeared. Wynne showed up at the courthouse for questioning and, as he was leaving, he was asked about his close association with Jack. "There's nothing in that," he responded. "I'm nothing but a farmer."[203]

The day ended with Alice facing yet another indignity from team Bennett. After her fruitless efforts at the various financial institutions in Greene County, she returned to Albany only to find that the attorney general, assuming that she was relaying messages from her husband to other gang members, had her barred from Jack's hospital room.[204]

That evening, investigators returned to their hotel to go over the papers they seized from the Cairo National Bank. With their work for the day finished, two of the investigators retired for the evening in an adjoining bedroom. Shortly after midnight, a prowler climbed down the fire escape and let himself into the suite. As he made his way across the room, he knocked over a chair and woke up the investigators who chased him from the room. Of course the Bennett team accused the Diamond gang of attempting to steal the papers back. "There must be something in them that someone is very anxious to get hold of," one of them told the press.[205]

The following day, Daniel Prior was able to get the order banning Alice from visiting her husband in the hospital lifted, but only on the condition that a state trooper would be present and within hearing distance during their conversations. During a visit the next day, Alice was served with a subpoena to appear in front of a grand jury for questioning. She showed up with Prior but refused to answer any questions "on the ground that it would tend to incriminate and degrade [her]." Other witnesses who showed up for questions included Grover Parks and James Duncan, Greene County beer runner Joe Coglianese, truck man Joseph Hoy (whom Scaccio and Dalton attempted to extort the previous January) and Aratoga Inn bartender Bob Lucas.[206]

The next order of business for Prior was to try to get Jack out on bail on the Sullivan Law weapons charge. On May 8, he and Deputy Attorney General John Cahill went before a supreme court judge in Schenectady. Cahill argued that Jack should not be released, saying in part, "The conditions that we have encountered in the investigation indicate that if Diamond is admitted to bail reprisals may take place and those witnesses who have tried to aid the state in this investigation might be exposed to danger. We feel that the only way we can break this ring is to keep Diamond in jail at this time. If witnesses come in to help us they must be protected."[207] To drive the point home, Cahill brought up the Hotsy-Totsy affair, where witnesses disappeared or were found dead. He also reminded the judge that the drive on Diamond had been ordered by the governor.

Prior countered by saying that the whole investigation was simply a publicity stunt with political motives. "Are they approaching this investigation with judicial calm, with open minds?" he asked, then answered his own query. "No, they are posing for the New York newspapers and are continuing in that spirit. Catskill is crowded with reporters and cameramen and the secrecy of the grand jury room is no more."[208] He concluded by saying that Diamond wasn't the real target; the real target was a Republican judge in Greene County that the Democrats wanted to oust. The judge didn't buy it; no bail for Jack.

On May 9, Quattrocchi's wife returned home to the Hollywood Inn after spending the day at the jail with her husband. When she pulled up, she noticed all the lights on. Knowing they weren't on when she left, she went into town to get the police. Three officers accompanied her into the inn and found that it had been ransacked. It was assumed that Jack had somebody break in to remove incriminating papers.[209]

Two days later, Jack got yet another dose of bad news. Seven more indictments came down against him and his cohorts. He took two for himself, violation of the Sullivan law and coercion. Marion and Scaccio were awarded three indictments in absentia, the former charged with second degree assault and the latter charged with assault and kidnapping. Quattrocchi's total increased threefold. In addition to his earlier indictment for assault he was charged with unlawful entry and extortion[210].

Twenty-four hours after the state laid the new indictments on Jack, the Feds did the same. Jack, Paul and Scaccio, who was still on the lam, were each hit with two Prohibition related indictments. They were charged with conspiracy to violate the Prohibition law, which carried a potential two-year sentence and $10,000 fine, and with possession, custody and control of a still, which carried a maximum penalty of two years in prison and a $1,000 fine. The indictment stated that the trio, "solicited, received and accepted orders for intoxication liquors of all kinds and that liquor was sold in conspiracy throughout Greene County and in other places unknown to the grand jurors."[211]

The Feds questioned the Hanna Brothers, owners of the farm where the fifteen-hundred-gallon applejack still was found. Daniel Prior, who wrote the lease for the Hanna farm, was also questioned, as were a number of road house owners.[212]

An interesting development in the shooting at the Aratoga was brought to light when a ballistics expert reported that Jack may have been shot by members of his own gang. At the Villa Pedro, where some of Jack's liquor was found, it was discovered that the barn there was used for target practice and that the shells found on the premises showed the same markings as those that were fired at Jack. Police were able to trace the shotguns used against Jack to a Philadelphia pawnshop. The proprietor could offer no information on the weapon purchasers other than they "looked like Filipinos".[213] The pistols found in the car were also traced back to Philadelphia where they were purchased at a hardware store.

In the early morning hours of May 23, a taxi pulled up to the corner of Marcy and Lexington Streets in Brooklyn, New York, and began to idle. In the back seat sat Gerry Scaccio deciding whether or not to get out. In a nearby doorway stood two detectives who had spent the last ten days searching for him. Little did Scaccio know, they had been tipped off by Vannie Higgins. The Brooklyn bootleg king had learned that Scaccio was meeting a girl at this intersection on this night and passed the info along.[xli] Not knowing exactly what time to expect the Diamond aide, the cops played it safe and showed up five hours earlier. Their patience was about to pay off, or was it? They couldn't catch Scaccio if he didn't get out of the cab, and so far he wasn't doing it. Finally, after ten minutes, the subject of their manhunt decided to exit the taxi. The decision cost him fifteen years. The detectives darted out of the doorway, guns in hand, and arrested him without trouble.[214]

---

xli After the arrest, the police told the press that they received the tip from a former Diamond gang member. A year later, after Higgins was killed, it came out that he was indeed the tipster. How he came about the info, whether someone told him or he learned it from Scaccio himself, is unknown.

Scaccio was taken to a Brooklyn police station where he was questioned by State Attorney General Bennett and Department of Justice agents regarding Harry Western and Diamond's bootlegging operations. Afterward, he was transferred upstate to the Catskill jail.

Still on the loose was James Dalton, who managed to stay out of sight while a rumor spread that Marion had been bumped off. It was assumed that she had been killed because she knew too much. Though there was no proof, the *Daily News* and *Daily Mirror* had no problem printing it.

☆ ☆ ☆

Meanwhile Jack continued his convalescence, and was soon able to walk around the hospital, accompanied by a state trooper of course. One month to the day after he was shot, he was examined by a doctor on behalf of Attorney General Bennett, and it was determined that he was healthy enough to be transferred to the jail at Catskill.

Fearing that Jack's gang might raid the jail and free him, Greene County installed numerous floodlights to light up both the exterior and the interior of the building. Lights were also set up to illuminate the surrounding buildings.[215]

Just before ten o'clock on the morning of May 30, Jack was escorted out of Albany Hospital by four state troopers and ushered into a sedan. The car containing Jack was sandwiched between two others. The first vehicle contained two troopers. A touring car holding four more troopers brought up the rear.

A large number of people hoping to get a look at Jack were loitering around the Catskill jail when the convoy arrived, and the troopers had to push him through the crowd. Weak from the trip, Jack needed assistance from the troopers to climb the stairs to the jail. Inside, he was booked and then taken to the hospital ward where he collapsed into bed.[216]

✬ ✬ ✬

As Jack was going through his troubles, back in New York City Dutch Schultz was winding up one problem and facing a much deadlier one. That April, Chink Sherman, the gangster who was wounded by Schultz and his boys during the Club Abbey fracas back in January, was released from the hospital. Since Sherman was out of mortal danger, the Dutchman came out of hiding and turned himself into police. He was put in a police lineup, but Sherman refused to pick him out. If Schultz thought that he was out of danger, he was sorely mistaken. There was unrest in his ranks and by the end of May, he, and his Harlem Mafia allies would be taking part in one of the bloodiest gang wars of the Prohibition Era.

Jack's transfer from Albany Hospital to the Catskill jail.
(New York Daily News)

10

JACK TALKS TO THE CITY

On June 1, both Diamond and Scaccio were taken from their cells in Catskill and brought before Justice F. Walter Bliss in the Greene County Supreme Court. Jack was arraigned on his new indictments, coercion and violation of the Sullivan law. Scaccio was arraigned on second-degree assault, two counts of kidnapping and carrying weapons. Jack showed up sporting a nice brown suit and was represented by Dan Prior. Interestingly, Diamond and Scaccio didn't speak to each other, nor did Prior have anything to say on Scaccio's behalf. Scaccio did tell the court that he had counsel but his lawyer was unable to make it to the arraignment. Jack's trial date was scheduled for June 8. Both gangsters pleaded not guilty and were led back to their cells.[217]

Due to a scheduling conflict with another trial, Jack's court date was knocked back a week to June 16. Prior went to work on getting a change of venue for his client. On June 6, Prior went before Judge Bliss and argued that Jack couldn't get a fair trial in Greene County. The state agreed to try Jack in any county, if Prior would agree to moving the trial date up. Bliss asked Prior if that was acceptable, and he agreed to it. When the state asked for June 12 to be the new date, Prior was non-committal. So June 16 it remained.[218]

While the change of venue issue was being worked out, Jack finally got a bit of good news. Prior managed to get him out on bail on the coercion and gun charges. At ten-forty-five on the evening of June 13, $10,250 bail was paid, and Jack was released from the Catskill jail. He was immediately taken back into custody. U.S. Attorney Medalie, in charge of the federal drug case against Jack, had given Catskill Sheriff Every orders to take Diamond to the town of Kingston for arraignment. This wasn't a surprise for Jack and Prior, who had an additional $7,500 in bail on hand.

Before leaving for Kingston, the press asked Jack if he had anything to say. "First of all," he stated clearly and concisely, "I'd like once and for all to correct the impression I'm one of those 'dose, dem and dese' fellows." He added, "I don't mind having the things I do broadcast, but I do object to being charged with things I haven't done. I'm going away for a few days, although I'll be ready to appear in court Tuesday (June 16) if necessary. It looks as if though I'll have at least a week and a half of sunshine and fresh air before I'm bothered again."[219] With that, Jack, Prior, four bondsmen and the police took the trip to Kingston, where Jack was arraigned at midnight. Bail was paid and Jack was released. However, he didn't get to "go away for a few days," as he was ordered to appear at a hearing taking place in New York City the following day in regard to his federal trial. [220]

Four hundred people were on hand at the federal court-house the next day when Jack arrived with his attorneys Prior and Isaiah Leebove. A dapper gray pin-striped suit couldn't hide the fact that Jack wasn't a hundred percent recovered. He looked pale and gaunt, and the dressing from the wound on his back puffed out the rear of his jacket. With his lawyers and two bodyguards in tow, Jack made his way to the front row of the courtroom.

"How are you feeling Jack?" one of the gawkers shouted out. All in the room hushed and pushed forward to listen for the response. "Not so good," he replied. He was arraigned and squeaked out a "Not guilty." Trial was set for June 22 (although the Feds let it be known they would wait until Bennett got through with him first). Then it was outside where a cordon of photographers was waiting for him. One of Jack's bodyguards used a straw hat to block the pictures, and the men jumped into a waiting taxi and took off. Their final destination was Albany[221]

The following day, June 16, Jack and Prior were back in Catskill at the Greene County Supreme Court in front of Judge Bliss for the scheduled start of the trial. Those arguing for the state demanded that the proceedings begin immediately. Prior argued that the stay he obtained for the change of venue was still valid. He also said that he received a change of venue application from a court in Albany which was valid until July 11. The state, frustrated in its attempts to put Jack away, just wanted a court date. In the end, Judge Bliss decided that Jack would be tried in Rensselaer County during the next trial term, which started on October 5. The state wasn't bothered by the decision because Governor Roosevelt had the executive power to call an "extraordinary special" session of the supreme court. Roosevelt did so. Instead of October 5, the trial was set to commence in the city of Troy on July 13.[222] The new date knocked Jack's federal trial back to August 4.

☆ ☆ ☆

While Jack was in the Catskill courtroom getting a change of venue, back in Manhattan Owney Madden's friend and business partner George Jean "Big Frenchy" DeMange was a captive of the Vincent Coll gang. At three o'clock that morning, DeMange was at his speakeasy, the Club Argonaut, when his phone rang. The person on the other end claimed to be a federal agent demanding a payoff. Big Frenchy climbed into his chauffeured car and started for the agreed upon site for the transaction. While DeMange's car was enroute, two sedans pulled up alongside it and forced it to the curb. Nine armed members of the Coll gang jumped out of the two cars and took Big Frenchy prisoner. DeMange was taken to a hiding place, and a call was placed to Owney Madden. If Madden wanted to see his friend and partner again, it would cost (depending on the source) between $25,000 and $75,000.

The ransom was paid within twenty hours, and DeMange was released. Word of the kidnapping spread around Broadway, and the press questioned Big Frenchy about it. He shrugged off the whole affair, telling reporters, "It was just a little business deal with friends."[223]

In his novel *Legs*, Diamond historian William Kennedy insinuates that Jack was the architect of the Big Frenchy snatch and that Coll and his gang were simply the gunmen that pulled the job. It has long been rumored that Jack and the Vincent Coll gang united in the summer of 1931 (mainly for the reason that will be discussed in the following chapter) but there may be some validity to Mr. Kennedy's assertion. Jack was, after all, in Manhattan the day before the kidnapping. But how would Diamond and Coll manage to come together? A link between the two is the Bifano Brothers. Dominick Bifano, Eddie's right hand man in Denver, who was almost killed with him, returned to New York City in early 1929. What part he still played with Diamond is unknown, but his younger brother Louis was part of the Coll gang. It's not difficult to imagine how a Diamond-Coll partnership could have been arranged. With Jack's inner circle either in jail or hiding, he would have welcomed some fresh blood. Seeing that Jack was strapped for cash and, as we learned from Charles Entratta, he would not have been above putting over a snatch. It is possible that Jack orchestrated the kidnapping and let Coll and his boys do the actual job.

✳ ✳ ✳

Times had changed since Jack's previous legal troubles. He was now looking at back to back high-profile trials, the first against the state attorney general and the second against the federal government. This time, there would be no Rothstein to pull strings for him, no judges on the payroll. Left to his own devises, Jack did what he'd never have dreamed of doing six months before. He went public. In an attempt to change his public persona he gave an in-depth interview to the *New York Daily News.*

Part of the reason he chose the *News* may have been the fact that he was friendly with its night editor Gene McHugh, one of the few newspapermen Jack trusted.[224][xlii] Jack and McHugh were close enough that, if somebody got bumped off and Jack knew who did it, he would let McHugh know if his newspaper was barking up the wrong tree.[225] The fact that the *News* boasted of having "The largest daily and Sunday circulation in America" didn't hurt either.

Sitting for the *News* was a shrewd choice. Jack and Dan Prior knew that the men who would be sitting in the jury boxes weren't the *New York Times* type. Plus, largest circulation gave the best odds. Of course the interview was self-serving and Jack, while pointing out some of the more ludicrous things written about him, did lie through his teeth at times.

Reading the interview, which ran in four parts, one can almost see Dan Prior coaching his client on what to discuss and what to avoid. Knowing that the prosecution would be painting him as a murderous racketeer, Jack hit all the points that probably would be brought up against him at trial, while presenting himself as simply a victim of circumstances, a regular guy, no angel mind you, who had to pay the price for the "mythical Legs" character dreamed up by the press. Journalist John O'Donnell and a photographer were sent to Albany to handle the interview.

"Certainly I'll talk for publication," Jack told O'Donnell. "All I'm asking is fairness. I haven't seen much of it in what's been written about me up to present."

The men had dinner in the hotel dining room and afterward Jack stood at a window smoking. Outside was a park and across that the state capital. O'Donnell pointed out to Jack that just across the way all the powers of the state were

---

xlii In addition to being pals, McHugh supposedly resembled Jack so much that there was almost an attempt on his life at the Club Madrid by some of Jack's enemies.

planning their war of extermination against him. "Against me, Jack Diamond," he responded, "or against this figure in the public imagination that they call Legs Diamond and stick all the other labels on?"

Walking back to the table, he put out his cigarette. "If you think that I've got horns popping through my hat, or wear a tail between my legs and have to curl up to sit down – well, go ahead and say so. But let's use common sense."

Back in his seat, he looked over his plate which had yet to be cleared. "I've read about everything that has been written about me, naturally." He continued, "Some of the things hurt. Others were just asinine. The things that hurt were the untruthful things about my family and my brother Eddie. After all, my folks were decent people. And then there were the asinine things – the ridiculous things they pulled out of the clouds to throw at me."

Jack switched gears and, in a humorous tone, said, "Why the boys who were writing some of the stories had me killing a half dozen men around Times Square every day." Adding with a smile, "If you swallow it all I must have used everything except airplanes and submarines. Every time I snapped my fingers a squad of supposed enemies would curl up and die."

O'Donnell brought up an example. "Now that's what I mean by the asinine things written about me," Jack responded. "This idea of pinning everything on me that happened from the time of the Hotsy-Totsy affair to the Vivian Gordon and Starr Faithfull [murders]. None of us may have wings sprouting from our shoulders but after all there's a limit and common sense ought to show that clearly enough. I might have been in a hospital. I might have been trying to get some fresh air in my lungs up in the Catskills. That didn't make any difference, if there was an important crime hanging around loose in New York, I would pick up a paper and find some writer had hung it on me. Now that's not common sense. That's why I've never talked to a newspaper reporter before for any length of time. If you want to use common sense, let's talk."

Jack, O'Donnell and the photographer continued the interview while taking a stroll around the neighborhood. Puffing on another cigarette, Jack said, "Tell me if this is the way you figure it out. I haven't been talking out of vanity. The fact that I've never given out my side before would show pretty clearly that I'm not publicity mad. But here's what I think. This stuff written about me has created a mythical figure in the public mind. I mean this mythical Legs Diamond. Now, I'm Jack Diamond, and I've got to defend myself against the mythical crimes of the mythical Legs." Tossing his cigarette butt into the street, he added, "I wonder how many thousand[sic] people think I'm a 'dese, dem and dose' sort of person, who talks out of the side of his mouth and swaggers around with that famous bodyguard."

While the men stood there pondering the last remark, they noticed that other people in the area had recognized Jack and were shooting glances their way. The trio crossed the street with Jack in the middle. "They probably got you two fellows figured out as the sinister bodyguard of Legs Diamond," Jack joked. As they re-entered the hotel, Jack laughed at the idea that their picture might turn up in an Albany newspaper the following day with them described as "Albany's underworld visitors."

Back inside, they took to some chairs and Jack continued with the bodyguard theme. "I've never had a bodyguard. All the trouble I've been in ought to prove that fact enough." It had been printed numerous times that he had pulled bodyguard duty for Arnold Rothstein and was acting as Little Augie Orgen's guard the night he was killed. That may have spurred his next comment. "Well to begin with, I'm not a muscle man and I never have been. I mean," he said while tapping his bicep, "I never had to use this. Probably the reason for that is that I could never keep my face straight long enough to put over the muscle man talk. I'd break out laughing at myself in the middle of it. I've heard the muscle line of course, but I never had any part of it."

Returning to his original line of thought, he added, "We were speaking of the troubles I've been in and why. I'll say this: I've always been a pretty independent sort of fellow. And because I was independent, because I wouldn't take a lot of hard talk from some of the boys who thought they were tough, it caused a lot of these accidents to happen to me. But you know we can't go into that now."

Commenting on Jack's ability to survive his "troubles", O'Donnell said,

"You're probably the luckiest man who ever walked in shoe leather to come out of those accidents."

"There must have been a lot of prayers said by somebody," Jack responded.

Jack mentioned the first time he was shot back in 1925, and O'Donnell responded with surprise because he was unaware of the shooting. "I wasn't Legs Diamond in those days," Jack retorted. "That's why you never heard of it."

Now that Jack had sent the message that he wasn't the evil, cold-blooded killer the press said he was, he moved onto his next phase, clearing himself of the extortion charges made by Greene County innkeepers and hotel owners. "Publicity helps the punk. Publicity helps the guy that is on the muscle. And I don't want it," Jack said. Lighting another cigarette, he gathered his thoughts. "Don't think I go around calling people 'punks' and 'guys on the muscle.' I don't. Of course if somebody started to call me those names I'd talk right back at him. But I don't like that hard talk. But here's what I mean. A lot of cheap people – men I wouldn't even bother talking to, people I don't know – have been going around for months, using my name and cashing in on the stuff written about me." So all those business owners testifying to Attorney General Bennett were, like Jack, the victims of con-men simply using Jack's infamy to scare the proprietors into paying up. They lost their money and honest Jack got the blame. "Even when I was in the hospital up here, after I got hurt down in the Aratoga Inn, they were working this racket. I found out a little while ago that this cheap crowd went around and said they were taking up a collection for me. Now I didn't know them, didn't want the money - never saw the money, but I heard from the people who were shaken down for it."

O'Donnell couldn't hide the fact that he thought it was humorous that Jack was playing victim to these supposed strong-arm guys. "How else have the boys been taking you over? Cashing in on your reputation?" he asked.

"Plenty," Jack responded, smiling at the fact that O'Donnell was humored. "How about this speakeasy racket? Didn't it ever occur to you that right at this very minute – right while you and me are sitting here smoking – that some of the boys I never even heard of might be going up to a speakeasy in New York, or here in Albany or down in Greene county and saying: 'Here you. This is Jack's beer and you've got to take it.' It's happened all right. Just one of those things. I don't happen to be interested in selling beer[xliii], but that's not going to stop anybody from crashing in on this Legs Diamond reputation."

In one fell swoop, Jack cleaned his slate of both racketeering and bootlegging. He closed the topic with another lament: "When I go on trial July 13 over here in Troy and down in New York later, it will be a mythical Legs Diamond on trial – not me, Jack Diamond."

Next, Jack tackled the idea of him being a notorious gunman and of his house being an arsenal. "I was supposed to be Little Augie's bodyguard at the time [of the murder] if I remember the stories correctly. It's funny that if I really am such a gunman as I'm supposed to be, or have all these bodyguards and guns that I get hurt so often – and that no one ever finds a weapon. That affair in the Hotel Monticello wouldn't indicate that I was much of a gunman. The only weapon I had was a bed pillow. Then consider that trouble at the Aratoga Inn – last April when I got hurt. Do you think that I had the foresight to hide all my guns because I knew I was going to get into trouble and the police would search me and my house? But what

---

xliii Apparently Jack forgot or didn't care about the statement he released from the hospital after the Aratoga shooting: "I was doing pretty well in the beer racket, but I never went in for extortion and shakedowns."

happened? I dropped with these slugs in me in the doorway of the Aratoga. The troopers were there in a few minutes. They found out quickly enough that I didn't have a gun. At the very same moment, another squad of police were searching my premises from top to bottom. There wasn't a gun there. Does that support the theory that I'm a dangerous gunman living in a stronghold or fortress or whatever they've been calling it?"

Next Jack would disassociate himself from some of the high profile murders his name had become connected with. "I want to tell you that I had nothing to do with killing Eugene Moran. Those stories mixing me up in that weren't legitimate." He told O'Donnell, "That Moran case was one in which all the newspapers were completely wrong as far as I was concerned."

O'Donnell reiterated what had been said in the press about the break with Rothstein and the attempt on Eddie's life in Denver as well as the subsequent murders that were all laid at Jack's feet. When Eddie was brought up, Jack's eyes swelled with tears. "All these troubles seem to have happened to me since Eddie died." Then, regaining his composure, he said, "But to get back to this Moran affair – what's wrong with the whole theory that has been printed about this murder is this. I never went after Moran and the rest. I didn't think they tried to kill Eddie in Denver."[xliv] He lied, continuing the tale with, "If you remember, you'll know that Eddie was only ten feet away from the men who drove up to his automobile and tried to shoot him. He saw the men. Saw them perfectly, he told me. Now Eddie told me that neither Moran or Walsh did the shooting. And Eddie knew. What my brother said satisfied me. I believed Eddie – why shouldn't I? As far as Moran was concerned he was neither my friend nor my enemy. He just didn't play any part in my affairs. And Fatty Walsh was killed down in Florida

---

xliv One of the "rest" that Jack was talking about was Frank "Blubber" Devlin who was found in New Jersey on March 5, 1929, with three bullets in his temple. The press labeled him as Moran's and Piteo's accomplice in the attempt on Eddie, so Jack got the credit for the kill. Chances are Devlin was included simply because he was killed the day before Fats Walsh, and the papers tried to link the murders.

in a fight over a card game. It hadn't anything to do with me or Eddie at all." Jack was correct about Walsh but Moran was another story. Chances are that Jack didn't kill him, but lying about Moran's part in the attempted murder would have made a politician nod in approval. If Jack had said, "Yes Moran was involved, but I didn't seek revenge." He would have looked like a cowardly gangster or a flat-out liar. He also couldn't say that Moran was simply a gun hired by Dutch Schultz to exact revenge for the Diamond directed murder of Noe. Nope, a lie was necessary.

There were some murders Jack conveniently forgot to discuss, namely Harry Western, Red Cassidy, Simon Walker, William Wolgast, Tommy Ribler and Hymie Cohen. Also notably missing was any discussion of Marion. She was still at large at the time of the interview and some of the papers, the *Daily News* included, insinuated that Jack had her knocked off. To assure readers that Marion, wanted by the authorities, was alive and well would be showing knowledge of her whereabouts, which would result in Jack having more charges thrust upon him. Better to remain mum.

Using the Denver episode as a segue, O'Donnell brought up Eddie again. "Everybody knows about your devotion to your brother," he stated. "Why shouldn't we have been devoted?" Jack responded. "All we had was each other."

Racketeering, gunman, murders. Was there anything else the press got wrong that Jack wanted straightened out. "I suppose one of the things that got under my skin was the way my Army record was interpreted- so as to make me look like a slacker, or to appear as if I stole from fellow soldiers. That simply doesn't happen to be true." He had to polish his military record should it be brought up in the courtroom. However these were irrefutable records, simple lies couldn't wash them away, so instead Jack tried to spin the story to make it stink less. "Right on the record it shows that I enlisted back in June 1916, in the Ninth Regiment. That doesn't sound like a slacker does it?" No, but he left out the part that it was right before an arrest and most likely a ploy to keep out of jail "And I didn't steal anything from other soldiers. It wasn't pointed out that I was in France from July 1918 to the following January. When I was sent back it was to stand a court-martial for an offense that took place in this country before I was sent over. I admit I went A.W.O.L. before we went across. And while I was A.W.O.L. in this country I was accused of stealing some clothes from a place I was staying. But that's not like saying I was a slacker or stole from members of my outfit." He stole items from the barracks, maybe not his outfit per se, but somebody's outfit. He also assaulted a superior officer.

Racketeering, gunman, murders, court-martial, any other misunderstandings? What about that whole European fiasco from the previous year, when he was kicked out of every country he entered? "Honestly the only thing I wanted was to get the same treatment for my stomach that I had taken before at those German baths. You know, these Germans are great people on stomachs. They make a specialty of it." And to end that lie with a happy spin, "But I certainly enjoyed the trip back on the freighter. Those days on that slow freighter coming back from Hamburg were perfect. There I was. All alone on the boat with a cargo of eight thousand canaries. Nothing to do but eat with the captain and first officer, sit in the sun and put on weight. I think I gained a pound a day." A perfect trip that ended with him snarling at photographers and threatening to punch any reporter that came near him.

What about his police record with over two dozen arrests for everything from attempted robbery to murder? "But take a look at that record and analyze it. Certainly I've been arrested twenty-five times. Certainly that looks bad. But were all these judges crooked who turned me out? Mightn't it be true that I was innocent? On the interpretations some of the newspapers have put on that police record of mine you would think that I was the most powerful guy in the world. If what they write about me is true, all I had to do in New York when I was arrested was to snap my fingers and some district leader would dash into court and say: 'Here judge, you've got to turn Jack Diamond out on that homicide arrest. Or turn him out on that grand larceny charge. And then according to the stories, the judge would probably stand up in the bench and bow at me and say: "Mr. Diamond, we're very sorry this happened. We never should have arrested you and we'll turn you out immediately."

"Then if a friend of mine comes out and tries to help me – and, after all, I do have friends, you know, good people – someone tries to say that's protection. There's a difference between affection and protection. If I were a neighborhood kid that happened to get into trouble, there are lots of friends who would like to help me out. But if I were actually this terrible Legs Diamond created in the public imagination, how could I ask any friend to help me?"

With his past taken care of, the conversation turned to why he was in Greene county and his current troubles. "As a matter of cold fact I bought that place in Acra for my brother Eddie when he was sick. Later I went up there myself and that's all there was to it – except I've had a lot of grief thrown at me."

"Does it add up and make sense to say that I wanted to take over Greene County- even if I could? Of course the boys were right on one count. They said I used my wife's name up there- calling myself Schiffer. As far as I know, you can use any name you want so long as you don't do it to defraud anyone." In case people thought that the fact that he went by an alias constituted criminality, he added, "If using a different name than the one you were born with is a crime, I think some of these writers ought to start right in on Times Square and expose these criminals. It won't be such a terribly tough job for them to dig up some theatrical owners, actors and, perhaps writers and publishers, who are using names that don't exactly match up with the ones you'll find on their birth certificates."

So, if everything about Jack was a huge misunderstanding, why then, O'Donnell wanted to know, were the charges of kidnapping and torture made against him?

"Because they're crazy," Jack replied. "Can anyone with a grain of common sense tell me what I'd want with Parks' five barrels of cider? And why would I do an insane thing like that torture story to find out where that applejack still is located? Particularly when everyone in Catskill with a nose on his face can't help knowing where it is? It's about as secret as the town hall. If you want to find out where this mysterious still is go down to Catskill and take a few sniffs of the breezes some night."[226]

Timing is everything. Jack's four-part series ran in the *Daily News* from June 28 through July 1. Just five days after his last installment of assuring New York that he wasn't a gangster, he had his named dragged through the underworld mud yet again when former friend and partner Charles Entratta was gunned down in Brooklyn. "Diamond's ex-henchman gets the works" said one headline, another in big bold letters declared, "Ex-aide of Diamond killed by gunmen." Just the type of publicity he didn't want prior to his trial.

By the summer of 1931, Entratta's parole board had allowed him to return to New York City. In addition to a house in Long Beach, Long Island, Charlie also took a suite at the Hotel Ogden, located at 50 West Seventy-Second Street. For appearances since the Hotsy-Totsy case, he became associated with two legitimate businesses, a dress manufacturer and a paper goods company.[227]

Around March of that year he, against the advice of the parole board, also took a "sales" position in a Brooklyn bottling company. (In actuality he owned a third of the company.) The parole board felt that in such an industry he would mix with bootleggers. Of course they were right and, using his underworld contacts, Entratta's business began to boom.

On the morning of July 6, Entratta left his Long Beach home in his chauffeured sedan and headed for New York City. His first stop was in Queens at the paper company he held an interest in. Afterward it was to the bottling plant.

His sedan pulled up to the plant and Charlie entered the office of Abner Traub, one of his partners. A few minutes after his arrival, three gunmen rushed into the office and opened fire on Entratta. Traub jumped under his desk as three bullets smashed into Entratta's head and two more plowed into his back. The murder was never solved, but it was speculated that Brooklyn gangsters felt that Charlie was encroaching on their territory.[228]

Jack's trial was scheduled to begin a week later on Monday, July 13. He moved into the Kenmore Hotel in Albany for the course of the ordeal and on Thursday, July 9 (the day following Entratta's funeral), a number of that city's detectives descended on the place to ensure that Jack didn't get bumped off in their town. The following evening, a local reporter was admitted for an interview. The reporter noted that during his conversation with Jack they were continually interrupted by phone calls. At one point, Jack also sent a guy to New York City on some business. The journalist asked Jack how he was spending his time. "I am resting up mostly," he replied. "I know that next week's trial will be a strain on me and I am trying to get enough strength together for it." He added. "I pass most of my time here in this room with an occasional automobile ride out into the country for fresh air."[229] Apparently Jack needed some fresh air late that night because at one o'clock he left in a car.

The next day, with Alice and a few friends, Jack quietly celebrated his thirty-third and final birthday. Sunday, when he wasn't busy with his lawyers, was spent at the Kenmore with Alice. He did manage to speak to the press one final time on the eve of the trial. "I'm not worried about the evidence they will present against me. I am certain I can prove I'm not an insane person, who wanders around the country roads, kidnapping people and torturing them, but what worries me is that the jury may think I'm the kind of a roughneck some of the papers said I am."[230]

Jack also hinted that he might take the stand himself. "I want to show these people," he said, reiterating his mantra, "I'm not a dese, dem and dose guy. That's why I want to tell my story myself and let them look at me and listen to me."[231]

So, in preparation of the trial, Jack asked the public to use "common sense" when it came to judging him. He was confident that he could prove he wasn't an insane bootlegger who went around torturing people in the middle of the night, nor was he a gangster who settled his scores with a gun. Misunderstood Jack felt that all he needed to be acquitted was a fair shake. To hedge his bets however Jack got a witness that would take the stand and lie through his teeth for him.

Under the watchful eye of his attorney Dan Prior (L) Jack gives his side of the story to Daily News reporter John O'Donnell. (New York Daily News)

11

ENTER MR. COLL

The story of the man behind one of the deadliest gang wars to plague New York City begins on April 12, 1909, when the *S.S. Columbia*, which sailed from Londonderry, Ireland, nine days previous, docked at New York City. Among those exiting down the gang plank were Toaly and Anna Coll along with their sixteen-year-old daughter Florence. Tagging along were sons Thomas, eleven, and Charles, five. Chances are Florence was carrying her younger brother Peter, then about a year-and-a-half old, while her mother carried the newest member of the family, six-month-old Vincent.[232] Although Peter would have his posthumous moment in the New York dailies it would be the youngest son, Vincent, who would cut a swath through gangland.

Toaly, Anna and Florence had been in America before, but it was the first time for the boys. Toaly first reached the U.S. more than two decades earlier and became a citizen in 1886. During his stay he met Anna Duncan, born in Illinois of Irish and Australian decent.[xlv] They married and had their first child, Florence, in 1892. After her birth, they returned to Ireland, where the boys were born.[233] Less than a year after Vincent's

---

xlv The 1910 census states that the father became a citizen in 1886. Although Anna's death certificate states she was born in Ireland, this was probably an error. The death certificates of Vincent and Irene list her as being born in the U.S. as does the 1910 census. This is further supported by the passenger list of the *S.S. Columbia* which labels the entire Coll family as American citizens. In regard to Anna's nationality her death certificate states that her father was born in Ireland and her mother Australia.

birth on July 20, 1908, they returned to the States. Once back in New York City, they made their way to the Bronx where they took an apartment on Courtland Avenue.

The young life of Vincent Coll mirrored that of Jack Diamond. Both would feel the pain of losing a mother and siblings at a young age. After their arrival in America, the Colls had two more children. A daughter, Irene, was born on January 9, 1911, but sadly she passed away seven months later on September 5.[xlvi] Five years later, two months shy of their seventh anniversary of arriving in the States, Anna died.[234] Without the family matriarch, the Colls seem to have come apart.

Known as a "lazy drunkard who never made any real effort to support his family,"[235] Toaly disappeared after his wife's death. Florence and Thomas stayed in the Bronx where the latter worked as a store clerk and the former got married and started her own family.[236] Like the Diamond brothers, the youngest Coll boys, Peter, Vincent, and possibly Charles, were shipped off to an institution. They ferried over to Staten Island and moved into the Mission of the Immaculate Virgin. Unlike the Diamond brothers, they didn't have an uncle to take them back out. The brothers stayed there for three years. Unhappy with his new surroundings, Vincent ran away a number of times. In 1920, Peter and Vincent returned to the Bronx to live with an aunt.[237] Charles remained on Staten Island, where he maintained a job as a waiter. At the age of seventeen, Charles contracted tuberculosis and died ten days before Christmas in 1920. If the pain of losing Charles wasn't bad enough, older brother Thomas, who had since moved to Middletown, New York, to work as an attendant at the Middletown State Homeopathic Hospital, died of the same affliction two months later.[238] Another thing Jack and Vincent shared was losing a brother to TB, or in Vincent's case two brothers.

---

xlvi According to a Coll family descendent, the other child was another daughter named Tessie, who lived a full life without bringing any attention to herself. There were two other siblings Toaly and Anna buried in Ireland. The first male son, also named Toaly died in 1896 at the age of two. There was a second son, Robert, who also died around the turn of the century.

Vincent wasn't any happier at his aunt's house than he was at the Mission and again ran away numerous times, sometimes living on the streets. It was during one of his homeless periods that he was befriended by another young man named Joe Iadoroli. Vincent was ill with an eye infection, and Joe, who went by the moniker of "Bar Rags", brought him home. Vincent was immediately accepted and cared for by the family matriarch Angelina. From that time on the Iadorolis and the Colls were close. In fact Florence acted as God Mother to the Iadoroli's youngest sister Rose. Just as Vincent and Peter were blossoming gangsters, so too were Joe Iadoroli and his younger brother Gennaro, a.k.a. "Chin."

Though Vincent Coll was capable of extreme violence, those who knew him remembered a much different young man than the one-dimensional, insane, uncouth character described in books and on film. To his friends, Vincent was a shy and polite young man, not to mention generous with his money.[239] [xlvii]

Good attributes aside, Vincent was a problem child and had the police record to prove it. His first arrest came in 1920, before he was even a teenager. By the time he was twenty-two, he had been arrested a dozen times, once for homicide. An arrest on November 7, 1924, for having a gun, resulted in his being sent to the House of Refuge on Randall's Island. Despite an escape that lasted only five hours (he was rearrested after he returned to his neighborhood), he spent a little over a year and a half on the Island. Since his behavior at the House of Refuge was bad, on August 10, 1926, three weeks after he became a legal adult, Vincent was transferred to the state prison at Elmira. There he stayed until being paroled the following year.[240]

Brother Peter was also a delinquent, although his rap sheet wasn't nearly as long as Vincent's. He was arrested twice

---

xlvii Years later Rose Iadoroli would tell her son John about how Vincent would flip her silver dollars. Once when she was sick, Vince and his girl-friend Lottie paid her a visit and gave her a box of candy.

in 1924 for auto theft and robbery and again in 1929 for imper-sonating an officer but was never convicted. At the time of his death, he was out on $2,500 bail for violating the Sullivan Law after cops received word that he and another gangster were in a Broadway apartment planning a murder.[241]

Had Vincent remained a run-of-the-mill punk, it is doubtful whether he would be remembered today. His path to infamy however was paved when he managed to get on Dutch Schultz's payroll. Exactly how Coll came to work for Schultz cannot be said for certain, but chances are it was through his best friends the Iadorolis.

Both of the Iadoroli brothers worked for Schultz, as did their father, who was a night watchman at one of the Dutch-man's buildings in the Bronx.[242] So it seems likely that Vincent and Peter rode the Iadorolis' coattails into the Schultz organi-zation by 1928. The raid on Schultz's headquarters on Decem-ber 13 of that year shows that Vincent was already carrying a gun for the Dutchman. This arrest violated his parole, and he was sent back to Elmira on January 12, 1929 to serve an addi-tional six months or so.

By the late summer of 1929, Coll was back on the outside and working as Schultz muscle. This job would cost Vincent one of his best friends, Joe Iadoroli, who was killed while ful-filling a labor racket contract. Fred Redkay, the superintendent of the Keystone Hosiery Company, was preventing his workers from unionizing. Some pro-union men hired Schultz to beat some sense into him. On the morning of August 27, 1929, Schultz sent Joseph, Vincent, Fats McCarthy (remembered by his contemporaries as a "crazy son-of-a-bitch. He'd go out and shoot a guy in the head and the next day walk [Iadoroli's mom] to church."[243]) and another guy known only as Chick the Jew to handle the contract[xlviii]

The group left the Bronx and headed for Brooklyn and their rendezvous with the superintendent. Driving along Seventy-Ninth Street, they saw their target walking to work and pulled up to the curb. Three of the guys, including Iadoroli, jumped out

---

xlviii Joe Piteo may also have been with the group.

and started to pummel Redkay with blackjacks and a baseball bat. The superintendent screamed for help and an off-duty cop named James Quigley came to his rescue. The gangsters made a run for the car as the wheelman fired a few shots at Quigley. The patrolman returned fire. Iadoroli dropped to the sidewalk, mortally wounded, as his confederates sped off.[244]

A few days later, a horse-drawn hearse pulled up in front of the Iadoroli house where the wake for Joseph was held. The casket was carried out and placed inside the hearse. Friends and neighbors joined the procession to St. Raymond's Cemetery, where Joseph was interred. Although he wasn't supposed to attend the funeral (detectives would probably be on hand), Vincent showed up anyway to pay his respects.[245] In honor of his friend, and as a gift to Iadoroli's grieving mother, Vincent had a special tombstone imported from Italy.

Over the next two years, Dutch Schultz, in addition to running his other enterprises, began to monopolize the Harlem policy racket. In this venture it was necessary to partner up with the locale's chief Mafia boss Ciro Terranova, so it wasn't uncommon for Schultz's boys to hobnob with Mafia guys.

In the spring of 1931, there was dissention in the Schultz ranks. Coll defected, leading a gang of disgruntled gangsters in a war against the Dutchman. The reason for the break is uncertain. The generally accepted version is that Coll and his cohorts wanted a bigger piece of the gangland pie, and Schultz wasn't interested in sharing. Iadoroli family lore suggest that the split was over a stupid argument, the cause of which is now lost to history. Whatever the reason, while Jack Diamond was upstate preparing for the Parks trial, New York City was about to witness one of the bloodiest gang wars of the Prohibition Era and Jack, most likely, was about to get a new mob.

Taking on the Dutchman would have seemed like an impossible, if not suicidal, task. However, when "The Mick" or "Irish," as Coll was known to his gangland brethren, broke off from Schultz, he took a formidable contingent of Schultz gunmen with him. The new gang consisted of at least a dozen or more young thugs, including brother Peter, Mike Basile, ace gunman Fats McCarthy, Dominick "Toughy" Odierno, Frank Giordano and Gennaro "Chin" Iadoroli.

The exact date the Schultz-Coll war began is unknown, but the first documented fatalities took place late in the evening of May 28, 1931. The victims weren't Schultz men, however, they were his allies; Mafia guys connected with Ciro Terranova. That evening's target was Joe Rao, one of Terranova's top guys. His car was parked on 116th Street, and he was sitting at the wheel talking with two of his men, Dominick "Louis Slats" Bologna and Frank "Big Dick" Amato, who were standing near his window. Why Coll wanted Rao dead is a mystery. Since he was a Terranova man, Coll probably had some sort of contact with him. All that is remembered is that for some long forgotten reason Vincent hated Rao with a passion.[246]

While Rao chatted with his two friends, a sedan pulled up alongside his car and a burst of gunfire erupted. As shots poured into Rao's car, a gunman jumped from the sedan and went after Amato and Bologna. The former ducked behind a car, but the gunman found him and shot him in his head and neck. With Amato down, the gunman turned his gun on Bologna, who was running across the street, and drilled him in the back with a single shot. Mortally wounded, "Louis Slats" stumbled into a restaurant and screamed for an ambulance then dropped dead. Rao slipped out of his car and escaped with a slight wound. [247]

Retribution was swift. In the early hours of May 30, Peter Coll was driving through Harlem when another car pulled up and opened fire. Instinctively Peter turned to the right as a number of bullets smashed through the windshield and slammed into the left side of his back. Losing control of his car he crashed into a divider. He died later at the hospital.

About twenty-four hours after Peter got his, the mob struck again. The victim this time was Vince's best friend Gennaro "Chin" Iadoroli. At one-forty-five in the morning, Chin walked down a stairwell and entered the subterranean Hub Bowling Alley. He approached the manager and told him that he was expecting a phone call. Then, seeing a group of guys he knew from the neighborhood bowling on lanes seven and eight, he walked over and took a seat. About twenty minutes later, mobster Trigger Mike Coppola and two other young men described as "hard-faced and well dressed" entered and began scanning all the patrons who were engaged in bowling or playing pool. The manager asked the three men if they wanted to play. "No. We'll just look around for a while. We want to see someone," one of them replied. The men strolled through the alley and situated themselves behind the lanes occupied by Iadoroli and his pals and watched the men bowl.

Apparently Trigger Mike and his boys didn't know their victim by sight and Iadoroli didn't seem to recognize them; if he did he played it cool. Some time passed and then one of the bowlers called Iadoroli by his moniker "Chin." Upon hearing the name, the trio of gunmen each pulled out a pistol and began blasting away in Iadoroli's direction. Bowlers and pin boys alike all dove for cover as the bullets flew. After about fifteen shots had been fired, the three gunmen took off, leaving four of the bowlers wounded and Chin dead on the floor.

Police believed that the phone call Iadoroli was going to receive was actually a trap. The three gunmen, according to the police, who didn't know the gangster by sight knew that the call was coming and they were going to get him when he answered the phone. Since they learned his identity beforehand they took the initiative and finished the job early.[248]

St. Raymond's Cemetery in the Bronx was the scene of much gangster mourning during the first week of June, as "Big Dick" Amato, "Louis Slats" Bologna, Peter Coll and Chin Iadoroli were all laid to rest there. If the opposing gangs ever crossed paths during their respective ceremonies, they kept their guns holstered.

In less than two days, Vincent lost his brother and a best friend whom he considered a brother. Those who knew him concede that the back to back murders may have had a psychological effect on the young gangster; afterward he "went nuts."[249]

Coll and the remainder of the gang didn't take much time off to grieve. Forty-eight hours after Chin was put on the spot, they descended on one of Schultz's beer drops and, at gunpoint, forced the laborers to destroy ten of the Dutchman's beer trucks, as well as one hundred and fifty slot machines.[250] If they couldn't hit Schultz, they would hit his pocketbook.

Blood could only avenge blood, however, and two days after the raid on the beer drop Louis DeRosa, said to be a Schultz lieutenant, was found in the Bronx with nine extra holes in his body, five in the head and four in the chest. The savagery of this hit leads one to wonder if Coll and his cohorts didn't hold a special grudge against DeRosa.

Five days after DeRosa was eliminated, the Coll gang struck again. This time their victim was twenty-four-year-old John Jacoporo, who was discovered in the back seat of a Buick, five bullets heavier. Jacoporo was one of those who had been picked up at the Schultz-Noe headquarters back on December 13, 1928, along with Coll, during the trouble with Diamond.

The next Schultz man to go was thirty-one-year-old John Saricelli, described as a superintendent of a fleet of beer trucks that transported the Dutchman's suds into Harlem and Bronx speakeasies. Saricelli was home asleep on June 21. At three-forty-five in the morning, he was awakened by his ringing doorbell. Groggy, Saricelli found his way downstairs and opened the door. On the porch stood two men.

"Good morning," they said.

Then each raised a .45 and fired one shot apiece into Saricelli. The bullets passed through Saricelli's body, one lodging in the wall behind him and the other piercing a wicker basket before slamming into a can of tomatoes. As the gunmen ran away, Saricelli stumbled into his kitchen. Hysterical, his wife went for the phone, but he stopped her and made her light him a cigarette before allowing her to phone for an ambulance. The cops arrived, and even though Saricelli knew he was a goner, he refused to answer any questions.

"Get away. Don't bother me. I know I'm dying but you get nothing from me," he grumbled, dying true to the gangster code.[251]

Two of the Dutchman's guns. (L-R) Joe Piteo sent to Denver to kill Eddie Diamond and Joe "Bar Rags" Iadoroli, Vincent Coll's best friend who was killed on the job. (Courtesy John Colasanti)

Gennaro "Chin" Iadoroli, Bar Rags brother and also a good friend of Coll, killed in a bowling alley during the war with Schultz. (Courtesy of John Colasanti)

Vincent "Mad Dog" Coll and the boys. (L-R) Coll, Mike Basile,
Pasquale "Patsy" Del Greco, Dominick Odierno,
Frank Giordano (Library of Congress)

"A crazy son-of-a-bitch" Edward "Fats McCarthy" Popke was a Coll gang
member and one of the deadliest gangsters of the era.

12

JUSTICE WILL NOT BE SERVED

Thanks to the New York City tabloids, by the time the trial in Troy rolled around, the citizens of Rensselaer County knew that Jack was a big-city gangster. They knew of his links to murders, whether real as in the case of Harry Western, or imagined as with Vivian Gordon. They knew that he had most likely tortured Parks. They also knew that they would be making up the jury pool, and they weren't happy about it. Fear was the overriding factor. As one possible juror put it: "[We] Don't want our barns and our homes burned down by that feller's gang."[252]

Conversely, because of the change of venue, Catskill citizens felt like they were being robbed. "As long as we have to pay for it, we might as well have had the show right on our own front steps," one of them said. "How much do you think this is going to cost our hotels? Diamond's trial right here where it belonged would have been worth a lot of money."[253]

On Monday morning, July 13, the "show" began. Security in and around the Troy courthouse was tight. A squad of Brooklyn and Manhattan cops was patrolling the courtroom looking for known gangsters from the Big Apple, while state troopers in plain clothes were seated throughout the room in the event of trouble. Seven county deputies were on hand at the court entrance, and a contingent of state troopers was there to escort the witnesses to and from the courtroom.

A crowd of over two hundred people milled around the courthouse waiting to get a glimpse of Diamond. They got their chance when, a few minutes before the proceedings began a taxi pulled up in front of the building and Jack and Alice got out. The crowd shouted to him, but Jack ignored them as he and Alice entered the annex.

At precisely ten o'clock the trial commenced. Presiding over the case was Supreme Court Justice James Cropsey from Brooklyn. Cropsey was renowned for taking decisive actions on the bench in order to keep a trial moving. He was also famous for publicly shaming citizens who tried to get out of jury duty.[254] Prosecuting Diamond was Attorney General Bennett's deputies Henry Epstein, John T. Cahill and August Merrill.

Jack's bail was revoked for the duration of the trial, so anytime outside the courtroom would be spent in jail. One hundred and fifty prospective jurors were on hand, and Cropsey got the ball rolling by saying that he would hear excuses. Over half of the group got in line. As each man stated why he felt he should be excused from jury duty, Justice Cropsey lived up to his sharp-tongued reputation and shot each man down.

"I have a market to run," said one.

"Well what about it? You've got work to do here. Next."

"I can't hear well."

"You heard me didn't you?"

"But my left ear isn't any good."

"How's your right ear? With your right ear you can hear and it will be right next to the witness stand."

The day wore on with Cropsey blasting those who tried to shirk their civic duty: "You're a faker;" "I don't believe you;" "I think you're lying." These retorts and others were heard throughout the morning and afternoon. At twelve-fifty everyone was given an hour lunch. Jack, Alice and some companions drove over to the jail, escorted by motorcycle cops and police cars, to have their meal.

Jury selection continued through the afternoon. By six o'clock only six jurors had been chosen, so Cropsey called for a night session. A recess was called until seven-forty-five, and after the judge left the room Jack lit a cigarette with a shaky hand. Alice came up and they spoke in quiet tones for a few minutes before heading back to the jail for dinner, again with the police escort. After the break, the trial reconvened. By eight-thirty the jurors had been picked. Then it was time for opening arguments.

The state opened by describing the attack on Parks. Prior then rose for the defense opening argument. "Maybe someone did assault Parks that night, but this defendant, John T. Diamond, did not do it," he told the jury. "Diamond was not there, nor anywhere near where the complainant says this thing happened. Not that night."

"What did happen there we don't know, but we will show by the highest kind of proof, that this man Diamond was not there"…

"We will prove who went with him that night, what he did, where he went, and what time he got home."

"You will find that Park's story has varied from time to time"…

"We will show that Diamond could not and did not take part in that assault"…

Prior wrapped up around nine o'clock, and court was adjourned for the night.

The following day, the courtroom was once again packed with spectators, and hundreds more stood outside. The trial reconvened, and the state put Parks on the stand to tell his story. He spoke slowly, and his testimony took a long time. Duncan followed him on the stand and corroborated the story. Parks' wife then testified, and the state rested.

It was now Prior's turn. The first witness for the defense was one of the owners of the New Kenmore Hotel in Albany, who stated that Diamond had called him on the evening of April 15 to say that he was coming in that night to have dinner with a doctor named Joseph D'Urgolo and a former Queens official named Michael Fornaro.

D'Urgolo was Diamond's ace in the hole. Though he called himself a physio-therapist, he admitted that he wasn't really a doctor. On the stand, he stated that he made the trip to Albany and stopped off at the State Education building to visit with the secretary of the State Board of Medical Examiners, Dr. Harold Rypins. He went on to say that, at the time that Parks was being tortured, he was with Jack and Alice in the New Kenmore's dining room. There they stayed until four in the morning, when he gave them a ride back home. Three other hotel employees backed up D'Urgolo's testimony. A photographer from the *New York Daily News* also took the stand to say that Parks had told him that he wasn't sure who was in the sedan that forced his truck to the side of the road and that he couldn't identify the men who worked him over.

The state countered by putting up three musicians who said that they had seen Jack in a Catskill speakeasy on the night of the attack. A former Greene county sheriff and his companion backed this up by saying that they had spoken with Jack at the speakeasy and had shaken his hand. Finally, no doubt to Prior and Diamond's chagrin, the state brought out Dr. Rypins, who testified that he wasn't even in Albany on the day that D'Urgolo said that they had met. With that, the state confidently rested.

Prior summed up the defense by saying that Parks was simply a publicity hound looking to get his picture in the paper and came up with his "fantastic" story to reach those ends. The state, in return, said that the defense was lying and the witnesses had perjured themselves. Then they asked that the jury show courage by helping put a gangster away.

"God give you the power and the courage to go out and do your duty like honest men," Deputy Attorney General Henry Epstein pleaded. "Return a verdict of guilty in this case."

Before sending the jurors off for deliberations, Judge Cropsey stated it was up to them to determine whether Jack was in Greene County or Albany on the night in question. The twelve men were sent off to decide Jack's fate. Eight minutes shy of the two-hour mark, the jury announced that it had made a decision. Jack, who was described as nervous during the break, stood and leaned forward to hear the foreman say the words, "Not guilty." With that, he fell forward on the table and then grabbed Prior's arm and gave a squeeze. A cheer went up through the courtroom at the verdict. Once the crowd outside heard the decision, they too began to cheer for Jack.

With applause ringing throughout the chamber, Alice ran up and congratulated her husband. She was followed by reporters looking for a statement from Diamond. "I'm sorry," Jack told the journalists, "You'll have to ask Mr. Prior. I can't." The newsmen turned to Prior who said, "Not now boys," as he led Jack away.[255]

Diamond and his entourage returned to Albany, where Jack had some of the press up to his suite at the New Kenmore. "I am feeling good over the verdict, but I am too tired and sick to enjoy it, celebrate it or talk about it," he told the reporters. But talk about it he did. "I owe it all to Dan [Prior] and his efforts," He said. One of the boys asked about any future plans. "I'm going away and try to get some rest first. You know, I had a pretty struggle in the hospital. Then before I had a chance to get back any strength they put me in jail."

"Since I got out on bail, I have been busy almost night and day in conference with my lawyers and getting ready for my trial. The trial itself was a heavy strain and I wasn't in any too good shape to stand it. As I said I feel good about the verdict though it was what I expected. I couldn't believe there was any chance of a disagreement or a conviction."[256]

After the press conference, Jack allowed the *New York Daily News* personnel into his suite for exclusive photos and a statement. Sitting there with Alice, her arms draped about him, Jack told the *Daily News*, "The cheers of the crowd outside that I heard coming in from the street showed I was vindicated by the people, which was as important to me as the verdict, that outburst showed what the people thought of the persecution of me by the politicians, who are looking for publicity and political advantage."

Jack the gentleman also expressed his gratitude to the jury and the cheering crowds. "I want to thank the people of Rensselaer County for the complete vindication they gave me. It was marvelous for one who has the reputation I am supposed to have to go into a county without a friend and to get a fair and just trial when every obstacle was placed in my way."[257]

✫ ✫ ✫

After his trial, Jack stayed in Albany. The house at Acra, which had been labeled a "fortress" in the press, was practically a tourist attraction, and he probably felt safer in a bigger city where he could melt into the crowds. Albany authorities knew he was staying in their town and a detachment of detectives followed him around to ensure he wasn't bumped off. Free bodyguards were a bonus for the cash-strapped Jack. The Albany police also had an ulterior motive for shadowing Jack, not only didn't they want him murdered in their city, they didn't want him operating there either.

✫ ✫ ✫

As was stated earlier, there has always been a rumor that the Vincent Coll gang teamed up with Jack. While Jack was beating the rap in Troy, the Coll gang was busy renting houses in the Catskill region. Six of the men, Mike Basile, Vincent Palumbo, Louis Bifano, Phil Gussow, John DeRosa and John Burnett were staying in a farm house about a mile away from the Aratoga Inn. About twenty miles away in the town of Coxsackie, Coll's sister Florence and her husband Joseph Redden were staying in another house with a guy named William King. Where Coll and the others were staying is unknown. The close proximity to Diamond, as well as the Bifano link, leads one to believe that there was indeed a merging of the Coll gang and what remained of Jack's crew. It was a perfect fit. Jack was a long time rackets guy without a gang, and Coll and the boys were muscle in need of leadership.

Whatever Jack and his new cronies may have been cooking up was doused less than a week after Jack's acquittal. Police learned the locations of Coll's mob and raided the dwellings on the morning of July 19. The house outside of Cairo was the first stop. Detectives managed to let themselves in while the gang was sleeping and, although some newspapers would print the opposite, they arrested all six gang members along with three molls without a fight. A few hours later, detectives raided the house in Coxsackie and arrested Florence, Joseph and King. More importantly, they captured the gang's arsenal, which consisted of two machineguns, five sawed off shotguns and a large number of handguns and ammunition. All gang members were lodged in the Catskill jail, where Scaccio was also cooling his heels awaiting his turn in front of a judge. "The Mick" and Fats McCarthy, however, were able to elude capture.

✫ ✫ ✫

Three days after the Coll gang was picked up, Joseph D'Urgolo, Jack's chief witness during the trial, was arraigned in Troy for perjury and held without bail. Meanwhile, back in Catskill, Scaccio was preparing for his trial. Representing him in front of Judge Bliss was an associate of Dan Prior's named Joseph Delaney. The trial was scheduled to start on July 22. Delaney requested a postponement as well as a change of venue, but both motions were denied. Delaney then withdrew himself from the case.

"Mr. Scaccio, stand up," Judge Bliss ordered the gangster after his lawyer quit. "You have heard Mr. Delaney state that he must withdraw as your counsel? Have you hired him to represent you in this case?"

"Yes, I have."

"Do you understand that he is telling you now that you are here without a lawyer?"

"Yes."

Bliss asked Scaccio if he wanted to get another lawyer and how long it would take.

"As soon as possible, a week."

"No, there will be no week. Can you get another lawyer by tomorrow morning?"

"I may. Probably not."

"Well I am willing to give you a short time. Have you money to hire a lawyer?"

"Yes, your honor."[258]

While Scaccio was going through his ordeal, the Greene County grand jury was hearing damning evidence against the Coll gang. Samuel Ostroff, an attorney from New York City, appeared on behalf of the gang and stated that the men were simply in town for the weekend. He also asserted that the guns that were taken into evidence weren't found in their possession and that they never attacked the police as some newspapers had printed. "They were awakened at five a.m., drowsy, rubbing their eyes, and several of them were maltreated," he told the court before asking for bail.

Ostroff was in the right place at the right time, as later that day he was hired by Scaccio and appeared with his new client the following day for the opening of his trial. At the start of the hearing, the gangster's brother, who was a doctor, stepped up and pleaded with the judge to delay the trial so that Ostroff could have more time. The prosecution contended that Scaccio knew that Delaney was going to throw in the towel thirty-six hours before it was announced. Since it was a Friday, Judge Bliss threw the defense a bone by saying that they would pick one juror and after that court would be dismissed until Monday.

The majority of the trial was spent picking the jury. Once it got underway, Grover Parks again took the witness stand and spent the better part of the day describing the ordeal from the night of April 15. Ostroff contended that the whole scenario was a fabrication. "Parks is more or less a dreamer," he told the jury. "His place is in a movie studio in Hollywood, where he can earn money for his tales."

Dreamer he may have been, but Ostroff was unable to shake him on the stand. The following day he tried again for an hour, but Parks was unmovable. James Duncan also did damage with his testimony. Since perjury worked for his boss, Scaccio's defense tried it as well. A baker was brought in from Brooklyn and testified that Scaccio had paid for some pastries the night before the assault, and his sister took the stand and nervously lied that he had spent the night of the attack in her Brooklyn apartment. The prosecutors brought out the same witnesses from Jack's trial that stated that they had seen him at the Catskill speakeasy. In his summation, Ostroff blasted the credibility of Parks and Duncan and stated that Attorney General Bennett's prosecution staff had, "No conception of fair play, but seeking a conviction at any cost." The state responded by saying, "Diamond himself could have come here to help and assist his bodyguard if the defense story was true. He could have told us from his own lips what happened on that night. Was Legs called to the stand? If it didn't happen as Parks said it did, where is Diamond?"[259] On July 31, the jury went in for deliberations and forty minutes later they returned with their verdict, guilty.

In future months it would be said that Jack abandoned Scaccio and left him to face the music without any support. The record shows, however, that Scaccio did have a lawyer, a colleague of Prior's albeit who quit, but when asked if he had the money to hire another, Scaccio said yes. It would appear that Judge Bliss' rush to begin the trial had more to do with Scaccio's downfall than anything Jack did or didn't do.[xlix]

✫ ✫ ✫

Prior to July 28, Vincent Coll was just another mobster to the public, not hated any more or less then the next hoodlum. The events of that summer afternoon would make him

---

[xlix] Another piece of evidence showing that Scaccio didn't necessarily hold Jack responsible is the former's receiving blotter from Clinton Prison. On it is listed "Accomplice" - Jack Diamond. Then, "Is prisoner on friendly terms with accomplice?" – Yes.

the most despised gangster of his time, as well as give him two knew monikers, one "Mad Dog" and the other "Baby Killer."

Joe Rao, the intended target back on May 29 when Amato and Bologna were killed, ran what was known as the Helmar Social Club in Harlem. While a man was lounging on the stoop of the building, a number of neighborhood children played nearby. Suddenly a sedan pulled up and gunmen began to rake the front of the building with pistol and shotgun fire. When the smoke cleared the gunmen and their intended victim, said to be Rao, were gone, but in their wake were five seriously wounded children ranging in age from three to fourteen. One of them, five-year old Michael Vengalli, died a short time later.

Police were quick to clear Coll and Rao of any wrongdoing, stating that they believed the shooting was the result of a "bookmakers feud." After a few weeks without any leads, they changed their tune, and Coll and his gang were named as the shooters. Immediately, a nationwide manhunt was conducted to bring in the "Mad Dog" dead or alive for what became known as the Harlem Baby Massacre.

After this episode, the Coll gang once again retreated to upstate New York, where they had a new hideout about ten miles east of Troy in the town of Averill Park. The "Mad Dog" may have returned to the city in late August. According to mob turncoat Joe Valachi, Coll was given a contract at that time by Mafia boss Salvatore Maranzano to kill Jack's old pal Charlie "Lucky" Luciano and Vito Genovese. That contract was voided when Luciano and Genovese struck first and had Maranzano killed on September 10.

A piece of evidence supports the fact that Coll may have been in town around this time and that the police may have thwarted an attempt on his life. On August 30, police picked up twenty-four-year-old Ernest Saricelli, brother of slain Schultz man John Saricelli, in the Bronx. He was armed with two handguns. Back at the station Saricelli told the officers, "If you'd waited a little longer you'd of got 'Irish' too."[260] This comment led police to speculate that Saricelli was privy to information that Coll was back in town and that he was out gunning for him.

Not Guilty! Jack and Alice pose exclusively for the *Daily News* in their hotel room after the Parks trial. (*New York Daily News*)

13

JUSTICE IS BACK ON THE MENU

Things didn't look good for Jack and Paul Quattrocchi in the approaching federal case. Attorney General Bennett and his team turned over their findings to the Feds and this, coupled with the Prohibition agents' own work, and the seemingly endless list of bartenders, innkeepers, tavern owners, not to mention Diamond's own employees, who would be testifying against them, assured an air-tight case. Changing attitudes toward Prohibition and bootlegging also were a factor. Just a few months earlier, bootleggers weren't necessarily looked down upon, as Prohibition was an unpopular law. However, with the July 28 Baby Massacre, gangsters became widely despised.

Jack would be tried on two counts, selling beer and liquor and owning the still that was found on the Hanna farm. Needing another ace in the hole, Jack and Prior once again turned to perjury. This time, however, Jack's duplicitous nature came out. The plan was to have Paul Quattrocchi, the man who struck Joe Coglianese when he said he hoped Diamond would die, take the fall.

Armed with the list of witnesses that would be taking the stand, Prior had his "investigator," a man named Alexander Green who had been accused of planting drugs in a U.S. senator's Albany hotel room back in 1924, visit a number of them and tell them, "When you get down there to the trial, throw it all on Paul; If they ask you who sold you the beer and the whisky, blame it on Paul."[261]

✩ ✩ ✩

As Jack was perspiring in Manhattan, upstate in Catskill Scaccio was also in a courtroom on August 5 for his sentencing. Though he kept a stiff chin when Judge Bliss handed down a sentence of fifteen years in prison, it was reported that his eyes filled with tears as he was led away. On August 17, he arrived at Clinton Prison in Dannemora to begin his sentence. Three days later, he was joined by Skunky Klein, who, after spending a year in the Catskill jail, was sentenced to a term of two-and-a-half to five years for possessing Western's car.

✩ ✩ ✩

Back in New York City the following day, nineteen witnesses took turns in the chair incriminating Jack and Paul. Ten of the witnesses were innkeepers who told of Jack forcing his product on them. To establish ownership of the still, prosecutors brought out Leonard Greco, the young plumber who helped to build it as well as do other side jobs for Jack and Paul. He identified some sales receipts from the local hardware store where he purchased parts for the still and charged them to "Mr. Schiffer's" account.

At one point, Jack was questioned outside the courtroom as to whether he had tuberculosis. Never one to miss an opportunity, Jack, knowing full well that he wasn't afflicted, responded, "Well, I've got lead in both lungs. Look at me and draw your own conclusions."[263] Perhaps Jack was hoping someone on the jury would catch wind of the story and think twice about sending a dying man to prison.

One evening after court was adjourned for the day, Jack once again sat for an interview with the *New York Daily News*. Instead of reporter John O'Donnell, Jack requested a female journalist named Grace Robinson, who had written about him in the past and wasn't very charitable. Jack had read everything printed about him, so he was aware of her articles. "I want to see you because you've lashed me so in your stories," he told her. "There must be some sunshine for me somewhere. But I'm not asking sympathy. And I'm asking no promises from you. Write what you like after you talk to me." Robinson agreed, and Jack told her what hotel he was at and what name he was registered under.

Robinson arrived at the hotel, and, knowing Jack was on the eighth floor and wanting to catch him off guard, went up unannounced. She was able to approach Diamond's room without any trouble and found the door wide open. She knocked and walked in. Jack was lying on the bed, tie off, collar unbuttoned. Alice was at the mirror applying lipstick. There were two other guys standing around, but they took a powder pretty quickly after she arrived. After some goading from Jack, Alice also left to join some family members [most likely Kitty and her son John] on the roof.

"Will you have something to drink, Miss Robinson?" Jack asked once they were alone. At the time newspapers were full of stories about Al Capone muscling into the New York City beer racket, so Robinson cracked wise, "Yes, but I don't want any of this Al Capone beer. This Capone beer from Brooklyn – I had some the other night and it made me sick. If you have some good Diamond beer I'll drink that."

Jack laughed, "I assure you Miss Robinson there is absolutely no such thing as Diamond beer." He then made himself a Gin Rickey. Robinson was a rye drinker so he sent out for some ("it was excellent") and made her two highballs over the course of the interview. Using room service, they ordered dinner. She had the chicken salad; he had the steak.

"I suppose you always have to eat in your room at hotels. Dangerous for you to eat in public. To many people with guns and a grudge," Robinson quipped, adding, "My office tipped me off what to do dinner-dating with you. Drop to the floor at the first sign of trouble."

"I've nothing to be afraid of," Jack replied.

"No? You've only been shot four times."

"Honestly I go about freely where I please. Except that if people recognize me and gather about, I leave. I hate to cause embarrassment to hotel or restaurant managers. I hate to have anyone suffer my presence."

"Do you mean to tell me you go about unguarded? Do you mean to say there's no bodyguard standing outside the door of this room?"

"None. You can look if you don't believe me."

Dinner was served and Jack spoke his normal piece about how newspapers give him a raw deal. The topic turned to the trial and he said that he thought the government's case against him was "absurd" using testimony from that day as an example. "The only car I own is a Lincoln. Does it seem reasonable that I would risk confiscation of a $5,000 car to deliver a case of booze at $57.50 as that witness testified today?"

"Well how about your Troy trial? The torture of Grover Parks, the truckman. I thought your alibi witnesses weren't so good."

"If I were to frame an alibi don't you think I'd frame a good one? Why should I pick simple hotel clerks to whom I might have given a few tips? I'm sure Dr. D'Urgolo, my chief witness, accused of perjury, will be vindicated if he ever goes to trial."

As Diamond's trial was taking place the New York authorities named Vincent Coll as the perpetrator of the Harlem Baby Massacre. Since Coll's gang was tied in the press with Diamond, Jack's name was brought into the matter. A headline that day stated, "Harlem Baby killers traced to Diamond's lair."

"Look at that," Jack said referring to the headline. "Linking me with the murder of that poor little child. And me on trial in federal court. The jury passing a newsstand in a hotel lobby could see that headline, and without breaking faith with court about not reading newspapers, could get the idea I had something to do with that baby murder."

"True enough. But tell me, how about your big beer merger with Vincent Coll?"

"I don't even know Coll. Honestly Miss Robinson, I have no gang. I'm not a gangster. I haven't a thing to conceal."

"Then tell me, if you're not a gangster, what have you been living on all these years? How do you make your living? You don't pound a typewriter as I do."

"I could tell you. You'd be amazed if you knew. And knew how little I have in the bank. But just one favor. In case the income tax people question me, I'd rather not answer that just now. It might embarrass me."

Robinson then switched to another topic Jack had no intention of discussing.

"Well, how about your affair with Kiki Roberts? You had her living at your Acra home. Will you go back to her?"

"Now on that –I tell you she was never at my Acra home. I can't talk about her. Miss Roberts must speak for herself. She is under indictment, you know. I don't want to say anything that might embarrass her. If she comes to trial."

Striking out with Kiki, she returned to the Parks case.

"Then about your trial at Troy. I thought the state's rebuttal witnesses were most convincing. To my mind, they proved you were in a Catskill speakeasy on the torture night and not in Albany as your alibi witnesses said you were."

"About that Miss Robinson, some other time. You see, it's just possible the attorney general may want to try me on another count in that indictment. If I go into that now, it might prove embarrassing."

With three strikes, Robinson then went philosophical.

"How about your future life? What do you think will become of you? Not your church belief. Your individual conviction. Where will you go from here?"

Jack thought about the question, and a grave look came over his face. He knew that it was just a matter of time before the killers got it right and he went the way of Little Augie, Entratta and all the other gangsters before him. One wonders if Jack ever lied awake in bed wondering how he would get it. Would he be walking down the street and get cut down by sawed off shotguns? Would a "friend" give it to him up close in the back of the head and leave his body in a burning car like Eugene Moran? Maybe he would simply vanish like Harry Western. Sack murders were gaining popularity. Perhaps he'd be found in a big burlap bag, garroted, his body folded in half.

"Fate. The future," Jack finally answered. "I don't dare look ahead. I don't even ponder on it. We don't dare wonder what is in store for us. We wouldn't dare."[264] It is not clear if the "we" in his response was intended to refer to him and Alice or gangsters in general.

The interview wasn't all business and gallows, however. There was some bubble gum, of the sort that one would expect to read about their favorite matinee idol in a magazine like *Photoplay* or *Modern Screen*. "He proudly receives hundreds of fan letters daily – most appeals for help. Feels proudest when he can help a friend in a trouble." Jack's favorite color? Brown. "Although he likes [Alice] in blue, his custom made clothes are mostly brown. Except his handkerchiefs, those are white. Shaves himself, but gets a manicure. Gets a regular haircut and is not concerned with turning gray. 'It's a little gray already; shows most after a shampoo.'"

"Daily menu: tea and toast for breakfast, sandwich for lunch and a steak for dinner. When in Acra drinks two quarts of milk a day. Smokes Ramses large size. Likes going to Al Jolson movies. Wears pajamas at night (both tops and bottoms) and has no moles." What does he do in Acra for entertainment? "In the hills you rest. That's all."

Why Jack agreed to do the interview is perplexing. His earlier sit-down with the *Daily News* was basically a public relations stunt designed to delude people into thinking he was just some poor misunderstood guy prior to going on trial. The Grace Robinson interview, conducted while Jack was in the middle of a trial, promised no such reward. Chances are the only thing he had to gain at that moment was money. Perhaps Jack and Prior knew he was going down and would need some money for bail, legal fees and of course living expenses. As will be seen later, the *New York Daily News* seemed to be on hand whenever Jack needed some jack.

✥ ✥ ✥

On the final day of the trial, there were half a dozen witnesses to bolster the government's argument regarding the still. One of them was Jack's beer runner/handy man Nick Fusco. When Fusco took the stand, he gave Jack and Paul an uncomfortable grin. They in turn shot back smiles of their own. At first it looked as if Fusco's testimony would benefit the defendants, as his answers were "I don't know" or "I can't recall." However, when his grand jury testimony was shown to him, he reluctantly admitted to taking beer orders from both Paul and Jack. On cross examination, Prior was able to get him to admit that he lied to the grand jury out of fear.

Since Quattrocchi, still oblivious to the plot against him, didn't have a police record, he briefly considered taking the stand in his own defense. He decided against it out of concern for Jack. "...I didn't take the stand because he didn't. How could I take the stand? I don't want the newspapers to say I'm a rat," he told reporters. In a day or so, he would regret it.

There appeared to be some growing tension between the two partners as the trial went on. There were reports of the two of them arguing and, according to the *New York Times*, the cause may have been Jack's suspicion that Paul was going to turn state's evidence against him. Both men denied it. Whatever the reason, relations between the two had cooled, as they didn't speak for the rest of the trial. The only thing Paul had to say about it was, "I told him to mind his own business and that I would mind mine."[265]

Wrapping up for Diamond, the best Prior could do was show that with Jack's trip to Europe and all the time he spent in the hospitals and recuperating at home, he really didn't have the time to run a bootlegging empire. Not a bad argument, considering that Jack's attempted takeover of the Greene County liquor trade started a few weeks before he left for Europe, he was home for three weeks before getting shot at the Monticello and spent the next four months recuperating. Then he got gunned down again in April and arrested right after that.

Paul's lawyer simply brought out three character witnesses to say what a good guy Paul was. One of the witnesses was Thomas Carazzo, the owner of the Villa Pedro, home to one of their beer drops. "Do you know Quattrocchi's reputation for being a peaceful, law-abiding citizen in the community where he resides?" the judge asked Carazzo.

"Yes sir. It was good," The innkeeper replied.

"Does it affect a man's reputation in that community if the man sells beer and liquor?"

"Not to my knowledge."[266]

With that, the case wrapped up, and Judge Hopkins charged the jury. "Most of the evidence in this case remains undisputed…," the judge stated. "Even though they [the witnesses] are in the liquor business, [they] tell stories that are corroborated and that dovetail…"[267] After the charge, the jury was sent in for deliberations.

While the jury was out, Diamond spoke to the press. He said that, whatever the verdict, "I'll take it with my head up."[268] After two hours, the jury returned. Jack, sweaty and nervous, and Paul, looking a little more in control, rose to hear the verdict: Guilty.

Witnesses said that the back of Jack's neck turned red as he tried to squeak out a grin. Paul managed a smile.

Both men were allowed to remain free until sentencing. Jack left with Alice and his attorneys, and Paul went off with a couple of his sisters. During the trial, some of the witnesses had informed the authorities about Prior's "investigator" Alex Green, and he was arrested and arraigned before Judge Hopkins after the courtroom had cleared.

As soon as Paul got back home, a number of the witnesses who testified against him stopped by to tell him about Alex Green. Speaking with reporters, Paul said, "I should get the double bank from that guy [Diamond]. That's what I get for being a good feller and not taking the stand. I never seen a man without no pride like him. He ain't got no pride and he ain't got no principle. He should have taken the rap. He was on the same ticket with me, like Republicans or Democrats or someone [who] are on the same ticket but there's no principle in that man."

The tirade continued, with Paul discussing the witnesses who broke the news to him. "They're friends of mine. They didn't do what that investigator said. When they got on the stand you heard what they said. They told the truth. And that's what I told them to say before I went down there to be tried. I said, 'Tell the truth; don't be afraid. I ain't got nothing to hide.' And that's all I told them."

Then he went back to cursing Diamond. "I'm glad now that I know him in his true color. I'm glad I know what a rat he is… I'm through with him. He was a racketeer and I was a business man. It was a fine thing for him to do. He's no bargain. If you know a man and he helps you out I don't see why you should try to make him ride."[269]

On August 12, Jack boarded a train for New York City to receive his sentence. On the ride down, he was approached by an older man. "Hello Legs, remember me?" "No," Jack replied. The man, Joseph Boyle, now head of the New York Central Railroad detectives, reminded Jack of his arrest in Cliffside, New Jersey, back in 1922. "Oh yes," Jack remembered, "you're the dick that picked me up there. It was a bum rap though. You didn't have anything on me."[270]

Later he was back in the courtroom with Paul but, because of the "double bank," the two former partners weren't speaking to each other. Before the sentences were handed down, Paul's lawyer tried to get a mistrial because of the attempted jury tampering. His motion was denied. Then the time came.

"Has the defendant Diamond anything to say [as to] why the judgment of the court should not be pronounced at this time?" Jack gave a slight shake of the head "no." The judgment of the court will be, John Diamond, that you be imprisoned in the federal penitentiary at Atlanta, Georgia, on the first count, two years, and pay a fine of $10,000. And on the second count of the indictment, two years, to run consecutively, and a fine of $1,000." While the words were being spoken Jack blushed and Alice went white. Some said they saw tears in Jack's eyes, although others denied it. Paul was only found guilty on the conspiracy charge and received two years and a $5,000 fine. He was then released on bail pending appeal. Jack's lawyer asked that his client also be released on bail pending appeal. Against the arguments of the prosecutors, Judge Hopkins agreed and Jack paid $15,000 to walk out of the courtroom.

14

THE WAY OF ALL GANGSTER FLESH

After the federal trial, Jack returned to Albany. He reportedly moved in with a local beer magnate in an upscale neighborhood. The police knew he was there so always had squad cars cruising the neighborhood to make sure the East Coast's most famous gangster didn't get bumped off in their city. Soon neighbors tired of the constant surveillance and started to complain. "We can't afford to take any chances," Albany's Police Chief David Smurl responded, justifying the around the clock police attention. Smurl drove the point home with a reminder of the Harlem Baby Massacre. "We don't want any baby killings in Albany. A machinegun fusillade means that innocent bystanders, even children, might get hurt."[271]

This was too much attention for Jack, and he took off. A week later on September 11, he was back in New York City with his attorney J. Arthur Adler. Paul Quattrocchi and his lawyer were also in the city to file their appeals.

Jack's movements that fall are not known in detail. He probably stayed in Albany and possibly some of the nearby towns, not remaining in one place too long. For money, one source had him selling dollar gin in the town of Watervliet. It is also possible that he was doing some bootlegging with a gang of Albany gangsters headed by brothers John and Francis Oley.

In addition to his and Alice's upkeep, he was also taking care of Marion who had been on the lam for six months. With little or no money coming in and no friends in high places

up in the middle of the street with our brains kicked out. But I never do a thing like that. I prey on thieves, big thieves. I walk in on them, tell them I want so much on the line, in a hurry and to get it up or else. That's my racket."

"I'd like to print that." O'Donnell said.

"You can," Jack said, "after I'm dead."

O'Donnell observed his wishes.

✧ ✧ ✧

The following day the *Daily News* was able to scoop the rest of the dailies with the headline "Kiki to Surrender." To throw off any suspicion that Jack and the paper were in cahoots, the story said that Marion was recognized by a "representative" of the *Daily News* while she was driving on an upstate highway and that this reporter had "halted" her. Weak, but that's what they went with. How he recognized her, especially since she no longer had red hair (it went back to its natural brown while she was in hiding) or why Kiki didn't just keep going instead of answering a bunch of questions wasn't brought up. It was just a coincidence that the *Daily News* correspondent happened to flag her down the day before she planned to turn herself in.

Why had she decided to turn herself in, the "representative" queried? "I know I'm innocent of all these charges in the indictments and I want to get it over with. At least the authorities were wrong when they figured that I had been killed by gangsters' vengeance, as I read in the papers. I am tired of reading of my tragic death and I'm just as tired reading that I'm the person who put Mr. Diamond in the hands of his enemies. And you can also say that I'm tired of staying away from Broadway and being fearful of talking to my family. I want to get it all over with so now I'm going to walk up to them, say 'Here I am' and what would they like to do."

O'Donnell asked her about the Parks case. "I don't know anything about the kidnapping and all this racketeering talk in

Greene County is merely so many words in newspapers," she said. "I simply don't know what Mr. Bennett and his friends are talking about and I'm curious to hear what they are going to say. Why don't you say that –that I'm giving myself up just because my woman's curiosity couldn't stand the suspense any longer."

O'Donnell asked her where she had been staying the past five months. "That is one of those questions that I'm not going to answer until I talk to a lawyer."

Fair enough, then at least why did she stay in hiding if she didn't know anything about the Parks affair? "I just stayed away because I knew that there were a lot of people who wanted to get publicity and advertise themselves, and one of the ways that seemed handy was to put me on trial. I just didn't intend to be used that way. If they can get into the headlines all right, but I don't intend to let them use my name as a way of getting there."

"There are two things I'm looking forward to when all this trouble is over," she continued. "The first is being able to call up my mother and family or visit her without thinking Mr. Bennett's men are going to arrest me. And the second is getting back to Broadway. I'm a dancer. I like dancing and as soon as all this is over, I'll be ringing Mr. Ziegfeld's and Mr. Carroll's doorbells. A vacation is all right but too much is enough."

O'Donnell asked where she planned to surrender. "I can't very well tell you all my plans when all these people are looking for me. I'm just trying to figure out the best thing to do, and the best thing is to get it all over with as quickly as possible and give Mr. Bennett a chance to prove all these things he's been saying about me. I happen to know that they are all ridiculous. The best thing to do is to have a showdown."

Then taking a page out of Jack's book, Marion played the misunderstood ingénue. "They call me a gun moll in some of the stories. Do I look or talk like one of those girls in a gangster talkie? Everyone who knows me knows that isn't true." Following the Jack method, she then put forth the evidence to bolster her case. "For six years I have worked and worked hard on Broadway for the Ziegfeld and George White shows. Does that look as if I could fit into the picture that the authorities have built for me? If Mr. Bennett wants a character reference for me, I will refer him to the people who hired me and paid me for years.

"Right up to within two weeks before all this racketeering stuff in Greene County came up, I was working in 'Flying High' right up to when the show closed in Chicago. If I am supposed to be so bad, does it seem likely that I would be out working hard every day in the week? That is something the authorities can answer. I can't"

Did any of this in anyway contradict that she was a gangster's girlfriend who sat in a car while her boyfriend kidnapped two people and then sat in the house while he tortured one of them? Of course not, it was transparent fluff just like Jack had peddled in his self-serving piece a few months earlier.

On October 8, as the lunch hour was ending in the town of Watervliet, Marion clambered off a streetcar with a suit case in tow and headed over to the police station. Inside she approached Chief of Police Maurice Keenan, who had just finished lunch with Sergeant Frederick Broderick. She asked if he was a cop. Keenan replied in the affirmative, and she introduced herself and said she wanted to turn herself in. "They've got a warrant for me down in Greene County," she told him.

"Well if they want you down in Greene County on this Diamond matter why don't you surrender down there?" the chief replied.

"Because I might be arrested if I went down there and I don't want to be arrested. My photographs are in the newspapers today and everyone is looking for me. Why can't you arrest me? I want to give myself up to you."

Keenan thought it over for a few minutes and then grabbed the phone. He called Catskill Sheriff Harold Every and told him he had Marion. Every got in touch with the attorney general's office and a bench warrant was sworn out. Word also made it to Dan Prior, who was in court at the time (as if he didn't already know). Turning the court case over to his assistant, Prior went to Marion. In the meantime, word spread of the surrender and journalists from Albany and Troy started to pour into Watervliet to question Legs Diamond's now infamous mistress. She sat in the station chain smoking and evading questions. All she revealed was information she already had told O'Donnell in the exclusive.

Sheriff Every and a state trooper picked up Marion and took her back to Catskill, where she was fingerprinted and photographed. Unbeknownst to the police, however, there was no Greene County judge on hand for arraignment. They drove her to Albany, where she was released on $2,500 bail.

Bennett didn't have any immediate plans to go after Marion; he still had Jack in his sights. Though the Parks case had been a fiasco the attorney general would get another shot that December when Jack would be tried for kidnapping Parks' young assistant James Duncan.

Why did Marion surrender in Watervliet? Most likely because Jack had friends in the police department there. As has been mentioned, there is a report of him selling booze in that town. More telling is the fact that Sergeant Fred Broderick was on hand when Marion surrendered. As will be seen, he and Jack most likely had a relationship on some level.

Since it contained the interview with Marion, Jack undoubtedly read the October 8 edition of the *Daily News*. His eyes also must have been drawn to the story in the adjoining column.

"2 Tortured by Mob, Sewn in Bags to Die."

That story was about two former members of Vannie Higgins' gang, who were beaten, stabbed and trussed up jack-knife style and stuffed into bags where they died from self-strangulation. Knowing that he was on the spot, stories like this must have affected Jack on some level. He could relate to the victims. Chances are he knew them to some degree. One wonders how reports like this may have shaped Jack's stated philosophy on things yet to come: "Fate. The future. I don't dare look ahead. I don't even ponder on it."

✿ ✿ ✿

On October 2, around the same time Jack returned to New York City to work out Marion's surrender, the Coll gang also returned to the Big Apple to continue the war against Dutch Shultz. First, two Coll torpedoes, Dominick "Toughy" Odierno and Frank Giordano, stopped off at one of the Dutchman's beer drops and killed a worker named Joe Mullens. Unfortunately for the killers, some utility workers witnessed the murder from a manhole.

A few hours after the Mullens murder, a bomb went off at another one of Schultz's beer drops. This was the final overt action on behalf of the Coll mob, because within forty-eight hours practically the whole gang was behind bars.

The roundup began the following day when, acting on a tip, police raided the gang's Averill Park hideout and arrested Coll's sister and brother in-law and three others. One of those picked up, Agnes De Lucia, told the police that her husband Vincent, or "Jimmy" as he was known, could be found at a garage in midtown Manhattan. They found him, along with the car used in the previous night's bombing. De Lucia most likely sang after his capture, because in a matter of hours detectives began to round up the rest of the gang.^{li}

The next stop was the Ledonia Hotel, where detectives found Mike Basile and Patsy Del Greco sleeping in their room. From there, police went to the Mason apartments and arrested Frank Giordano and confiscated five pistols. Finally, on Sunday, the police learned that the object of their two-month-old nationwide manhunt and his girlfriend, Lottie, were at the Cornish Arms Hotel registered as Mr. and Mrs. Moran. Also at the hotel, registered as Mr. and Mrs. Stein, were "Toughy" Odierno and his moll Betty White.

Five detectives checked into the room across the hall from Coll and began a stakeout. After about three hours, "The

---

li The fact that De Lucia was released when the rest of the gang was behind bars also leads one to believe he was the squealer.

Mick," now sporting a mustache which, like his hair, had been died black, and "Toughy" stepped out into the hall and were immediately surrounded by the detectives. Assuming that the men with guns were rival gangsters, Coll and Odierno froze as the blood drained from their faces. When the guns didn't go off, Coll realized that they were detectives and, breathing a sigh of relief, said, "It's the law boy. It's the law." After the detectives informed Coll that they had been searching for him for a long time, he replied, "I know it. If I had any information of value I would have called you."

Fats McCarthy was at the Cornish Arms as well that night but escaped over the rooftop, a feat he would repeat two weeks later.

Down at the station, Coll congratulated the police on their capture, saying, "It was good work to get me and the rest of the boys without someone getting drilled." He added, "I've been under a heavy stress and I'm sort of glad to get it over." He also had a complaint. "Everything that's happened around here has been blamed on me. As a matter of fact I've been up in Albany and Cairo most of the time. I just got back Friday."

"Toughy" Odierno and Frank Giordano were both indicted for the Mullens murder and, because of the utility workers' testimony, both were found guilty and placed on death row. Then came the indictment everyone was waiting for. The police declared that both Coll and the already doomed Giordano were the gunmen who killed five-year-old Michael Vengalli and that Basile, Del Greco and Odierno were also in the car with them. "There are the baby killers!" Assistant Chief Inspector John J. Sullivan told reporters, referring to the five gangsters who were in the police lineup. "We have information that each and every one of them was in the car that dashed through East 107th Street on July twenty-eighth and shot down five children at play." Trial was set for December.

✳ ✳ ✳

On October 19, a gangster named Enrico Battaglia, who was wanted by the police for the murder of a policeman dating back to 1928 (Fats McCarthy was also considered a suspect), was spotted by officer John Broderick while walking his beat on Manhattan's Upper West Side. He watched Battaglia enter a brownstone and then called the station for backup. Three detectives, Edward Willi, James De Ferraro and Guido Pessagno, were dispatched to help bring the wanted man in.

The officers arrived at the brownstone and rang the doorbell. When the landlady answered, the detectives identified themselves and explained why they were there. The landlady, perhaps hoping to tip off her murderous tenants, exclaimed loudly, "No police are coming in here to search my place." The detectives and officer entered anyway and searched the parlor before starting up the stairs. As they were ascending the steps, the landlady called out, "Well can't you shut the door?" At this, Officer Broderick returned down the stairs and shut the door, a move that most likely saved his life. Before he had a chance to rejoin the detectives, they had already arrived at Battaglia's apartment and knocked on the door. There was no answer, so Detectives Pessagno and Willi forced the door open with their shoulders. As the two detectives rushed inside, Battaglia, Fats McCarthy and another unknown gunman all opened fire simultaneously. Pessagno and Willi dropped to the floor wounded, Pessagno mortally. De Ferraro, a step behind his companions, rushed in with his gun blazing, but he too fell in a rain of lead fired from the trio of desperados. With the detectives down, Fats and the unknown gunman leapt over their victims and ran for the roof, followed by Battaglia. By this time, Broderick had made his way upstairs. Before Battaglia had a chance to get to the roof exit, the police officer dropped him with a single shot, killing him. Fats and his accomplice managed to escape over the rooftops.

☆ ☆ ☆

While Coll and his boys sat in prison, Jack continued moving about in Albany. In mid-November, the Albany police received a tip that Fats McCarthy, who had been red-hot since the shootout, was hiding out in a cheap rooming house on State Street. At one o'clock in the morning on November 19, police raided the house. They searched the place from the cellar up to the attic but found no sign of Fats. The raiding party was a bit surprised when Dan Prior showed up and asked if they were searching for his client Jack Diamond and, if they were, he offered to produce him on the quick. The police informed him that they were looking for McCarthy not Jack, so Prior bid them farewell. As the authorities were leaving, Jack was loitering out front waiting to get back inside.[272] Now that everyone in Albany knew where Jack lived, he was no longer safe; time to go. A report has him and Marion moving to a place on Hudson Avenue. After spending a short time there they moved to an apartment on Lancaster Street.

☆ ☆ ☆

As winter approached, Jack was preparing for his third trial of the year. Even though the Parks case was a debacle, the state was going to try to get him for kidnapping Parks' young confederate James Duncan. In addition to his legal problems, Jack had personal troubles. Marion wanted out of the relationship. She was tired of being shuttled around from rooming house to rooming house and longed to return to the stage. Jack was able to talk her into sticking around for a while, but both agreed that as soon as the Duncan trial was over she would return home to Boston and then try to revive her dancing career.[273]

To add to Jack's financial and legal troubles that fall and winter, Alice got into a car accident with the aforementioned Sergeant Broderick of the Watervliet Police Department. Broderick, we are told, sustained some injuries and was going to sue. Jack placed a series of calls to the officer to see if they couldn't work something out and settle out of court.

After Jack had left a few messages for Broderick, the sergeant finally met with him on December 6 at the apartment on Lancaster Street in Albany. When he arrived, he found both Jack and Marion packed and ready to move. He joined them as they drove to an apartment located at 21 Ten Broeck Street.

As a favor to Diamond, Broderick went up to the landlord and inquired about the apartment. It was still available. Broderick returned to the car, while Marion inspected the place and went about the business of renting it.

While Marion was unpacking in her new place, Jack and Broderick drove to the train station to pick up Alice. She, along with Kitty and John, would be moving to Albany to be with Jack during the upcoming trial. Once Alice was there, Jack assured Broderick, they would work out the settlement.

They pulled into the train station, and the police sergeant sat in the car while Jack went in to pick up his wife. The train pulled in and the passengers got off. As the train emptied, Alice was nowhere to be found. When the platform emptied, Jack went to a pay phone and found Alice still in New York City. She said that she would be delayed two or three days. Jack returned to the car and told Broderick he'd have to wait a few more days.

With some extra days at his disposal Jack probably returned to Marion's new place before moving into the boarding house where he would stay for the duration of the trial. Posing as "Mr. Kelly," Jack took three second-story rooms at a boarding house located at 67 Dove Street. One would be shared by Kitty and her son John, Alice had her own bedroom and Jack took the room at the front of the building looking out over Dove Street. Though she didn't let on, the proprietress, Mrs. Wood, was aware of who her new tenants were.

Jack hired an Albany taxi owner named Richard Storer to be his chauffer for the duration of the trial, which, like the first one, was held in Troy. Monday, December 8, found Jack in the courtroom with Dan Prior, who asked for a trial postponement.

It was granted and the trial was put off for three days. The following day, Broderick paid the Diamonds a visit at their Dove Street rooms and an agreement was settled on. Jack told him that he would pay him after the trial.[274] For some reason, possibly as a bodyguard, Broderick stuck around Diamond for the duration of the trial.[lii]

On Friday, December 11, court convened. Prior moved for a dismissal arguing double-jeopardy since Jack had already been acquitted of the same charges during the Parks trial. Judge Bliss denied the motion, and jury selection began. Perhaps it was because they'd seen it before or maybe because it was winter and close to Christmas but, for some reason, the crowds at the courthouse were smaller than the previous summer. Some New York City detectives were on hand to prevent any New York City gunmen from putting Jack on the spot.

It appears that it was no secret that there were a couple of guys in town to kill Jack. Even his chauffer, Storer, was aware of the rumors. He told Jack that he heard that, "a couple of Brooklyn mugs" were in town to rub him out. "What the hell do I care?" Jack responded.[275] Jack also may have been tipped off by one of the New York detectives who were on hand. Supposedly he saw two men he recognized as Brooklyn gunmen and alerted Diamond to the situation.[276]

It was Jack's habit during the trial to have Storer drop him off a block or so from the court house and walk the rest of the way on his own. This fact wasn't lost on the gunmen, who planned to shoot him down as he approached the court

---

lii There seems to have been more to the Diamond-Broderick relationship than an accident. Broderick stayed with Diamond throughout the trial and appeared to be part of his inner circle the last few weeks. Although he would subsequently say that the only reason he stuck around Jack was to make sure he could collect his money before Jack left town, it looks like he may have been pulling bodyguard duty or at the very least just being a friend. If it was a simple case of keeping an eye on Jack, he could have done that from a safe distance and it is doubtful Jack would have treated him like an insider had the relationship just been about the accident, if there ever really was one.

building on the final day of the trial. Luckily for Jack, on that day Dan Prior walked up and started talking to him and the two men entered the court together. Not wanting to kill Prior, the assassins gave Jack a momentary reprieve.[277]

The Duncan trial was basically a rerun of the Parks trial with the same witnesses telling the same stories. On Thursday, December 17, the case went to the jury. While they were out, Jack spoke with the press. One of the reporters commented on the fact that he had been wearing the same suit every day of the trial.

"Why, I was acquitted of torturing Grover Parks in the suit and I wouldn't take it off for a million dollars. I'm superstitious about it."[278] he said. Another thought is that he was broke and couldn't afford to maintain his former wardrobe.

Looking over the courtroom, Jack saw a couple of faces he didn't care for. Suddenly the gunmen rumors rang true. Sidling up to Broderick, he nodded toward the rear of the room and said,

"Do you see those fellows back there?"

The officer looked back and saw a couple of "young, slender, swarthy well-dressed men" sitting.

"Do you know them?" Jack asked.

Broderick said that he didn't.

"Well, they're a couple of $100 a week killers. They'll kill as many as you want, as often as you want, as long as they're on your payroll for $100 a week."[279]

During the wait, Jack walked out into the corridor. While he was standing there, some guy walked up, jabbed a finger into his ribs and said, "You rat. You're going to get it anyway, whether the jury convicts you or not. You might as well take it now." Back in the courtroom, Jack told Prior about the exchange. Prior went to one of the New York detectives and relayed it to him.[280][liii]

---

liii There are many variations of this exchange. Most papers relayed it as discussed above insinuating that a gunman made the threat. The *New York Evening Journal* however, claimed that the guy who uttered the threat was simply a local wise-ass trying to be funny. Jack however didn't appreciate

After the finger-poking incident, Jack spoke to some of the boys from the press. "I'm heading south if the verdict is not guilty," he told them. "I don't know just where I'll go, but it will be somewhere in the Carolinas. One of my lungs has a pretty bad condition from one of the slugs in it and my nerves are kind of shot. You know, three trials in four months is too many for any man, even for a tough one like me."[liv][281]

Finally at eight-fifty in the evening, after five and half hours in deliberations, the jury returned with a verdict. A cheer went up through the courtroom when Jack was once again found not guilty of kidnapping and torture. "We all felt that Parks and Duncan were bootleggers just as well as Diamond. They are all racketeers. The case was a 50-50 proposition and there was nothing else for us to do but find Diamond not guilty," a juror told the press.

As "not guilty" was ringing in the air, Alice ran up to Jack, followed by Kitty and her son. All congratulated him with hugs and kisses. Jack, Alice, Kitty, his nephew John and Storer walked the couple of blocks to the car. As they were pulling away, Storer noticed a car with Brooklyn license plates and brought it to Jack's attention, speculating whether or not it might be the gunmen out to get him. With the elation of the acquittal, and dismissing the guys he made out earlier as hundred dollar-a-week killers, Jack laughed and said, "Oh, I don't think they would come way up here to get me."[282]

Storer drove the group back to the Albany rooming house. John was put to bed, and Mrs. Wood was given the number to Young's Café, the speakeasy where Jack's acquittal party was going to be held, and told to call if there were any

---

the joke. The *New York Time* reported that the man approached Jack after the trial, when Jack was leaving the court, and that he told his lawyer who in turn told the detective. Seeing that the detective didn't do anything of note, it would appear that the *Evening Journal* was probably on the mark.

liv One has to wonder about the final line "…even for a tough one like me." Jack always down played his gangster persona, so it seems as if the journalist either added it himself or perhaps it was a misquote of something closer to, "even for a tough guy as I am supposed to be."

problems. Storer drove the group over to Young's and, as they were entering, Jack pulled him aside and told him to run up to Marion's apartment and tell her the news. Storer did as he was told. Marion was happy about the news and told Storer to let Jack know that she was going to go to Boston the next morning as they had discussed.

Storer returned to the party and, when he managed to get Jack alone, he relayed the message. Jack told him to grab some booze and go back and keep Marion company. He also told him to call back in an hour saying that he was "Fred" and had to see him on a business matter. That was going to be his excuse to slip out. Not wanting to be party to Jack's scam, Storer declined. "What the hell," Jack said, "do it for me. I'll be up as soon as you call."[283] Storer acquiesced and, as he was leaving, he ran across a pal named Sylvester Hess and took him along with him. They arrived back at Marion's and partied with her.

Meanwhile back at the speakeasy, two uninvited guys crashed the party. One was a priest and the other a loud-mouthed guy who worked as a New Jersey motor vehicle inspector and walked around handing out summonses to everyone as a joke. He tried to get invited over to Jack's table. "Who is that guy?" Jack asked Broderick. The officer said he didn't know. "Well, he doesn't look good to me."[284] The invite never came.

At about twelve-forty-five the phone at Young's rang. It was a call for Jack. Jack took the call and then returned to his table. It was Fred, and he needed to run out and meet him. To throw off suspicion, he asked Alice if she wanted to go with him. Alice said no. Jack then bid farewell to everyone, saying that he would be back in half an hour. It was the last time they ever saw him alive.

Storer drove back to the speakeasy and picked up Jack and brought him back to Marion's, arriving at about ten minutes to one. Jack told him to wait and went inside. A few moments later, Hess came out and joined Storer in the cab. Time passed. After two hours, Storer and Hess dozed off.

Twenty minutes later Storer woke up and saw that Marion's lights were out. Thinking that Jack may have come out and grabbed another cab, he drove back to the speakeasy and asked the bartender if Jack had returned. The bartender said no, so Storer hurried back to Marion's apartment. It was about four o'clock in the morning. When he arrived, he honked his horn a number of times trying to get Jack's attention. Luckily, a cab pulled up and a woman who lived in the same building let herself in. Storer walked in behind her and went up to Marion's room. He knocked on the door, and Jack answered. "Jack, come on get out of here before Alice starts looking for you."[285]

Jack, who had drank a lot, wobbled out of Marion's room and down to the car. Hess jumped into the backseat, while Jack rode shotgun. Jack didn't want to go back to Young's, so he told Storer to take him back to his Dove Street room. Storer took back streets to the rooming house, dropping Hess off along the way.

They pulled up to the Dove Street house. Jack got out of the car and weaved up to the front door. He took out his key, but was too plastered to make it work. Storer came to the rescue and unlocked the door for him and then escorted Jack to his room. Once Jack was safely in his room, Storer let himself out of the house and locked the door. He pulled away from the house and headed back to Young's Café, not noticing a maroon sedan parked just down the street.

Alone in his room, Jack peeled off his brown chinchilla coat and matching fedora and let them drop to the floor. Next he stripped down, folding his shirt and hanging his pants over the back of a chair. No fancy monogrammed pajamas tonight, he climbed into bed in his skivvies.

Back at Young's, Alice was furious. What was supposed to be thirty-minutes had turned into three and a half hours. Assuming the truth about where and with whom her husband had been, she yelled at Storer to tell her where Jack was. Storer lied and said that he had taken him to see some friends and then took him home. "Don't try to kid me!" she hollered at him.

"Where is he?"[286] After some back and forth, Storer finally convinced her that Jack was back at home in bed.

While Storer was getting the third degree from Alice, back on Dove Street two figures emerged from the maroon sedan. One was armed with a flashlight, the other a .38. They approached the rooming house and either picked the lock or let themselves in by some other method. They quietly made their way up the stairs and approached Jack's room. Letting themselves in, they crept up to the bed and stood over the man who had, to that point, seemed un-killable. Just inches from the face that graced thousands of newspapers, both here and abroad, the man with the .38 placed his weapon a hair's width from Jack's left ear. He pulled the trigger three consecutive times and then twice more as they dashed from the room.

Mrs. Woods awoke with the shots and heard the killers run into the hall. One of the men questioned whether they had fired enough bullets into Jack. "Oh hell that's enough for him," the other replied and they raced out the door to their waiting car.

Mrs. Woods ran to the front window just in time see one of the men get into the car before it sped off. A mile or so away, they threw the gun and flashlight out the window.

Assuming correctly what had just happened, Mrs. Woods slowly made her way up the stairs. The smell of gunpowder was still thick in the air, as she peeked into Jack's room. There, her lodger, Mr. Kelly, lay on the bed, his arms at his sides, head tilted to the right. Not needing to see anything else, she ran to the phone and called Young's Café and asked to speak to Alice. Alice came to the phone. "I think there's been a shooting upstairs," Mrs. Woods told her, "You'd better hurry over."[287]

Alice was hysterical from the get-go but Storer managed to get her into his car and drove her to the house. Once inside Jack's room, she became even more hysterical. Grabbing a towel she wiped the blood from his face. "Help me somebody. They shot Jack," she sobbed, "He's dead. They killed him."[288] Storer called Dr. Thomas Holmes, the physician who treated Jack after the Aratoga shooting, and asked him to come right over. The doctor arrived and verified what everybody already knew. Everyone stood around and watched Alice weep and rub Jack's face. Not until six-forty-five, approximately an hour and half after they arrived back at the rooming house, did anyone bother to call the police.

Four cops responded to the call and, upon entering saw Alice at the top of the stairs by Jack's door. "He's shot! He's shot!" she screamed to them. "Who's shot?" one of the officers replied. "My poor husband, Jack Diamond." The officers tried to remove Alice from the room, but she refused to go, grabbing onto a bedpost. "I didn't do it. Let me alone! They've killed Jack. They've killed him,"[289] she screamed as they literally dragged her out of the room, her arms swinging at them. It took three men to get Alice out of the house. She continued to fight and they had to drag her down the front steps and force her into a car.

Alice was hustled over to the Fourth Precinct for questioning. "Oh why didn't I go with him last night?" she sobbed to anyone who would listen, (her feelings of guilt were a sad result of Jack's duplicity. She declined his invitation to join him, as he knew she would.) She asked to go to the ladies room and was escorted by Chief Smurl and Sergeant Kelly. On the way, she lunged for a phone. "I want to call Dan Prior," she screamed, but Smurl and Kelly blocked her and rudely informed her she couldn't use the phone. "I have privileges." she yelled. "I have a right to call my lawyer." Kelly pushed her away from the phone and ordered her back into the detention room. "Don't lay your hands on me!" she screamed at the sergeant. Ignoring her, Kelly and some others jostled her back into the room.[290]

Eventually, Prior showed up and upon seeing him, Alice slowly walked up to him and placed her head on his shoulder. "Oh Dan. Oh Dan," she moaned while he tried to comfort her. The police questioned her until the afternoon, and then she was released.

While Alice was getting manhandled at the Fourth Precinct, Marion was waking up to the sound of newsboys outside her window yelling, "Extra, Extra, Jack Diamond killed."

Her head still foggy from sleep and booze, she assumed the boys were yelling that he had been acquitted. Then, hearing the boys correctly, she ran and opened a window to make sure. Hearing the truth, she fainted. Or so she said.[291] Since she planned on leaving anyway her things were already packed. The only inconvenience was that her ride to the train station was currently getting an autopsy. This was easily remedied, however, and before the police could get to her flat, she was on a train headed for Boston.

The owners of the *New York Evening Journal* and *Boston American* located Marion before the authorities. Would she be willing to sell her story to the papers? You bet! The first installment of her story appeared the very next day, while the man she claimed to love was room temperature in an Albany morgue.

Grover Parks even made it into the act. He testified against Jack two days earlier and happened to be in Albany delivering a truckload of freight. With him was State Trooper Frances Hill-frank, who arrested Jack the previous April after the attack on Parks, and was now assigned to protect the truck driver in the event of gangster retaliation. When the men arrived in town, they heard about the shooting and headed over to the mortuary to take a gander at Jack on the slab. Parks was silent as he gazed down at the bullet-riddled head of the man who eight months earlier strung him up and burned his feet.[292]

15

AFTERMATH

If the man who held the flashlight was worried about Jack surviving, he need not have. As his cohort said, it was indeed enough. In fact, the first shot was enough the second and third simply gratuitous. Each bullet perforated the left side of Jack's head. One of them entered under his ear, passed through his neck and exited the right side of his neck at the base of his skull. Another entered in front of the ear and took an upward course through the brain but stopped on the other side without piercing the skull. The third entered at the top of the ear and went straight through coming to a halt just above the right ear.[lv]

After the autopsy Jack's body was removed to an Albany funeral parlor, where curious bystanders hung around day and night. When authorities were finished with Jack's remains, Alice was given charge of the corpse. Late in the evening of the nineteenth, it was placed in a hearse for the drive back to New York City. In the wee hours of the morning what used to be Legs Diamond traveled along some of the same Catskill roads where earlier in the year the gangster was king.

While Marion was busy promoting herself with her serialized memoirs, Alice went about the business of burying her husband. It was no secret that the Diamonds were broke, so the question of who was going to pay for the funeral was put

---

lv Some reports vary as to where the bullets entered. This account comes from the police record that quotes the coroner who performed the autopsy.

forth in the daily papers. Reports had Alice running around town hitting up the underworld for cash. The rumor spread that Jack's one-time pal Owney Madden would be flipping the bill.

As for Jack's killers, the top suspect was Salvatore Spitale, who had an airtight alibi. He attended a hockey game at Madison Square Garden that night and then went to Lindy's and stayed until after four o'clock. Since Jack named him as the guy who wanted him dead in his interview with John O'Donnell, the *Daily News* tracked him down before the police had a chance to speak with him.

"Did I kill Diamond?" he asked the reporter. "Why don't make me laugh. Why I never harmed a hair on that fellows head. I've helped him plenty of times though and it has cost me money."

He went on to say that his piece of the Monticello Hotel was worth $35,000, but after Diamond was shot there he "couldn't give [it] away". As for whether or not he was one of the gunmen. "Say, do you suppose, if I did want to shoot Jack, I'd have picked a spot where it would have cost me that kind of money?"

Was he upset about the demise of his one-time friend? "I'm not sorry that Diamond was killed. He had it coming to him and he'd been living on borrowed time for a long while." Realizing that the last statement sounded like he could have been holding a grudge or was privy to some inside information regarding Jack's death, he added, "He never did anything to me, you understand, and I had no reason to want him knocked off, but that guy didn't have enough friends to use as pall bearers." Spitale went on to echo Police Commissioner Mulrooney's assessment of the image created for Jack by the press. "He was the most overrated guy I ever knew. The newspapers built him into a great big shot when he was just a punk. And the worst part of it was that he read those papers and believed everything you fellows said about him. Why, he couldn't get his hat on with a shoe horn, he'd been on the front pages so much."

"You know what I think?" Spitale continued, "They shouldn't lock up the fellow who killed Diamond. No, they should give him a big reward, because he performed a real service to the community." An interesting comment coming from someone who had no reason to want Jack dead.

Did Spitale have any thoughts on who this public bene-factor was? "Who do I think killed him? Well as I say, I don't know. But my guess is that it was some insignificant little punk who wanted to get a reputation for himself as a real tough guy. Either that or some of those local boys in Albany got sore because Diamond was muscling in on their rackets, and they decided to tuck him away permanently."

"You don't blame a guy for getting sore at some stranger who begins to play in his backyard, do you? How do feel when some of those other reporters try to crash in on your game –you burn up, don't you? Well, then, there you are! Those rack-eteers have got feelings just like you."[293]

Jack's first wife Katherine was found and asked her feel-ings about the murder. Now remarried and living in Maspeth, Queens, she said, "I am sorry he has met his death the way he has but he means nothing to me, living or dead." Jack, she assured all, had "passed completely out of my life. I had com-pletely forgot about him."[294]

About a half mile away from where Katherine wasn't grieving, gawkers began to congregate around the home of Lawrence O'Brien.[lvi] Inside the abode, Jack was laid out in an $800 casket, dressed in a black tuxedo with a black rosary in his hands. Soon the flowers began to arrive: a blanket of roses from sister in-law Kitty and nephew John, another rose ensem-ble baring the ubiquitous underworld inscription, "From your pals." Other settings included a broken wheel made up of arti-ficial flowers, a standing cross and many smaller tributes. From

---

lvi This was described in the press as being the home of Alice's sister and brother in-law. However 1930 census data states that O'Brien's wife, Anna, was of Austrian decent. Alice's parents, per her death certificate, were Irish. Her sister may have been living there as a boarder.

Alice, came the biggest arrangement, a large empty chair with the inscription, "To my own. After all – Your loving wife."

Any lingering questions as to where Alice got the money for the funeral were cleared up when, on the day Jack was buried, his old newspaper benefactor, the *New York Daily News*, printed exclusive photos of the dead gangster in his casket, with and without Alice posing beside him.[lvii]

The curious who thronged the house saw Jack's family members from Philadelphia arrive to bid farewell to their wayward relative while Alice remained inside. She unsuccessfully tried to arrange a church funeral, so the only praying done for Jack was by the family. On the morning of his funeral, Jack's cousin, Marie Hart, knelt at the head of his coffin and recited the Lord's Prayer while Alice and other members of the family knelt around her.

At about eleven o'clock on December 22, after prayers had been said, loved ones all took their last look at Jack and the casket was closed. A heavy rain fell as the coffin was carried out to the hearse that would transport it to Mount Olivet Cemetery. While this was taking place plain-clothes detectives circulated through the crowd in front of the house in hopes that they might find James Dalton, who was still on the lam.

---

lvii That the *Daily News* paid for the funeral is speculation based on the facts that they were the only paper with a reporter and photographer allowed inside the O'Brien home and the improbability that Alice probably let them in for photos and a story out of kindness. After the funeral, she denied the rumors about Owney Madden and others flipping the bill, stating that she paid for it herself. Where she got the money she didn't say. Coincidently the *News* also scooped the rest of the New York press with Jack's death. While the other newspapers first editions trumpeted Jack's acquittal, the *News* broke the murder story. According to night editor Gene McHugh, one of Diamond's boys stopped by his office while Jack was partying in Albany and told him that "Jack is hotter than a blow torch" (meaning that he was on the spot) and not taking any precautions. In the event that the visitor was correct, McHugh had his team write up some obituary copy on Diamond that could immediately go to press if and when word of his murder came in.

An uncle of Jack's escorted Alice to the car that would tail the hearse to the graveyard. Alice told the others that she was going to remain strong during the ceremony so that, "I can act the way today that Jack would want me to be."[295]

Nine cars were in the cortege behind Alice, including the car containing Jack's floral tributes. During the drive to the cemetery, a number of other cars not associated with the funeral fell in line and joined the procession to the gates of Mount Olivet. Probably due to the weather, the funeral party was asked to remain at the gate –the grave diggers had yet to finish shoveling out Jack's final resting spot. The delay was somewhat welcome, as the car carrying the pall bearers was held up in traffic. Taking matters into his own hands, the chauffer of the hearse went and got four cab drivers to serve the purpose, but Alice lit into him and demanded that they wait until the proper bearers arrived. The wait afforded the police another chance to peruse the bystanders in search of Dalton.

The graveside ceremony, if it can be called that, was quick. With the rain still falling, a couple hundred gawkers with umbrellas watched as the casket was carried to the spot and lowered into the hole without any fanfare. "Goodbye boy!" yelled Alice, as the box was planted into the ground.[296] Those were the only words spoken. Once the coffin was down, mourners tried to get Alice back to the cars, but she insisted on staying. Not until her husband's grave was filled in and all the flowers placed on top did she agree to leave.

☆ ☆ ☆

While Jack was still on the slab in Albany, theories as to who killed him began to circulate. There was no shortage of suspects. We will most likely never know with any certitude who was behind the murder. Possibilities thrown around at the time were friends of Scaccio, who felt that Legs didn't do enough to help him out. Fats McCarthy was also listed as a top suspect. Even Alice was considered the culprit. A story goes that she found out that her husband was yet again with Marion and, in a fit of rage, placed a call to some gunmen and gave the go ahead to take Jack out. Fingers also pointed at Dutch Schultz as the architect, and his number one gun, Bo Weinberg, has been a top contender as the actual triggerman for years.

In the last few decades, another theory has surfaced that the killers were members of the Albany Police Department, namely Officer William Fitzpatrick, because Jack was planning on operating in their city. Author and Diamond historian William Kennedy sites a conversation he had with Albany political machine boss Dan O'Connell, who personally told him that it was Fitzpatrick who pulled the trigger.

The author believes it was Salvatore Spitale finishing the job he started at the Monticello Hotel fourteen months prior and has given time to that theory. It doesn't seem likely that the Albany police would go to the trouble of killing Jack, as he was down and out and looking at a federal prison sentence. If they really wanted to take him out they could have done so in a much less public fashion. A simple ride job could have been arranged: "C'mon Legs you're going down town," with his body dumped outside city limits. As has been mentioned, it was no secret that men were in town to kill him. Finding out where he was staying wouldn't have been a problem. They simply had to follow him home from court on the first day of the trial. Performing the job would have been as simple as spending a long, cold night in the car after the last day of trial, waiting for Jack to return from his celebration.

Who killed Jack is a wonderful debate and most theories have their strong points. In 1938, the New York Parole board said it was Spitale; O'Connell said it was Fitzpatrick; Dutch Schultz's lawyer Dixie Davis said it was Bo Weinberg; and on and on. Regardless of who orchestrated the murder, there was probably only one person who was truly sorry to see Jack go, and that was Alice.

The early Thirties was a bad time for the big racketeer. Reform was in the air and high profile gangsters were being targeted by federal authorities. Jack was on the ropes professionally and looking at four years in federal prison. He knew enough about the New York underworld to make things hot for crooked politicians, policemen and gangsters alike. Could anyone be certain he wouldn't open his mouth for clemency? It was time for him to go.

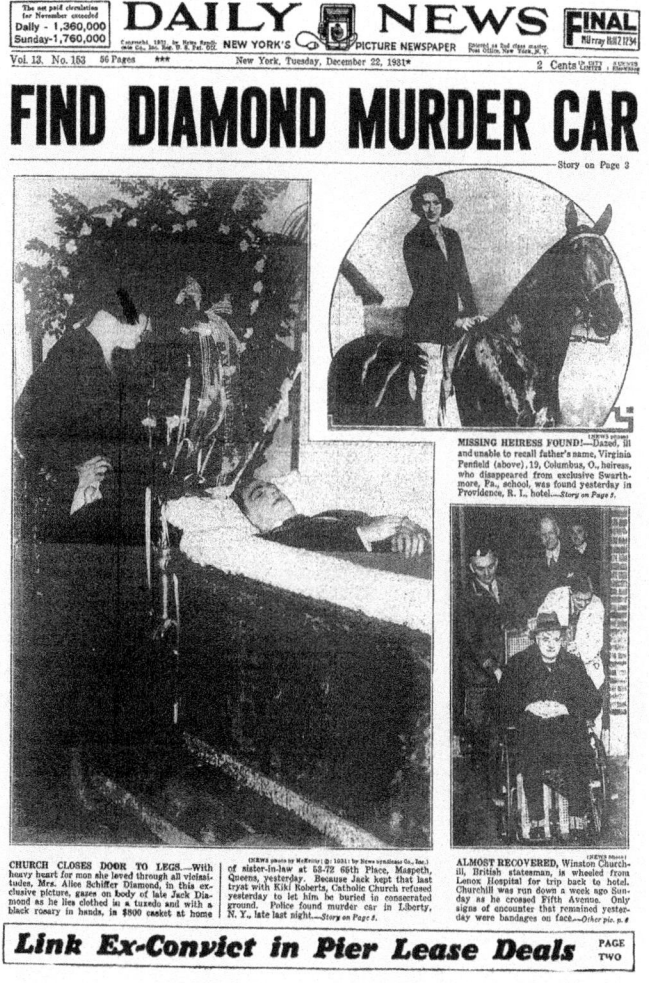

Jack reposes in his coffin while Alice looks on
in their final *Daily News* exclusive. (*New York Daily News*)

16

POST JACK

Marion's self-serving memoir ran in the *New York Evening Journal* every day for almost three weeks. On January 2, 1932, she returned to New York City to sign a contract to headline an act at the Academy of Music starting on January 5. If she was a hit there, the show's producers had numerous engagements lined up in other cities. There was only one problem. She was due in court back in Catskill on January 8 to answer for her part in the Parks-Duncan affair.

"I don't know anything about Jack Diamond's affairs," she told the press, complaining about the court date. "I don't know who shot him, or who he shot, or anything. And I told that to John Delaney, Albany's district attorney, a few days ago. I wish they'd let a girl alone, especially when she is trying to make good."[297]

While her mother sat next to her nodding approvingly, she also stated that she was past Jack. "My love for Jack Diamond is dead, just like poor Jack himself."[298]

At about the very same time Marion was preparing to cash in on having been Jack's moll, Alice paid a visit to a theatrical manager named Sam Burger. Was there any chance that people might pay to see the late, great Jack Diamond's wife? Burger felt yes, there indeed was. Alice did mention that she didn't think she was much of a performer, but Burger assured her that the public would be willing to pay just to see her.

On January 8, while Marion was in a courtroom learning her fate, Alice held her own press conference at the O'Brien home in Queens, where she had been staying since the funeral. She informed those gathered that she would be making her theatrical debut in a series of skits showing how Jack's enemies had framed him.

"I want to make people see that Jack was not the person he has been pictured. I want them to understand the sort of man he really was and know the facts about him. Jack was never a gangster. He wouldn't know how to be."[299] In other words, the show would be an act of fiction.

"Just what part of his life will be portrayed in the sketch which is being written for me, or who will play the two other characters, I don't know yet. But I do know that this is the last and only thing I can do for him now."[300]

A couple of weeks later, on the eve of her debut, Alice spoke to reporters during a rehearsal break.

"Grease paint and footlights won't lessen my loss or soften my grief," she told them, "but having something to do will give me less time to think about it all."[301]

It would also give her some much needed money. According to Burger, she was paid $1,000 a week for her engagements. First she played in the Bronx at the Central Theater and then Harlem. Both bookings were successes, so Burger took her on the road to Allentown and Reading, Pennsylvania. These were followed by an engagement in Paterson, New Jersey, for a Sunday show. Local clergy, however, protested the idea of a gangster's widow as entertainment on the Sabbath, and that engagement was cancelled. With this, her show folded.

Alice blew through whatever money she made and was soon broke again. Burger got her a job that summer as a Coney Island sideshow attraction. For ten cents, one could take a break from the sun and listen to Alice say what a great guy her husband had been. Each "performance" began with her walking to the center of the stage and announcing, "Mr. Diamond was a loving and devoted husband. Much that was said and printed about him was untrue."[302]

She did twenty shows a day[lviii] and after a month told Burger she couldn't stomach it anymore and quit. Later that

---

lviii   Burger said twenty. A newspaper report claims eight to ten.

summer, she moved to 1641 Ocean Avenue in Brooklyn, not far from Coney Island. She lived on the main floor but after six months moved upstairs to a small flat consisting of a living room, a kitchenette and a bedroom. Her bedroom archived all of her Jack memorabilia –photos, newspaper clippings, note-books. Above her bed hung the sign that advertised her show from the previous summer.

Socially, Alice spent a lot of time in speakeasies. One man she hung out with was a guy named James Dolan. Whether or not Alice and the thirty-two-year-old Dolan, who was also known by the moniker "Iron Man" and who ran a small speak-easy, were romantically involved or just friends isn't known. She is also said to have been friends with Lester and Florence "Three Fingered Flo" Flynn. Lester was a dock worker probably involved in the waterfront rackets. It would come out later that Flo lived with Alice for a short time, but the two got into a tiff because Flo was fooling around with an ex-con gunman named Edward Kenny whom Alice didn't like.

How she was supporting herself at that time isn't known for sure. Whatever she was doing wasn't bringing in much money. Foreclosure took the house in Acra that spring, and by June 1933, she was already behind in her thirty-five dollars a month rent.

Things were looking up though. Somehow she raised the necessary capital to go into business with a friend. Together they were going to run a drinking establishment on the Coney Island boardwalk called the Gypsy Tea Room, which was to open on July 1. More good news came around June 21, when her old manager Sam Burger got in touch with her again. A publisher of a horse racing tip sheet wanted to use Alice's name and title his paper, "Mrs. Jack Legs Diamond tips".[lix][303] Alice met with Burger at a Midtown Manhattan speakeasy and agreed to lend her name in exchange for a percentage of the profits. Burger drew up the contracts and all parties involved were to meet on Wednesday, June 28, to sign the papers.

---

lix This was the title given by Burger. Some others gave a variation of that name.

On Tuesday evening, Alice went down stairs to the super-intendent's apartment to play cards with him and his wife. A little after midnight, she went back to her apartment. At about the same time across town her friend Lester Flynn was in a tavern. Another man came in and ordered a drink. While the bartender was getting it, the man pulled a gun and, without warning or provocation, blasted Flynn into eternity and then escaped.

The following afternoon, Burger called Alice to remind her of the appointment they had that evening to sign the contracts. She didn't answer the phone. He tried her sister's place, but she wasn't there either. The appointment came and went. Frustrated, Burger tried all the next day to reach Alice to no avail. Friday found the theatrical manager vainly trying to save the deal. Finally at six-thirty that evening, he called her apartment and a man picked up the phone. Burger asked to speak with Alice, but was told that she was in the superintendent's office and couldn't come to the phone. Burger asked that she call him back at once. The man said OK and asked for his number. A short time later, two detectives showed up at Burger's office. Alice was dead, and they wanted to talk to him.

Alice hadn't been seen since the card game broke up early Wednesday morning. Neighbor's noticed that her lights were on all that day and night, as well as Thursday. Iron Man Dolan also stopped by a handful of times ringing her buzzer and leaving after no answer. On Friday evening (a half hour before Burger called), the superintendent let two painters into Alice's flat. Walking in, they saw her lying on the floor between the living room and the kitchenette.

She was wearing only socks and a robe. Sometime on Wednesday morning, she had a couple of visitors. They had some coffee and crackers and smoked a few cigarettes. Before leaving, one of them pressed a .38 to Alice's right temple and sent a bullet through her brain. Her house coat was torn, so she probably struggled at the last moment as she realized she was on the spot.

Just as when her husband was killed, the whodunit rumor mill went into overtime. Some believed that she was about to spill the beans on who killed Jack, so she was bumped off. Another theory was that it was remnants of the Vincent Coll gang. Other's pointed fingers at some of Jack's old cronies. There were reports of her getting drunk at a speakeasy the Saturday before the murder and saying that she "was tired of doing favors for mugs who didn't pay."[304] Oddly, even though no gun was found, some authorities claimed her death was a suicide.

None of Alice's acquaintances could shed any light on the murder –Iron Man Dolan suggested that he knew who did it and assured the authorities that he would avenge the murder himself. In early August Edward Kenny and Three Fingered Flo were arraigned for the murder of Lester Flynn. (They got off.) The theory was that they killed him for his $5,000 insurance policy. Police also theorized that, after the murder of Lester, Kenny and Flo popped by Alice's apartment. During the ensuing conversation regarding Lester, it was determined that Alice wasn't a team player and was dispatched accordingly. Since evidence condemns killers and not theories, Kenny and Flo were never charged with Alice's murder though they were questioned and suspected of it.

After the coroner was finished with Alice, her body was removed to a Brooklyn funeral parlor where the handful of mourners that showed up, namely her sister Mae and some friends of the family, cried and prayed beside her casket illuminated by a red electric crucifix. Just as it was a year and a half before when Jack was buried, the day of Alice's funeral was rainy. Outside the mortuary, hundreds of people showed up to hopefully catch a glimpse of the proceedings. Inside, the funeral party consisted of Mae and three other women who listened to the assistant funeral director give Alice the last rites. At about one-thirty that afternoon, her casket was carried out to a hearse and transported to Mount Olivet and placed into a vault for later burial.[305]

EPILOGUE

Death didn't keep Jack out of the press. In fact, death is the main thing that kept his name in the papers. On and off through the remainder of the decade, journalist routinely referred to Jack whenever anyone connected with him, no matter how tenuously, was killed.

The first to go was Vincent Coll. The twenty-three-year-old gunman was in his cell on December 18, when some guards informed him that Jack was dead. Later in the day, a visiting reporter called out to him asking if he heard the news. "Yes, I heard Diamond was killed," Coll yelled back from his cell, "The keepers told me about it." The reporter asked for Coll's thoughts. "I feel sorry for anybody who is bumped off, particularly so soon after he has just beaten a trial,"[306] he responded, not knowing he had only fifty-two days to live.

Four days after Jack was rubbed out, the Mad Dog went on trial for the Harlem Baby Massacre and beat the rap. On February 1, rival gunmen got word that Vince was at an apartment in the Bronx. The killers forced their way into the flat and sprayed the room with bullets, killing two Coll gangsters and a woman. Their intended target was not on the premises.

A week later on the evening of February 7, Coll prepared for what would prove to be his last hours on earth. Since the near miss on February 1, he and Lottie spent each night in a different hotel in Mid-town Manhattan. One of Vince's objectives that final night was a phone call, supposedly, to Owney Madden. Having hit the crime lord up the previous summer for the Big Frenchy snatch, rumor had it that Coll was threatening to kidnap Owney's brother in-law if he didn't pony up another small fortune. If the score paid off, Vince and Lottie planned to skip to Ireland for the remainder of their lives.[307] Unfortunately for Coll, he had a traitor in his midst. Seeing that there was no future in the Coll gang, this person made a deal to get out with his own skin intact by betraying his leader. So Madden not only knew what time the phone call was coming but also where it was coming from. All he had to do was wait until the designated time.

Dressing for the evening, Vincent put on an undershirt and underwear both made of silk and then buttoned up a blue shirt. That evening's attire would be a gray suit and vest topped off with blue overcoat with a velvet collar and a gray Stetson fedora with a black band. As the man assigned to kill him loaded .45 caliber bullets of the full metal jacketed variety into the drum of his Tommy gun, Vincent went out for his last meal, which consisted of spaghetti, vermicelli and chicken.[308]

At about one o'clock the following morning, Vincent and a companion walked into the London Chemist drugstore at 314 West Twenty-Third Street. Inside were two employees and three other customers. The gangsters made their way to the rear of the store where there was a bank of three telephone booths. Coll headed into the first one, while his confederate took a seat at the soda fountain. Vincent placed his call. As he was talking, a sedan pulled up out front of the drugstore. Three men alighted from the car. Two of them took up guard duty outside the front door, as the third entered. He calmly strode to the rear of the store. "Remain cool," he ordered everyone, while producing a machine gun from under his coat. As he approached the phone booths, Coll's buddy stood up and was allowed to leave the store. Taking up a position in front of the booth containing Coll, the gunner raised his Thompson to about shoulder level and pulled the trigger. A heartbeat later fifteen bullet casings lay on the floor. His job complete, the killer calmly exited the store.[lx]

---

lx The gunman may have been a West Side gangster named Thomas Protheroe based on the fact that in 1933, ballistic analysis proved that the

Chances are Coll never knew what hit him. The booths were designed so that anyone using the phone would be facing the right corner of the booth. All fifteen shots hit their target, leaving eighteen holes. The first two shots pierced Vince's fedora and entered the rear right of his skull, plowing through the brain to the left side of his head. The third bullet entered in front of the right ear and blew a two inch hole in his cheek, taking off a bit of his nose midway down. Ten more shots mangled his right arm, and his left arm was perforated by four. Three of the slugs that hit his right arm passed into his chest. Amazingly, only three of the eighteen wounds were determined to be fatal. There weren't a whole lot of people who felt sorry for Coll being bumped off, even after having beaten a trial.

The next to go was Jack's enigmatic confederate Lefty Joe Burke. Though the two were never linked in the press during life, the police stated that Burke worked with Diamond for ten years, including up in Acra. On the evening of April 1, 1932, Burke hopped into his Cadillac[lxi] and drove to a Brooklyn speakeasy that was hopping with about fifty people inside. Early the next morning, three men entered the speakeasy and drew guns. Unlike his former boss, Burke saw it coming, and there was nothing he could do about it. The gunmen ordered all the speakeasy revelers away from Burke and then let him

---

machine gun used to kill Coll was used in another West Side murder. Police stated that Protheroe was the man who wielded the gun in that murder. The main target of the shooting refused to identify him, however, and he went free. The *New York Daily News* stated that, at the time of the arrest, police said that Protheroe was actually found with the weapon in his possession. It is quite plausible that Owney Madden, a West Side crime boss, would use a gunman from his own base to take care of Coll.

lxi The Caddy used to belong to Jack. Burke bought it off of Alice after Jack was killed.

detectives approaching. He grabbed a shotgun and made a run for his car. Outside, he saw Detective Harold Moore and cut him down with a blast from his gun. Though wounded, Moore was able to get off one shot, which drilled Fats in the forehead killing him instantly. Kelly tried to escape through the rear but was wounded in the knee by a trooper. Mrs. Fats and Basile tried to fight it out, but after the former was slightly wounded the latter surrendered.[313]

✵ ✵ ✵

The summer of 1932 saw another of Diamond's cronies join the line-up in the sky. The next was his right hand man Paul Quattrocchi. It wasn't bullets that sent him over, however, it was the dreaded consumption. At some point around the previous year's federal trial, Paul was diagnosed with tuberculosis. He had never been sent to prison, having been able to have his sentence deferred a number of times because of his health. Finally on August 1, he cheated the government out of two years and five grand by succumbing to the disease at home in the Hollywood Inn.[314]

✵ ✵ ✵

A little less than three months later, a bullet and some sash cord brought Diamond's name back out. This time it was Dominick Bifano, Eddie's right hand man in Denver, who got the big send off.

After the murder attempt in December of 1928, Eddie Diamond returned east, but Bifano stayed in Denver and was arrested in early 1929 for vagrancy, for which he was fined $100 and sentenced to sixty days in jail. On appeal, the court agreed to drop the sentence on condition that the gangster left the state which he did.

Back in New York, Bifano managed to stay out of police hands until Christmas day of 1931 when he was arrested for firing two shots at a man. At the time of the arrest, he told the police that he was working as a chauffeur. The felonious assault charge for the shooting was dismissed in March of 1932, and that was the last the cops saw of Bifano until the morning of October 21.

William Carnastra, an ice deliveryman, left his apartment to make some deliveries and noticed a seemingly abandoned car with the motor running. In the back seat was a large burlap sack. Three hours later, Carnastra returned from his deliveries and noticed that the sedan was still there and the engine was still running, so he summoned a policeman.

The burlap bag was sliced opened and out popped Bifano, folded in half like a jackknife. Unlike some of the other sack victims of the day, Bifano had been shot in the back of the head prior to being stuffed in the sack and so was spared death by self-strangulation.

When detectives went to his home, they questioned his father who backed up the story that he was only a chauffeur. This, however, the police were disinclined to believe, because the dead gangster was dressed in snappy gangster fashion with a powder blue suit and red neck tie with white polka dots. Close examination also showed that he was the recent recipient of both a manicure and a pedicure, hardly the dress and comforts one would associate with a chauffeur.

With ties to both Diamond and Coll, there were probably safer locations for Bifano than New York City. Seeing that he threw a couple of shots at some guy less than a week after Legs bought it, perhaps he was eliminated on behalf of the Diamond haters or maybe it was the Coll busters doing some final house cleaning.

✡ ✡ ✡

"I'm gonna get the fellow who killed her," James "Iron Man" Dolan told detectives who questioned him following the murder of Alice Diamond.[315] Unfortunately for Dolan, he was got first. Exactly a month after Alice was killed, Iron Man and a friend entered a Brooklyn beer garden, took a seat and ordered a couple of beers. While the waiter was fetching the brews, two men approached the table and started talking to Dolan. One of them said something that greatly angered Iron Man, and he stood up to do something about it. By this time, the other man had slipped behind Dolan and fired a bullet through his back before he had a chance to do anything. Not called Iron Man for nothing, Dolan managed to chase his killers from the place before dropping dead with the bullet lodged in his heart.

✧ ✧ ✧

At around seven-thirty on the morning of August 22, 1934, the caretaker of a brownstone on Manhattan's Upper West Side found a trunk out front by the curb with some blood pooling around it. Opening it, he made a grisly discovery and Legs was in the news once again.

Inside the box were three pieces that, when put together, made up one Bernard McMahon. Police said McMahon had been a confederate of Jack's back in the early days before the latter was a successful hoodlum. How the two supposedly knew each other wasn't divulged. It came out a few years later that McMahon was part of the robbery team that stole $427,000 from an armored car in Brooklyn. The plan called for some of the bandits to escape by boat, and while McMahon was climbing aboard, he accidently bumped his sawed off shotgun against the side and blew off a kneecap. His confederates took him to a safe house and did their best to nurse him but he cashed in about three days later. A trunk was procured for his removal, but they couldn't squeeze him in, so they sawed off both his legs just above the knee. With one leg

wrapped in brown paper and the other in a coat, they were
packed in the trunk along with the torso.

☆ ☆ ☆

The evening of October 23, 1935, found Jack Diamond's
old pal/enemy Dutch Schultz conducting business in the rear
of a Newark, New Jersey, tavern called the Palace Chop House.
Also in attendance were his bodyguards Lulu Rosenkrantz and
Abe Landau. Rounding out the group was the gang's financial
wizard Otto "Abbadabba" Berman.

The years following Diamond's death were both good
and bad for Schultz. Good in that, by forcing many New York
City restaurants to join his Metropolitan Restaurant and Caf-
eteria Association, by controlling a number of unions and, by
organizing the Harlem policy racket, he made more money
than Jack Diamond ever dreamed of. (The policy racket itself
was said to be worth twenty-million dollars a year) Bad in that
both the federal government and New York State government
wanted to take him down.

Uncle Sam took the first swing in January 1933 by bringing him up on charges of tax evasion. After seeing the out-
come of Al Capone's bout with the tax man, Schultz took a
powder and went into hiding for nearly two years trying to
work out some sort of deal. Accepting the fact that there
would be no fix, the Dutchman surrendered on November 28,
1934. His trial the following spring resulted in a hung jury. The
retrial took place in August, and he was acquitted. Not willing
to accept defeat, the Feds went for him again on a lesser tax
charge, and Schultz surrendered in Perth Amboy. While preparing for the trial he set up shop in Newark staying at the
Robert Treat Hotel and conducting gang business each night
around the corner at the Palace Chop House. The main reason
he picked Newark was because of its close proximity to New
York City, where his enterprises were currently being threatened by both gangsters and Manhattan's special prosecutor

drew a gun and killed the hulking desperado with one shot. Not wanting any police trouble in their restaurant, the three brothers who ran the place dragged the 240-pound gangster down the block and left him on the sidewalk. They failed to wash away the blood trail, however, and police had no trouble finding the murder spot.[318]

The following year, bullets once again brought Jack's name back into print. Oddly enough, this time it wasn't a fellow gangster that was gunned down but his old mouth-piece Isaiah Leebove. Counselor Leebove continued representing the New York City underworld for a few years after Jack's death, but by the end of the decade he had relocated to Michigan where he headed an oil company. On May 14, 1938, Leebove was drinking in a hotel bar with some friends when a former partner with a gun and a grudge showed up and pumped four bullets into the former lawyer.

A month later on June 13, 1938, Edward Kenny, the probable murderer of Alice Diamond, was himself snuffed out in a bar on Manhattan's West Side. He entered the tavern at about eleven o'clock, followed by a well-dressed young man. Kenny ordered a drink and took a seat in a booth. A few minutes later, the well-dressed young man walked up and fired three bullets into his face. As Kenny plopped to the ground, the gunman waved his pistol at the bartender and patrons and beat a hasty retreat.[319]

※ ※ ※

It wasn't all blood and gore that kept Diamond's name alive. Salvatore Spitale and his partner Irving Bitz made quite a bit of copy during the 1930's, most notably for being appointed by Charles Lindbergh to act as go-betweens between himself and the kidnapper(s) of his child. In the press that followed, there was usually reference to their being suspected of killing Diamond. In 1939, Spitale was found guilty of bilking a guy for $1,000 and sentenced to five years in prison. During sentencing, the judge referenced a public report made by Irving Halpern, chief of the General Sessions Probation Bureau, which stated that police were convinced that Spitale and Bitz had Jack killed because he failed to return the $200,000 that they invested in the ill-fated European excursion.

It was Marion more than anyone else who kept Jack's memory alive. She managed to survive in showbiz until the close of the Thirties, working periodically in burlesque shows and by the end of the decade as a fan dancer. The advertisements for her show usually mentioned Jack in some capacity. She also made the papers a few times a year in non-advertisements as well, usually because a show she was in was busted for lewdness or she was asked to leave town. She also did a screen test in Hollywood but supposedly Will Hays forbade anyone to sign her.

On March 14, 1935, she married a twenty-three year-old guy named Joe Ross in Easton, Pennsylvania. Ross belonged to a local family and worked for the beer distribution company his brother owned. Apparently the couple only spent a few days together before tying the knot. Their honeymoon was spent in Columbia, New Jersey, where Kiki had a three-week dancing gig.[320]

It appears that after the job in Columbia, Kiki continued with touring and Ross went back to Easton, and the marriage fizzled out. About a year later in 1936, she was married in New

York City to a guy named August J. Savarese under the name of Frances Peterka. In an article from the *Syracuse Herald* in March of 1936, the priest who was going to perform the wedding ceremony stated that the Peterka woman said that she was also known as Kiki and that the couple was going to move from the Bronx because of publicity. The marriage was postponed for three months, perhaps because of the press, and the couple was actually married on June 4, 1936.

Why would Marion use a fake name to get married again? Well, possibly because she was still married to Ross. At the very least because she told the church it was her first wedding. As for the first possibility the *Morning Call*, the newspaper for Pennsylvania's Lehigh Valley, reported that on March 3, 1937, just before going on stage in a Northampton County theater, Kiki was served with divorce papers sent by lawyers for Ross.[321] This was a year after she married Savarese.

Weddings aside, she continued getting the occasional blurb as the years went on. In early 1937, she made the papers because, while performing in the "Pepper Pot Review" at a Boston burlesque theater, a frat boy entered her dressing room on an initiation dare and stole some of her underwear. The pledge was caught trying to leave the theater. Marion forgave and forgot, probably happy about the press. The same year, she was hospitalized for the flu and had to cancel some performances. After 1940, where she went and how she fared nobody really knows and nobody really cared. Walter Winchell gave a possible scenario in his piece from May 26, 1948:

…Locals report that Kiki Roberts, famed during the "Legs" Diamond era, is now running a Bridgeport luncheonette…[322]

PERTINENT ADDRESSES

Philadelphia
2628 Lehigh Avenue – John Diamond's residence 1896.
2671 Tulip Street - Sarah Hart's residence 1896.
Family residences
2336 Albert Street - 1900.
2220 East Cumberland – Circa 1906 -1907.
2157 East York – 1910 the boarding house where Jack, Eddie and their dad lived.
New York City unless otherwise noted
1914
327 W. 20th Street – Jack's residence.
161 Bowery - Pawn shop where Jack, James Burns and John Doyle tried to sell stolen gold chains.
205 Bowery – Doorway where the trio was arrested.
1917
332 W. 19th Street – Residence at time of his first marriage.
509 W. 23rd Street –Residence of wife Katherine and in-laws.
346 W. 20th Street – Church where Jack and Katherine were married.
1918
341 W. 22nd Street – Residence.
211 W. 12th Street – Rooming house where Jack stole clothes.
429 W. 24th Street – Residence.
1921
360 W. 28th Street – Residence.
1923

322 Palisade Avenue Cliffside, New Jersey – Residence.
510 w 146th Street - Residence.
1924-25
593 E. 136th Street – Residence.
318 Lenox Avenue – Eddie's residence at the time of his wedding.
1926
378 E. 149th Street – Bronx Theatrical Club.
1927
300 Haven Avenue – Residence.
1928
348 St. Ann's Avenue, Bronx – Residence.
651 Madison Street, Denver, Colorado – Eddie's residence.
1929
254 W. 116th Street - Residence.
143 Cairo-Windham County Road (Rt. 23) Acra, NY – Residence.
6 Shepard Avenue Saranac Lake, New York – Eddie's residence at the Trudeau Sanatorium.
1930
134 W. 93rd Street – Kitty Diamond's residence where Eddie was buried from.
35 W. 64th Street – Hotel Monticello.
1931
67 Dove Street Albany, NY. – Boarding house where killed.

NOTES

Foreword

1. New York Times 9/15/1931
2. New York Times 7/10/1931
3. New York Post 4/4/1939
4. Albany Times Union 12/19/1931
5. Sunday Journal, 1930, UK
6. Boxing Father and Sons, A real life "All in the Family", Nagler, Barney, The Ring January 1981

Chapter 1- Young Mr. Diamond

7. New York Times 2/8/1914
8. Ibid
9. New York Times 2/28/1915
10. New York Times 9/6/1914
11. John and Sarah Diamond Marriage license #86205 (Sarah's death certificate list her birth year as 1875 and her place of birth Elk County, Pennsylvania)
12. John & Sarah's marriage license and both the 1900 & 1910 Federal Census list John's occupation as glass packer
13. Birth certificate
14. 1900 Federal Census
15. Birth certificate
16. New York Daily News 5/16/1931

17. Birth, death and reason for death from Thomas Diamond's death certificate #3730

18. Margret Diamond death certificate #562

19. Sarah Diamond death certificate #15292

20. Federal Census of 1880 list John Diamond's mother as deceased

21. New York Daily News 5/15/1931

22. Ibid

23. Ibid

24. From Diamond's interview with journalist John O'Donnell. New York Daily News 6/30/1931

25. NY Daily News 5/23/31

26. Marriage Certificate NYC Municipal Archives

27. New York Daily News 10/17/30

28. New York Evening Journal 10/16/1930

29. New York Evening Journal 12/20/1931

30. The People vs Michael Culhane, William Tobin, Timothy Cleary, John Diamond. #119460 NYC Municipal Archives.

31. People vs John Diamond #119972 NYC Municipal Archives

32. NY Daily News 5/23/31

Chapter 2-Roaring in the Twenties

33. File 1149 People -against - Jack Diamond Bronx Municipal Archives

34. Now I'll Tell, Rothstein, Carolyn

35. The Big Bankroll, Katcher, Leo

36. New York Times 11/17/23 & 11/22/23

37. New York Times 6/12/24

38. New York Times 6/15/24

39. Eddie & Katherine's marriage certificate

40. Dummy Corp and Canada a trans-shipment point - Strength of the Wolf: The Secret History of America's war on drugs, Valentine, Douglas

41. Ship passenger list Ancestry.com

42. The Big Bankroll, Katcher, Leo

43. On the shooting -New York Post 7/1/1925, "Greasers" – New York Times 12/19/1931

44. New York Times 9/13/1925

45. New York Times 3/10/1926

46. New York Herald-Tribune 3/10/1926

47. New York Times 1/26/1929

48. New York Times 2/7/1926

49. New York Times 3/10/1926

50. Kill The Dutchman, Sann, Paul

51. New York Times 3/18/1926

52. Ship Passenger list Ancestry.com

53. New York Times 12/22/1926

54. New York Times 12/30/1926

55. Eddie's death certificate

56. New York Daily News 5/18/1931

57. S.S. Toloa Passenger list Ancestry.com

58. New York Times 10/26/1927

59. New York Herald Tribune 10/16/1927

60. Ibid

61. From Diamond's interview with journalist John O'Donnell New York Daily News 6/29/1931

Chapter 3-Diamonds in Trouble

62. New York Evening Journal 2/3/28

63. New York Evening Journal 8/26/29

64. New York Times 2/1/1928

65. New York Evening Journal 2/3/28

66. New York Evening Journal 11/21/1928

67. Denver Post 11/5/1928 & 11/6/1928

68. Denver Post 11/16/1928

69. Ibid

70. Deed Catskill Recorder's office

71. Eddie's death certificate, Brotherly love showed soft side of the notorious hood, Mclaughlin, Bill, Adirondack Daily Enterprise 2/6/1985

72. House descriptions taken from The New Yorker June, 13, 1931, New York Daily Mirror 3/12/1931, "secret stairway" New York Herald Tribune 8/27/30
73. Ibid
74. 1930 Federal census
75. Jack "Legs" Diamond: Anatomy of a Gangster. Levine, Gary
76. Ibid
77. People of the State of New York –against- Paul Quattrocchi
78. Biographical information comes from Scaccio's admission sheet to Clinton Prison
79. Brooklyn Daily Eagle 6/20/1932
80. New York Times 5/21/1929
81. New York Times 5/22/1929

Chapter 4-Everything Is Hotsy-Totsy Now

82. Cumberland Evening Times 7/25/1967
83. Ibid
84. Rothstein: The Life, Times, and Murder of the Criminal Genius Who Fixed the 1919 World Series, Pietrusza, David
85. New York Times 2/7/1930
86. New York Times 7/14/1929
87. People of the State of New York v. John Diamond
88. New York Times 7/17/1929
89. New York Times 7/20/1929
90. New York Times 8/1/1929
91. Gangster City, Downey, Patrick Barricade Books 2004
92. New York Evening Journal 8/26/1929
93. Ibid
94. New York Times 8/29/1929
95. Ibid
96. Vizzini, Vizzini, Sal Pinnacle Books, 1972
97. Ibid
98. New York Times 10/18/1929
99. Vizzini, Vizzini, Sal Pinnacle Books, 1972
100. Eddie's death certificate

101. Two detectives stationed there, New York Evening Post 1/16/1930. Eddie's death certificate list Charles R. Higgins of 7901 4 Ave Brooklyn, NY as the informant. The 1930 Census shows Vannie Higgins at that same address.

102. People of New York State v Charles Entratta

103. New York Evening Journal 3/11/1930

104. New York Herald-Tribune 3/12/1931, New York Evening Journal 3/11/1930

105. New York Evening Journal 8/6/1931

106. New York Times 10/13/1930

Chapter 5-A Star Is Born

107. New York Times 2/19/1930

108. New York Evening Journal 12/31/1931

109. No Foolin' info from ibdb.com, Follies of 1925 original show program located at ziegfeldgrrl.multiply.com

110. New York Evening Journal 12/28/1931

111. Information on Whoopee! Ibdb.com

112. New York Evening Journal 10/14/1930

113. New York American 10/14/1930

114. New York Evening Journal 10/14/1931

115. New York Evening Journal 12/19/1931

116. Ibid

117. Ibid

118. Ibid

119. Appleton Post Crescent 9/10/1938 syndicated New York columnist Dale Harrison's In Old New York. In the article he refused to name the choreographer identifying him only as "Joe". Ibdb.com list a Joe Smith as a choreographer working at that time.

120. New York Times 10/29/30

121. New York Times 8/6/31

122. New York Post 8/26/30

123. Gangster City, Downey, Patrick Barricade Books 2004

124. New York Daily News 8/20/1930

243. Interview, Colasanti, John. How McCarthy was described to him by neighborhood contemporaries.
244. Specifics, New York Evening Journal. Who was in the car; interview with John Colasanti
245. Interview, Colasanti, John
246. Ibid
247. Gangster City, Downey, Patrick Barricade Books 2004
248. New York Times 6/1/1931 & one of those wounded during the shooting was 19-year old Michael Kohutencz known in the neighborhood as Mikey the Pollock, years later he told Chin Iadoroli's nephew John Colasanti that the hit squat was headed by Trigger Mike Coppola.
249. Interview, Colasanti, John
250. Gangster City, Downey, Patrick Barricade Books 2004
251. Ibid

Chapter 12-Justice will Not Be Served

252. New York Times 7/13/1931
253. New York Daily News 7/1/1931
254. New York Times 7/13/1931
255. New York Times 7/15/1931
256. Albany Evening News 7/15/1931
257. New York Daily News 7/15/1931
258. New York Times 7/23/1931
259. New York Times 8/1/1931
260. New York Times 8/31/1931

Chapter 13- Justice Is Back on the Menu

261. New York Times 8/9/1931 & 8/10/1931
262. New York Times 8/6/1931
263. New York Times 8/9/1931
264. New York Daily News 8/9/1931
265. New York Times 8/9/1931
266. Ibid

267. Ibid
268. Ibid
269. New York Times 8/10/1931
270. Albany Evening News 12/19/1931

Chapter 14-The Way of all Gangster Flesh

271. Olean Evening Herald 9/2/1931
272. Albany Times Union 11/19/1931
273. New York Evening Journal 12/19/1931 Kiki memoir
274. Albany Daily News 12/29/1931
275. New York Times 12/19/1931
276. Scoop! Paul Gallico, True November 1946
277. New York Herald Tribune 12/19/1931
278. New York World Telegram 12/18/31
279. New York Evening Journal 12/21/31
280. New York Evening Journal 12/19/1931
281. New York Times 12/19/1931
282. Ibid & New York Daily News 12/20/1931
283. New York Daily News 12/20/1931
284. New York Evening Journal 12/21/1931
285. New York Daily News 12/20/1931
286. Ibid
287. New York Times 12/19/1931
288. Ibid
289. Times Union 12/18/1931
290. Ibid
291. New York Evening Journal 12/19/1931
292. Times Union 12/18/1931

Chapter 15-Aftermath

293. New York Daily News 12/20/1931
294. New York Evening Journal 12/20/1931
295. New York Daily News 12/23/1931
296. Ibid

CPSIA information can be obtained at www.ICGtesting.com
Printed in the USA
LVOW04s2021211214

419840LV00022B/627/P